IMAGES
of America

PRESQUE ISLE, CARIBOU AND NEW SWEDEN

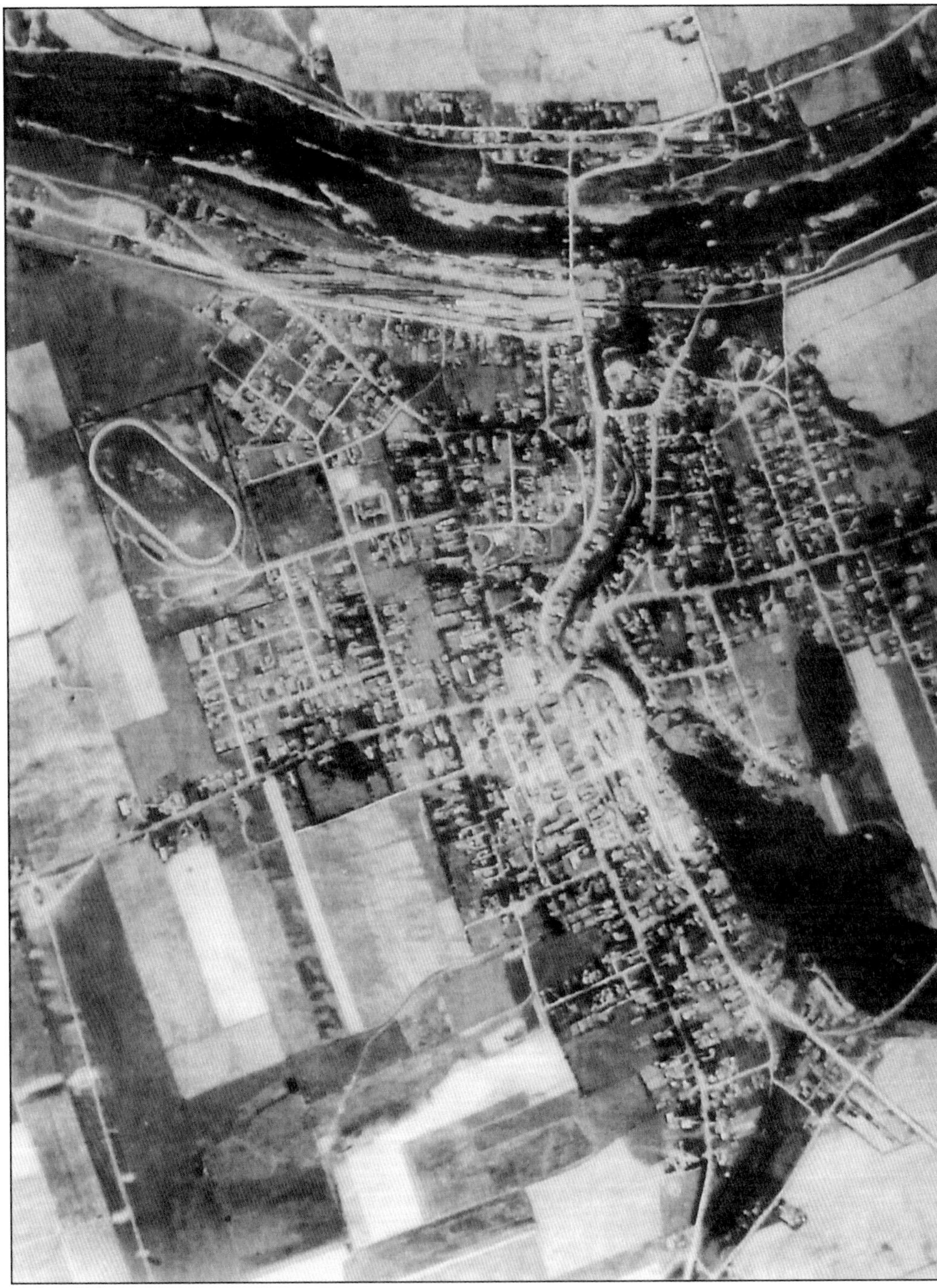

An aerial view of Caribou in the 1930s.

IMAGES
of America

PRESQUE ISLE, CARIBOU AND NEW SWEDEN

Compiled by
Jackie H. Greaves, Stan P. Greaves, and Frank H. Sleeper

ARCADIA
PUBLISHING

ISBN 978-0-7385-5715-1

Published by Arcadia Publishing
Charleston, South Carolina

Printed in the United States of America

Library of Congress Catalog Card Number: 2007941021

For all general information contact Arcadia Publishing at:
Telephone 843-853-2070
Fax 843-853-0044
E-mail sales@arcadiapublishing.com
For customer service and orders:
Toll-Free 1-888-313-2665

Visit us on the Internet at www.arcadiapublishing.com

Contents

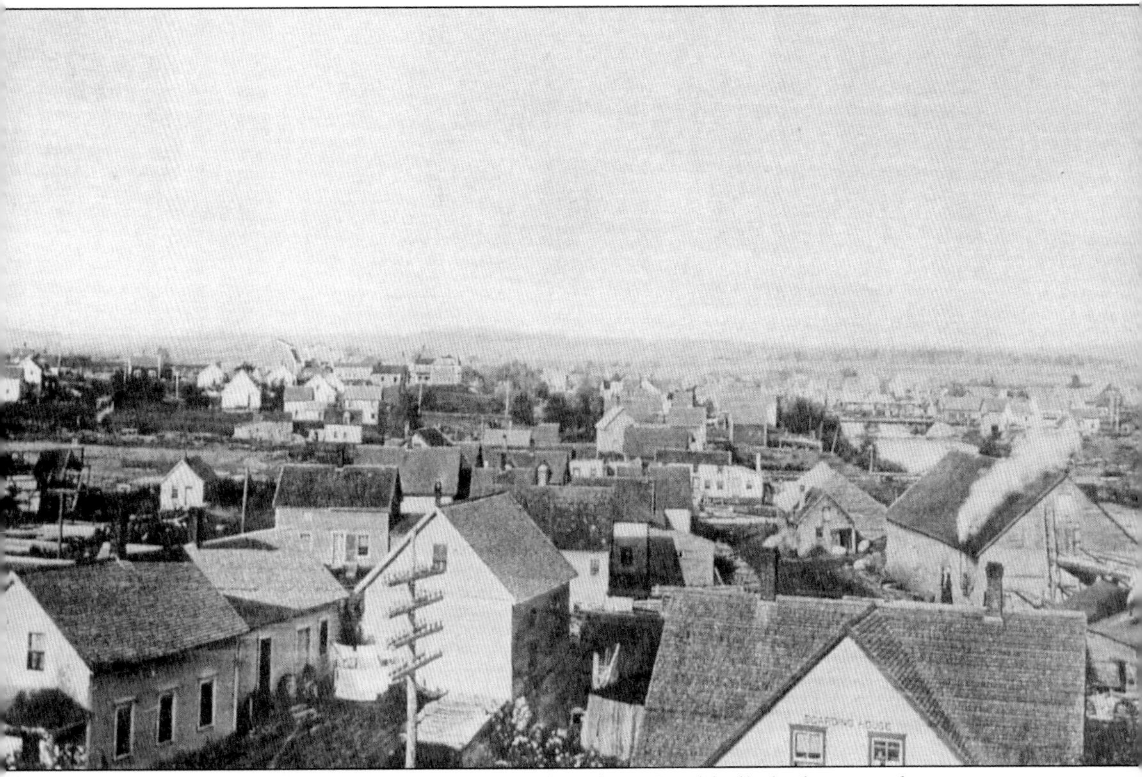

Panoramic view of Presque Isle in 1910, taken from Gouldville looking north.

Introduction

Madawaska in the far north of Aroostook County, Maine, was settled in the late eighteenth century. Houlton in southern Aroostook County was settled in 1807. In between these two communities stretched more than 100 miles of land almost devoid of any settlers until after the "Bloodless Aroostook War" of 1839 and the signing of the Webster-Ashburton Treaty of 1842 that permanently ended the dispute over this country's northeastern boundary with Canada. That dispute had kept settlers from moving into the large, fertile territory.

The settlement of the dispute brought people into the area. Those few who were in the area already came from both sides of the newly made-permanent border. The newcomers came from both this country and Canada, particularly from Maine and New Brunswick. The area has been called "America's Last Frontier." But there were no real gunfights here, no shootouts at the OK Corral, no Boot Hill cemeteries for dead outlaws and gunfighters, no cowboys, not very much in the way of cattle.

But there was the social mobility of the western frontier and there was a pioneer spirit, a spirit of adventure, a gambling spirit—all of which still exist to some degree. They did not disappear when the area moved quite rapidly and dramatically out of the frontier stage after the Civil War and especially after the development of the potato growing industry and the coming of the railroad to take the spuds to US markets. While the number of potato growers in the area has declined in recent years, those who remain have larger farms. And that means they gamble more each year—on how potatoes grow in Idaho, in the Red River Valley, and in other potato-growing areas of this country and abroad. As good gamblers do, these growers try to hedge as much as possible. But weather, blight, and other potato diseases can't always be hedged against—and they often control the price paid to the growers for their crop.

There are good years and bad years for potato prices. You could always see it in the yards of the farms, Cadillacs in good years; Model T's in bad. The gambling spirit of the frontier survived. So did the social mobility which brought a sense of true democracy to most things: the wealthy man will wear the same overalls, the same informal clothes as the man who just lost his shirt in potatoes.

Move in more closely on these three communities. Presque Isle was not incorporated as a town until 1859 and didn't annex neighboring Maysville until 1883. It became Aroostook County's first city in 1940. Caribou was not even under that name when it started out. The town of Lyndon had been incorporated in 1859. Lyndon annexed the Eaton Grant, Forestville, and Sheridan in 1869. The center of population had shifted and a dispute arose over whether the name should be Lyndon or Caribou. The official name change to Caribou was only made in 1877. New Sweden wasn't settled until the summer of 1870 when William Widgery Thomas of Portland, later to be US ambassador to Sweden and Norway, led about fifty Swedes from that country into the fertile lands north of Caribou. More Swedish families followed. It was a unique way to fill empty spaces in this last frontier and it worked, though New Sweden, Stockholm, and Westmanland will be hurt for a time by the closing of Loring Air Force Base in nearby Limestone.

New Sweden, because it was settled so late, is like a little laboratory for photographs of the Aroostook frontier. But Presque Isle and Caribou also provide photographs giving good examples of the character of that frontier. The environment was difficult—but the people, especially the Swedes, adapted rapidly to it. There was plenty of fun, both in winter and summer, to help counteract the trials of the fires, snow, and floods. There was also plenty of work, in raising potatoes, in lumbering, and in the retailing and wholesaling that grew up in the area. And, during and after World War II, a new element entered into the area which was about the closest continental place to the USSR—defense.

The Presque Isle Air Force Base was activated before World War II. For a short period at the end of the 1950s, it became a Snark missile base—but was closed in 1961. The area made a tremendous comeback from that closing. Presque Isle was named an All-American city as a result. The spirit of innovation that often goes with frontier life had carried on.

The area now has to cope with the closure of another large defense installation: the huge Strategic Air Force Command Base, Loring Air Force Base, at nearby Limestone.

It's hoped that some of these old photographs of Presque Isle, Caribou, and New Sweden will give people from outside some idea of just what goes into the makeup of these sturdy people. It's also hoped that people in the three-town region themselves will learn a bit more about their forebears: their joys, their sorrows, and their zest for life.

It's an excellent time to look back at the American frontier, wherever it was, and at the good, enduring values it left. And so, Presque Isle, Caribou, and New Sweden become a little laboratory for looking at the ways of the frontier and what it became—through the eye of the camera.

Some of that shines through in the faces of the people in the sections entitled "Doers and Shakers" and "Faces of the North." And some of it may be found in the towns themselves seventy-five or more years ago. The people of this three-community area struggle, survive—and win.

Frank H. Sleeper
Jackie H. Greaves
Stan P. Greaves
October 1994

One

The Last Frontier

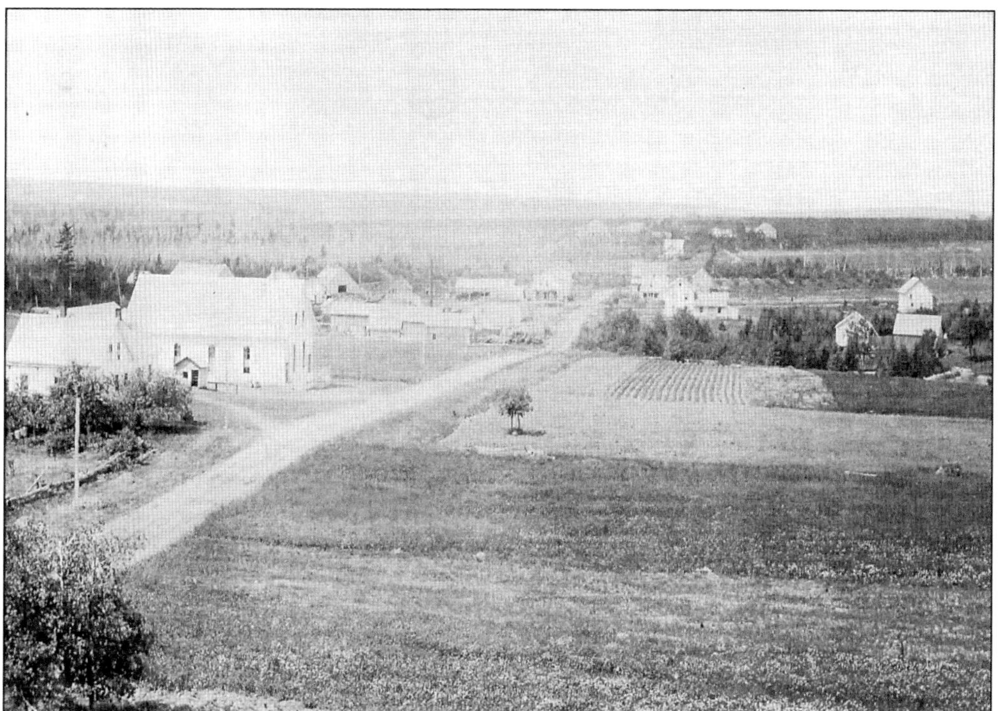

A look at the community of New Sweden in the 1900s. We are facing west toward the Free Mission (now Covenant Evangelic) Church. New Sweden was not settled until the summer of 1870.

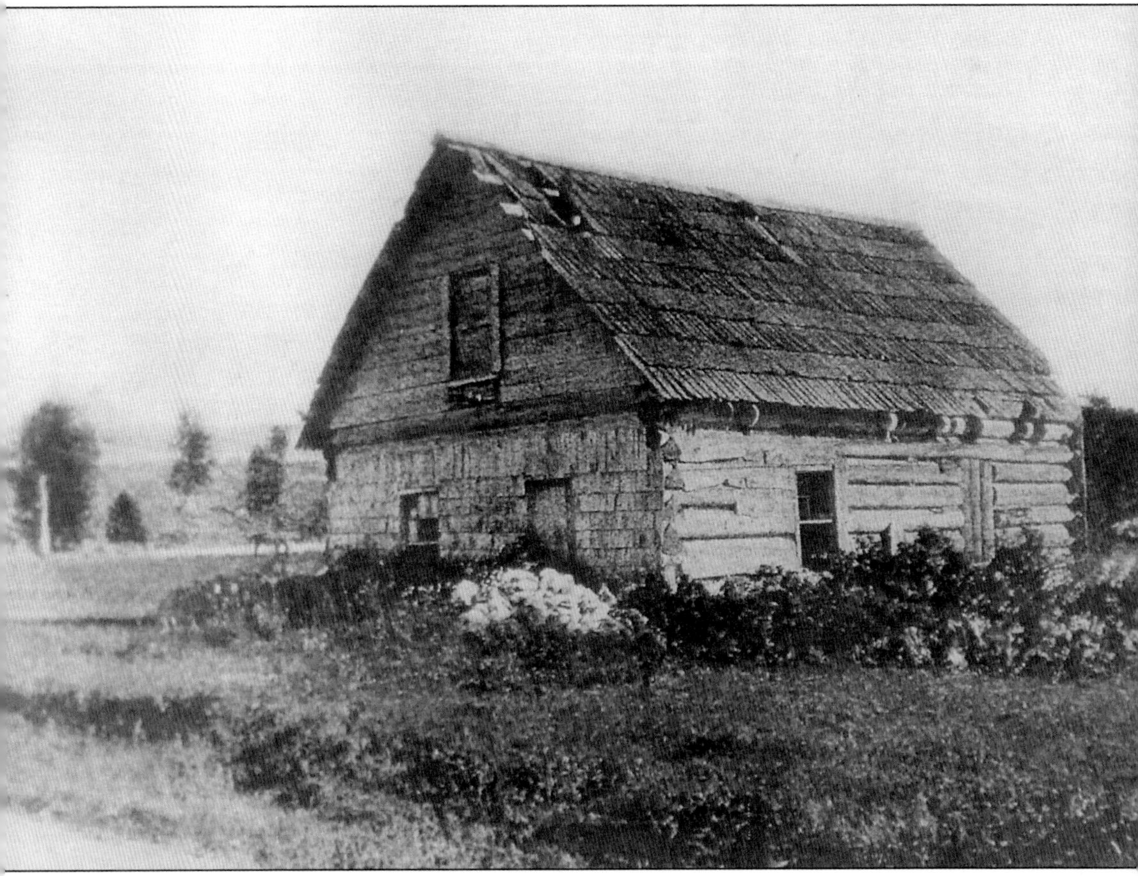

One of the first houses in New Sweden, a real look at what some have called this country's last frontier. The state was supposed to supply a log house and 100 acres of woodland for each Swede. Records indicate that only three such homes were built, though the woodland was supplied. With true ingenuity, the skills they had, and just plain guts, the Swedish settlers built their homes before winter came. It was a great example of the frontier ethic, imported from a country much like the Aroostook County region where New Sweden was founded.

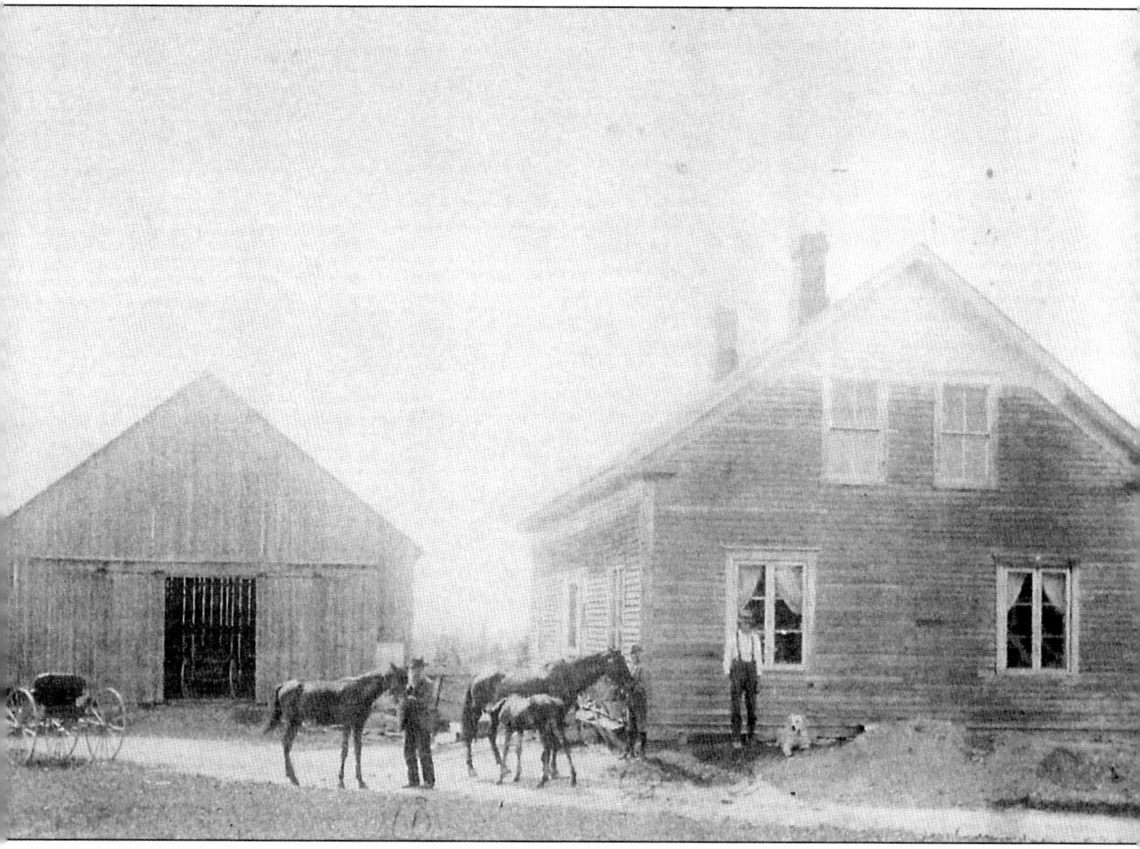

The Captain N.P. Clase house in New Sweden about 1910. Left to right are: Captain Clase, A. Percival Anderson, and Reinhold Anderson. Captain Clase's young daughter was the first of the settlers to die, even before she reached New Sweden. Captain Clase was a leader in the community for many years.

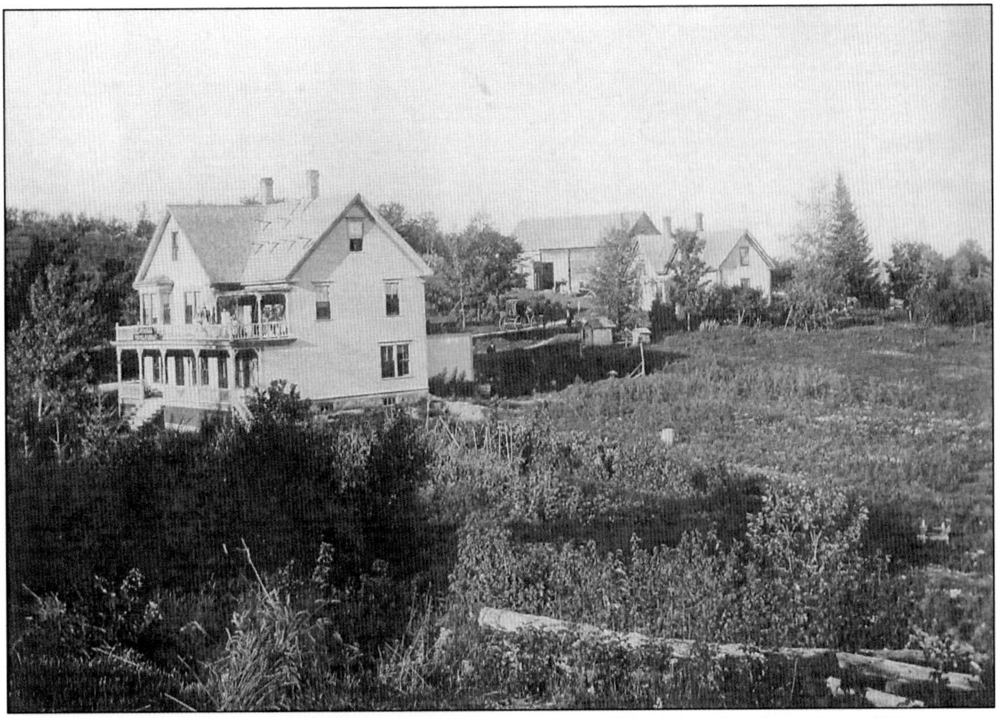

The Jemptland section of New Sweden about 1918. The area was about 5 miles north of the center of the town and had its own post office. This photograph is of Jacob and Ada Hedman's home.

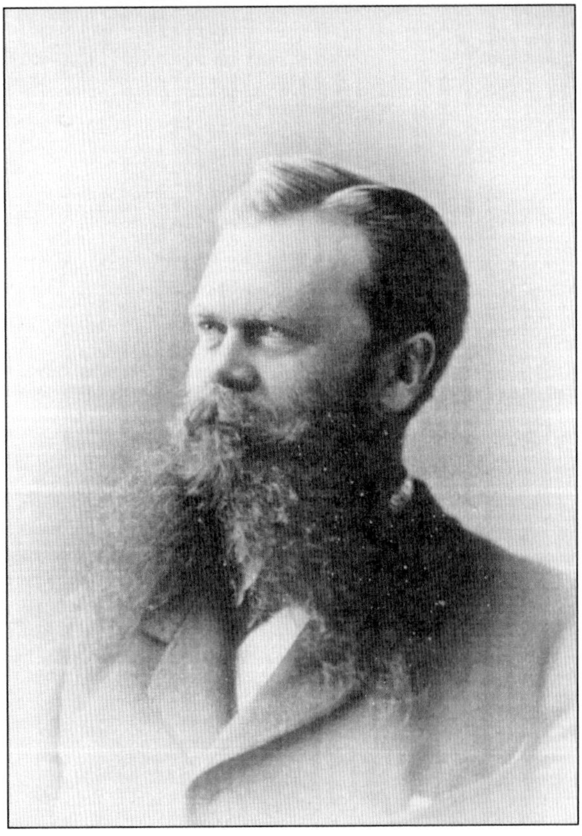

William Widgery Thomas of Portland probably looked something like this when he led the settlers to New Sweden. Named war consul to Sweden by Abraham Lincoln, Thomas fell in love with the country, married a Swedish girl, and felt that the Aroostook area was ideally suited for Swedes.

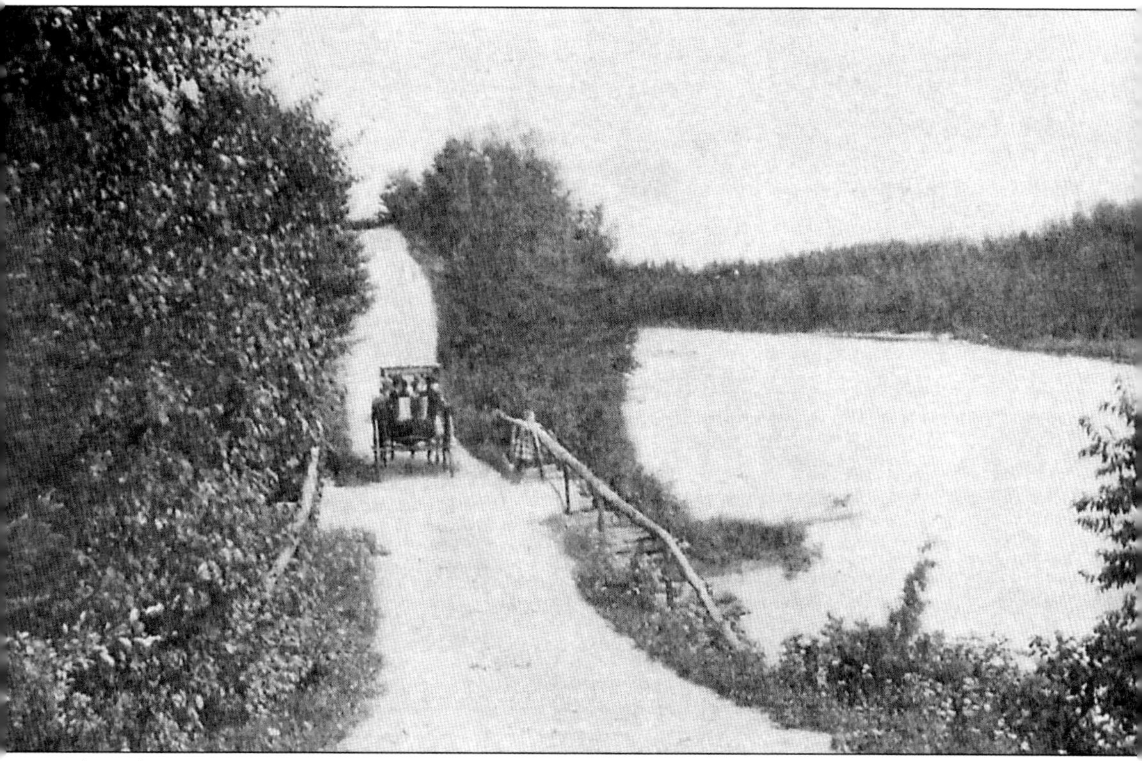

Madawaska Stream in Caribou about 1900. It was in this area that several New Brunswickers became the first settlers of Caribou.

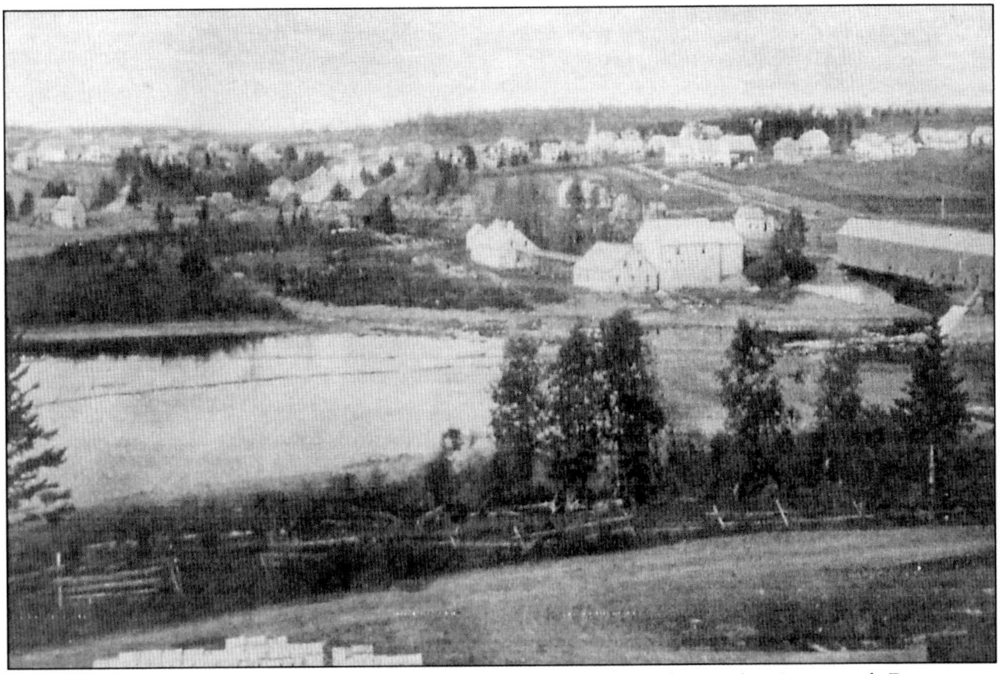

An early view of Caribou (before 1895). Caribou Stream flowed into the Aroostook River.

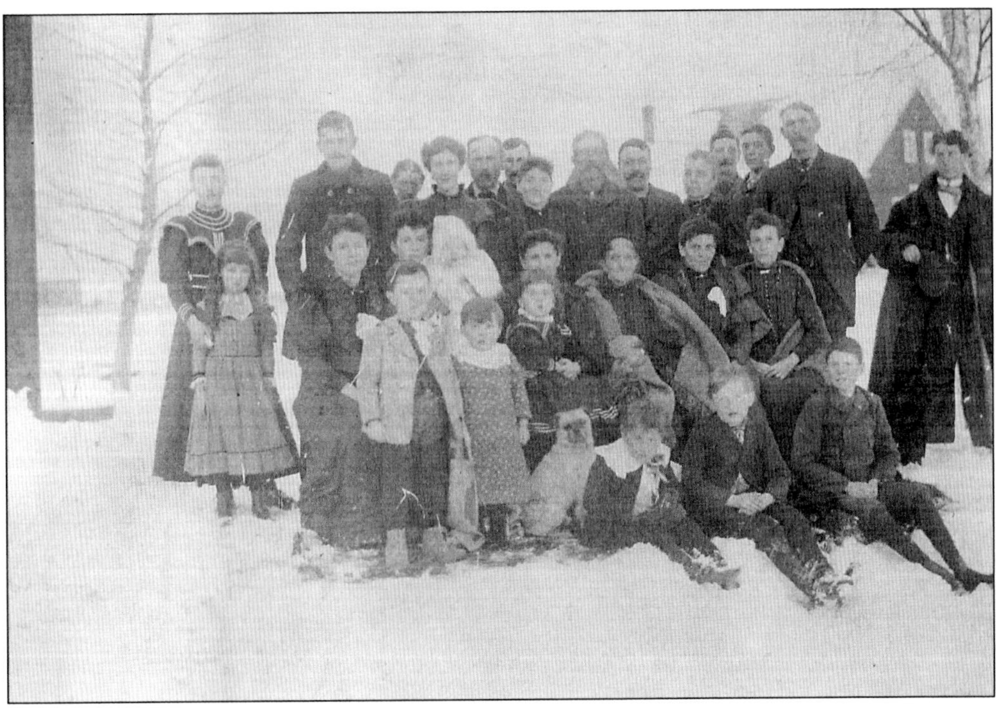

Thanksgiving on the old farm in Caribou in 1894.

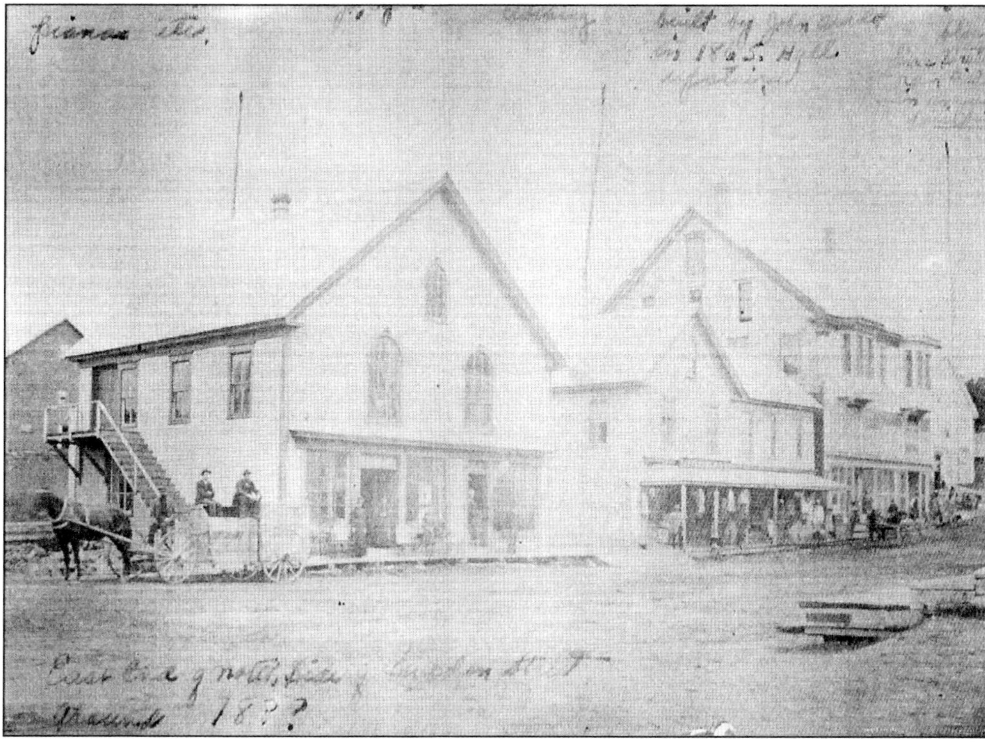

We go way back in Caribou. Sweden Street looked like this in the 1860s. A touch of the frontier?

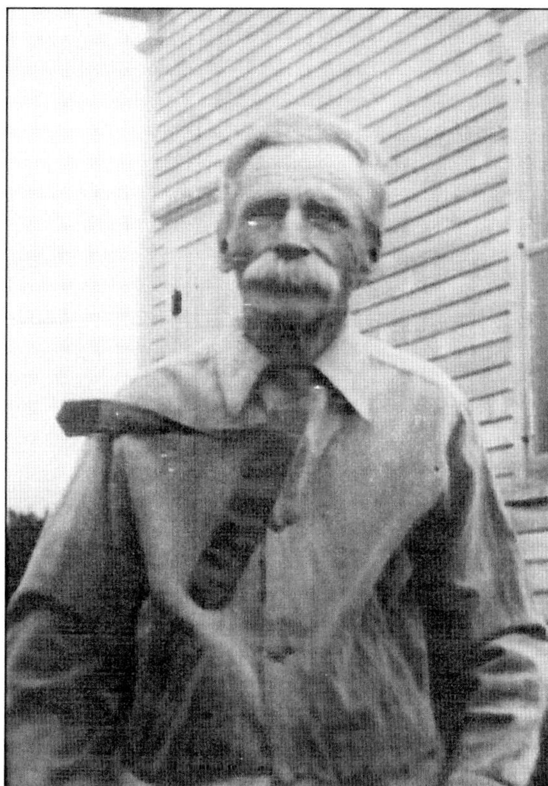

Israel Bodin, one of the first settlers of New Sweden.

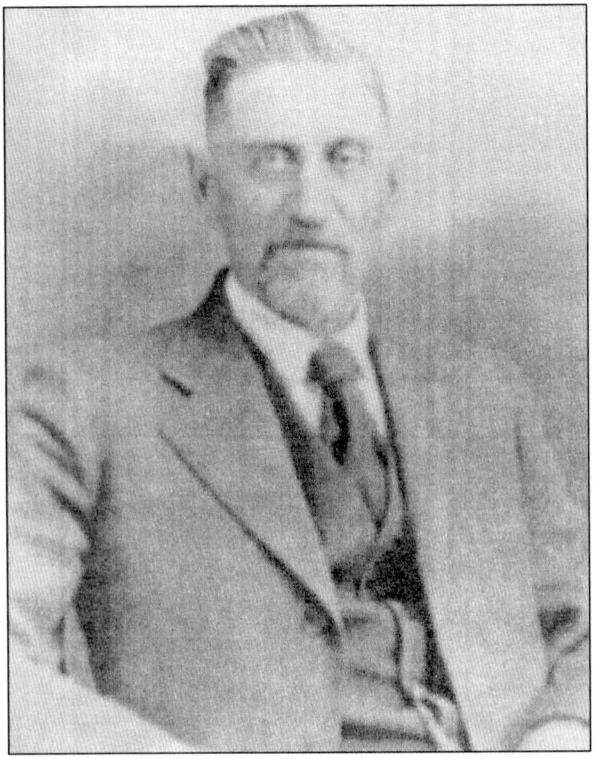

A frontier face—Lars Larsson ran a general store in the Jemptland section of New Sweden, was a first selectman and justice of the peace, and was treasurer of the Covenant for many years.

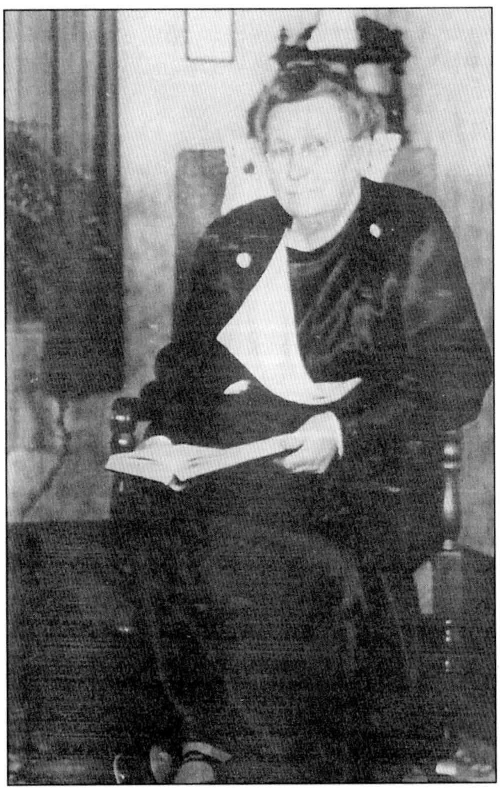

Mrs. Agnes Anderson, a daughter of Captain N.P. Clase of New Sweden. She was the last survivor of the first settlers.

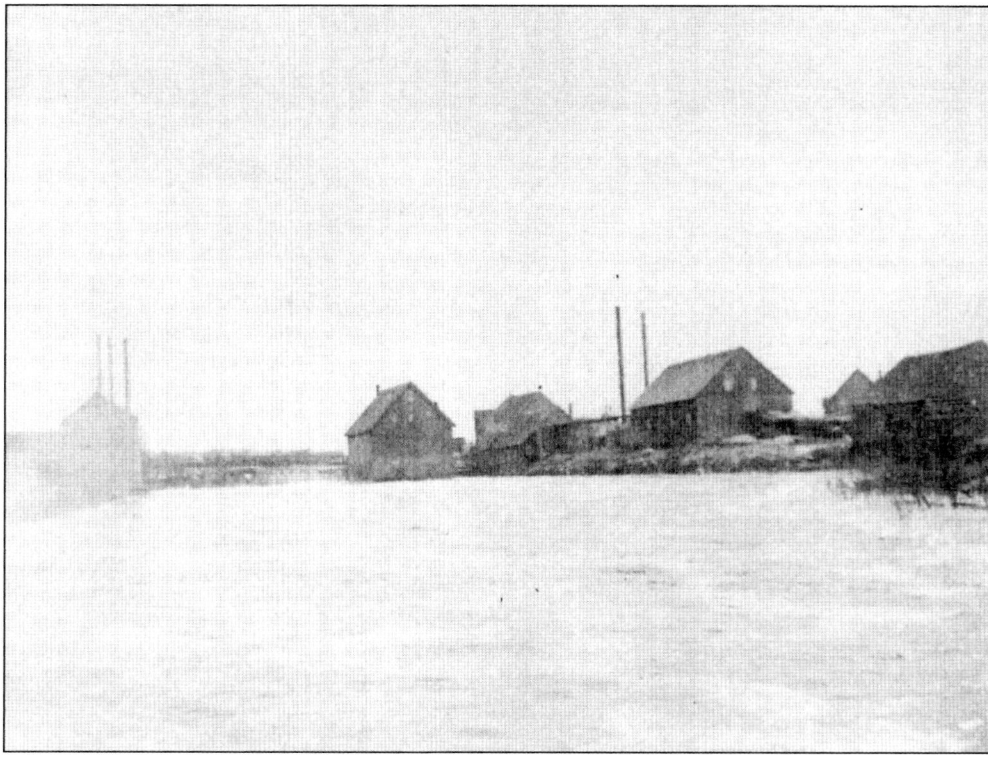

The Presque Isle mill dam about 1900, photographed from the first bridge. The starkness of the buildings seems to illustrate some of the loneliness of frontier life.

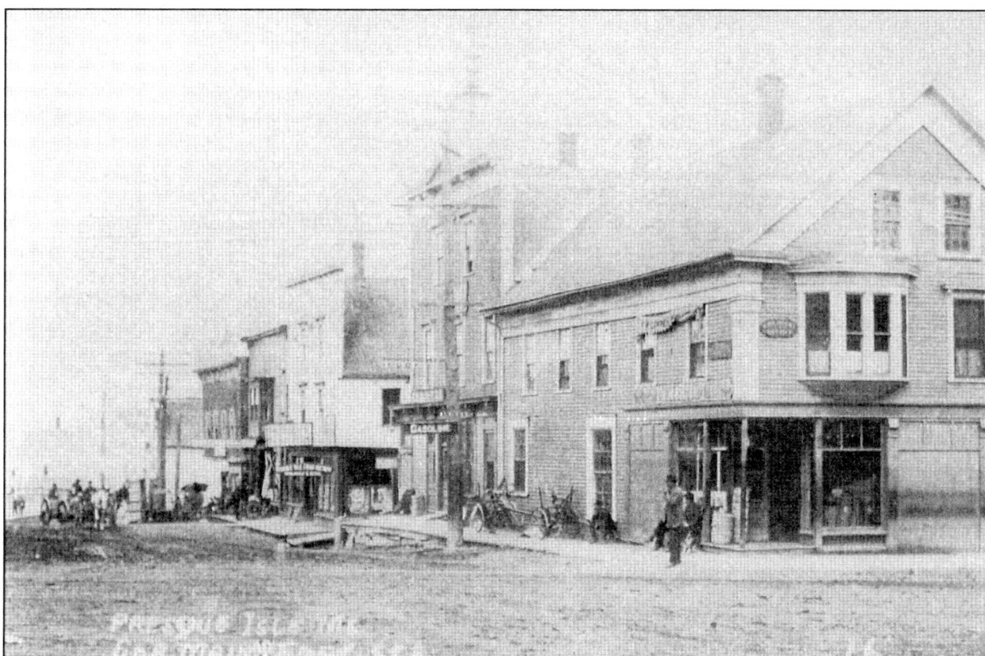

The frontier look was still there. This is the corner of State and Main Streets in Presque Isle about 1915. The old A.M. Smith Building is still standing.

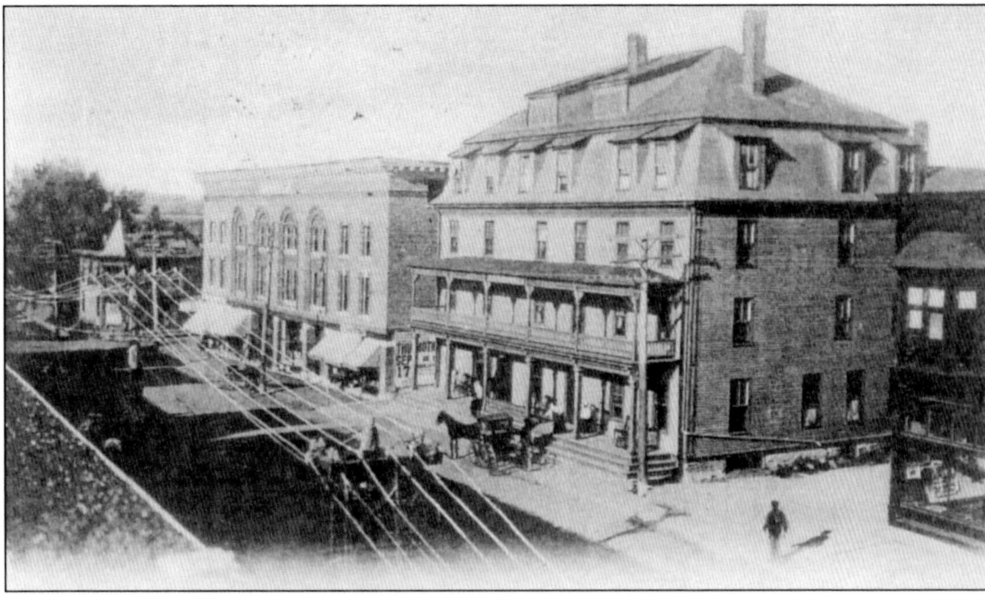

Another early Presque Isle view—the Presque Isle House and the Perry Block about 1900.

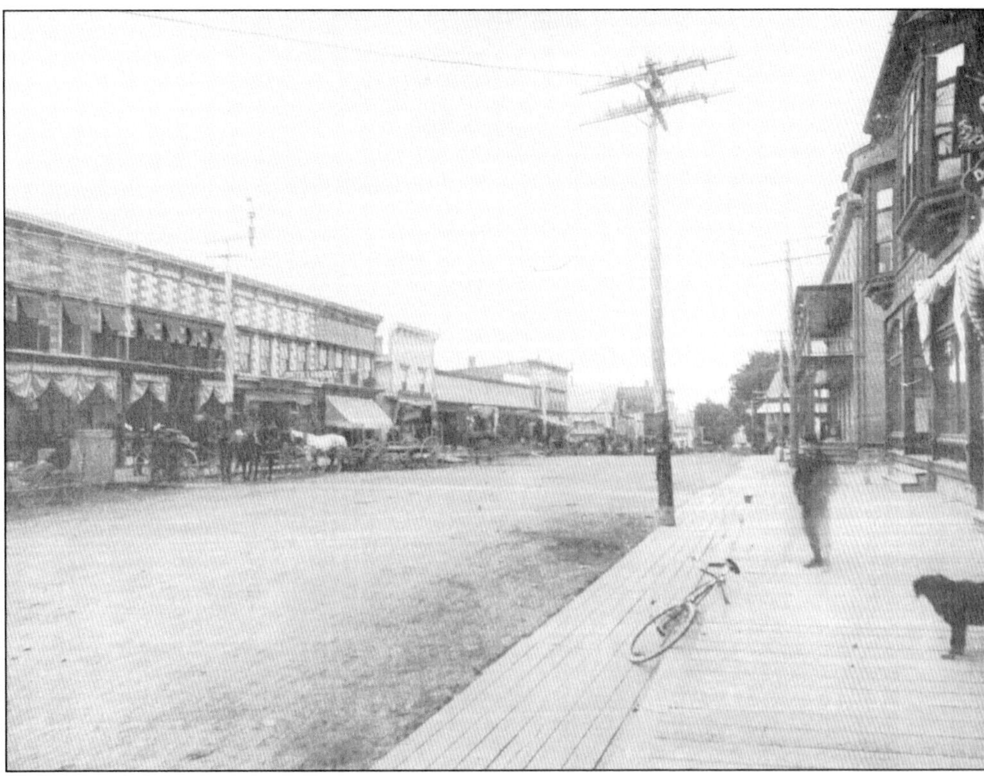

Main Street, Presque Isle, looking north, about 1900.

State Street and the Free Baptist Church clock tower about 1890. The clock tower was a local landmark for years.

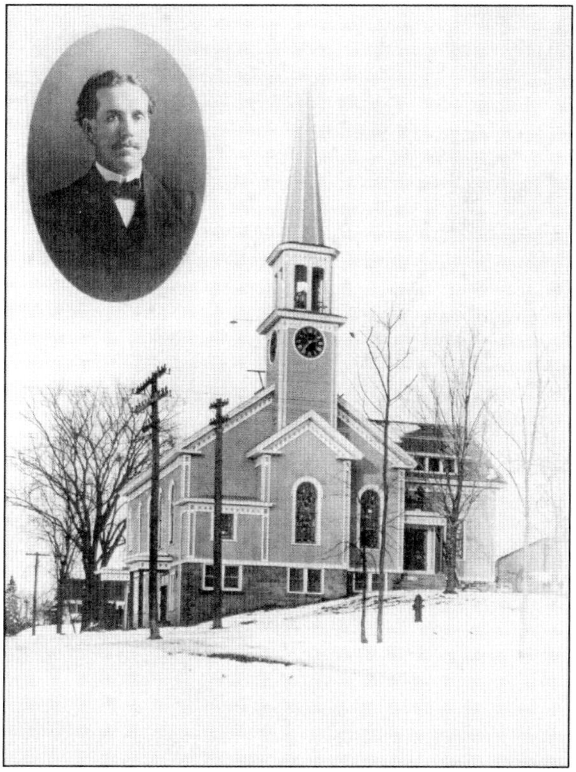

Another of the first houses in New Sweden. The settlers were quick to build better homes.

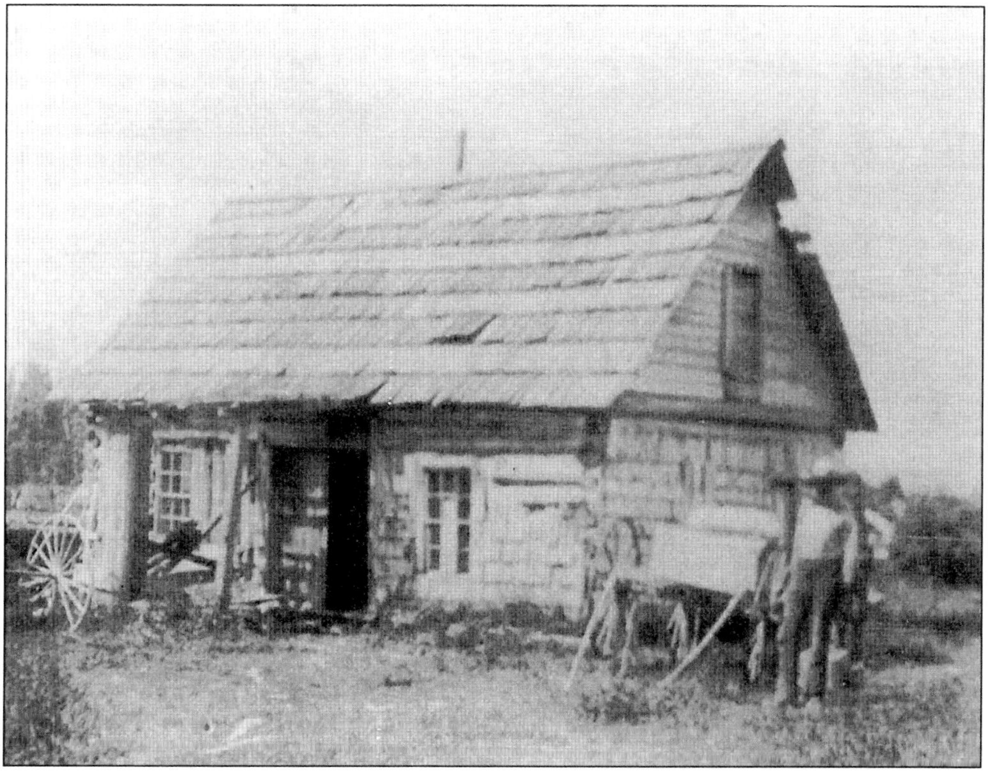

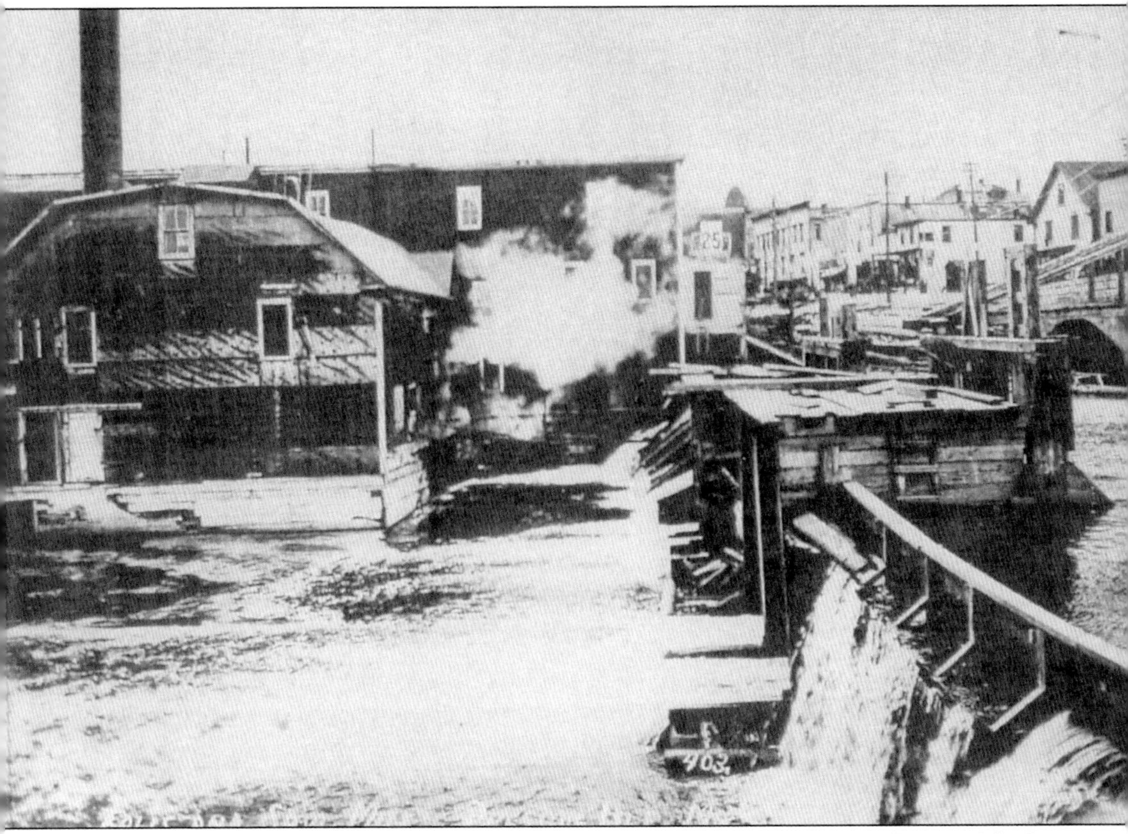

The lumber mill on the east bank of Presque Isle Stream at State Street in Presque Isle. It was operated by Charles F.A. Johnson and Thomas H. Phair until 1888, then by Arthur R. Gould as the Aroostook Lumber Co. until it burned in 1920. Lumbering was the principal business of the area until the potato industry took over after the Bangor and Aroostook Railroad came during 1894. Lumbering continues.

Two

A Difficult Environment

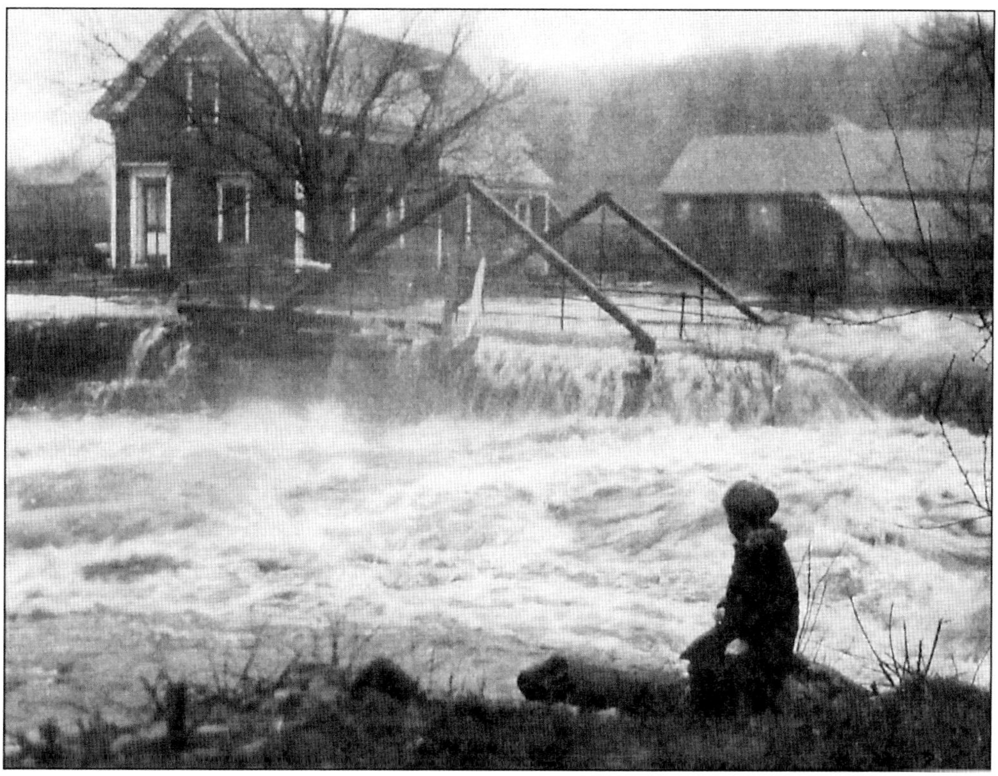

An Aroostook River flood in Caribou during the 1920s.

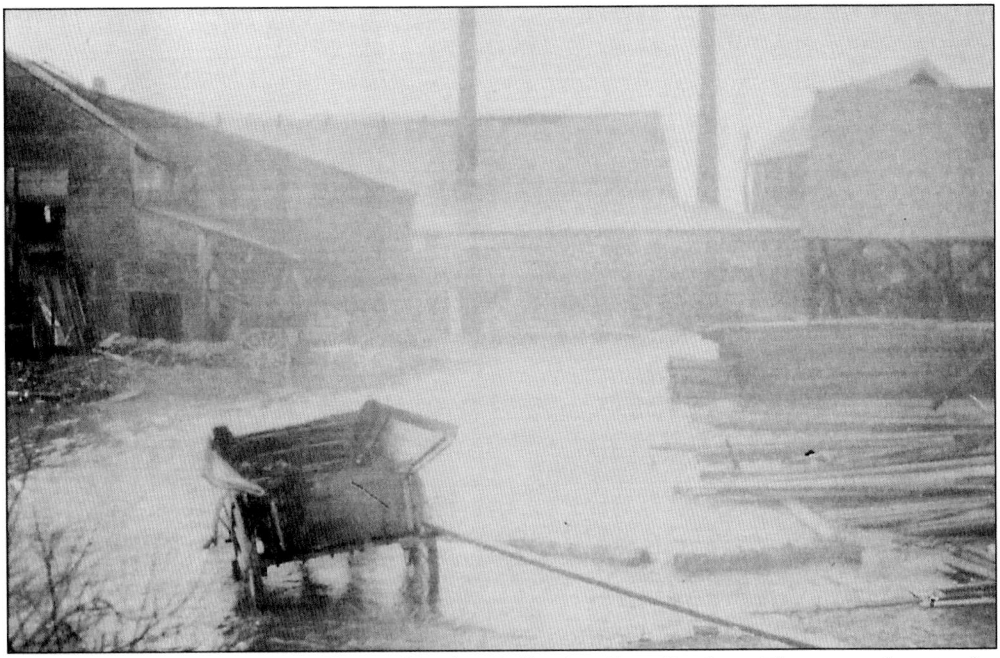

Another flood involving a mill, possibly the Collins' mill in Caribou. This was taken in the 1920s or earlier.

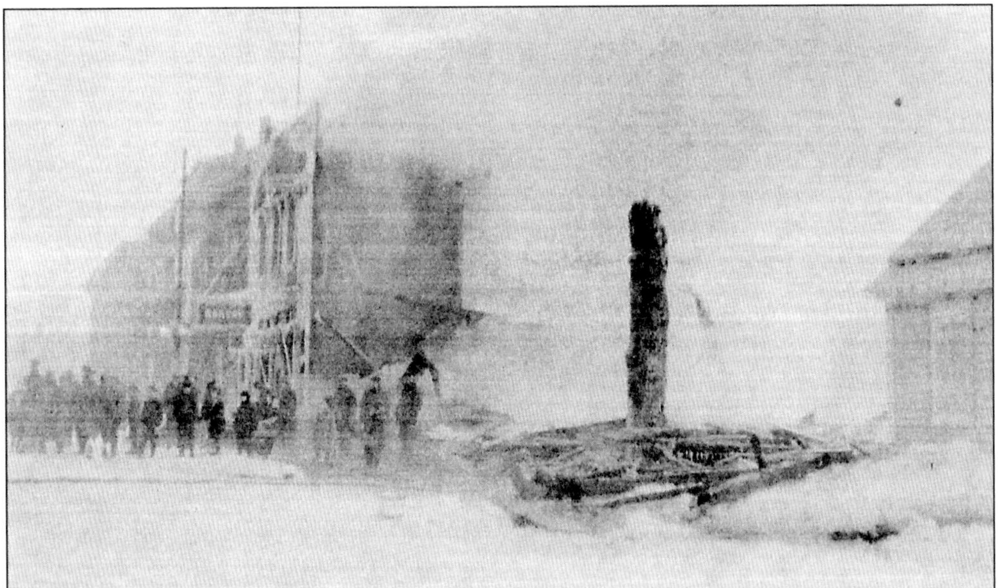

A very old shot of a fire in Caribou. The picture is so old that no other information was available.

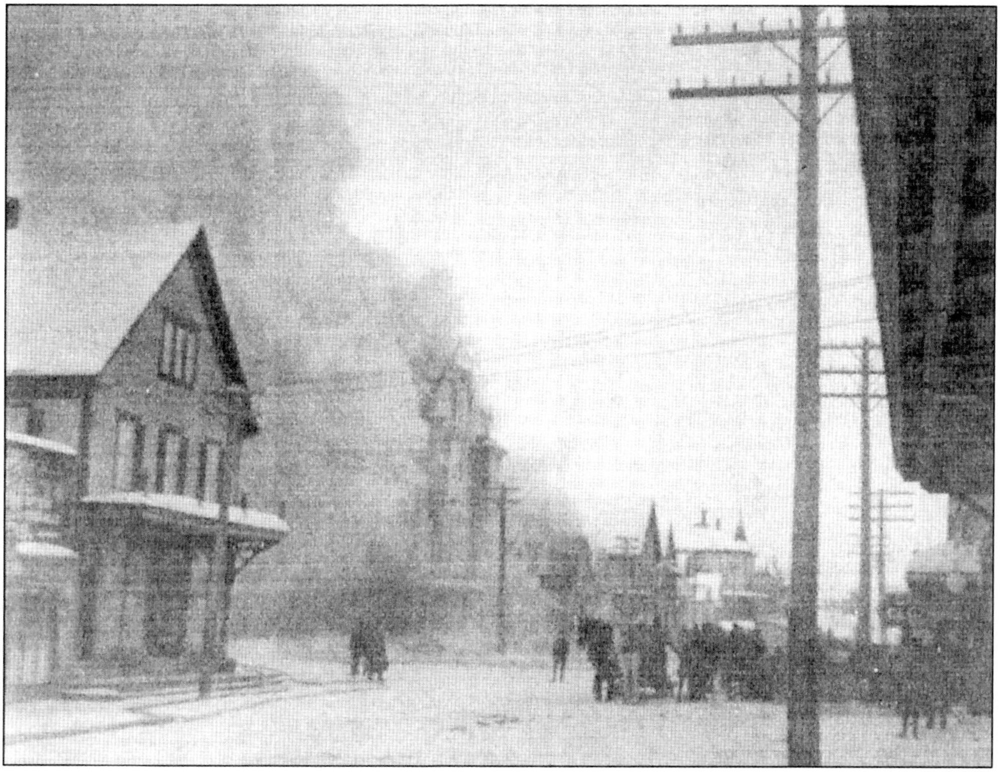

A fire on Sweden Street in Caribou in the 1920s or slightly earlier.

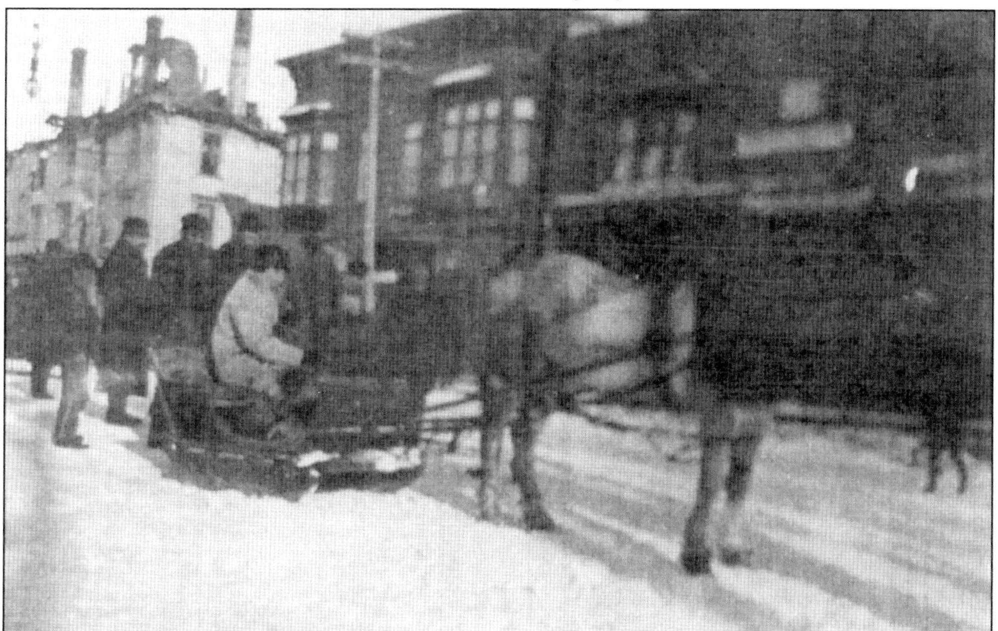

Thomas H. Phair, a prominent Presque Isle businessman, is pulled in a sled by his horse, Trotter, about 1900. Trotter, by the way, was trained to be a trotter in harness races but did the above when his racing days were over.

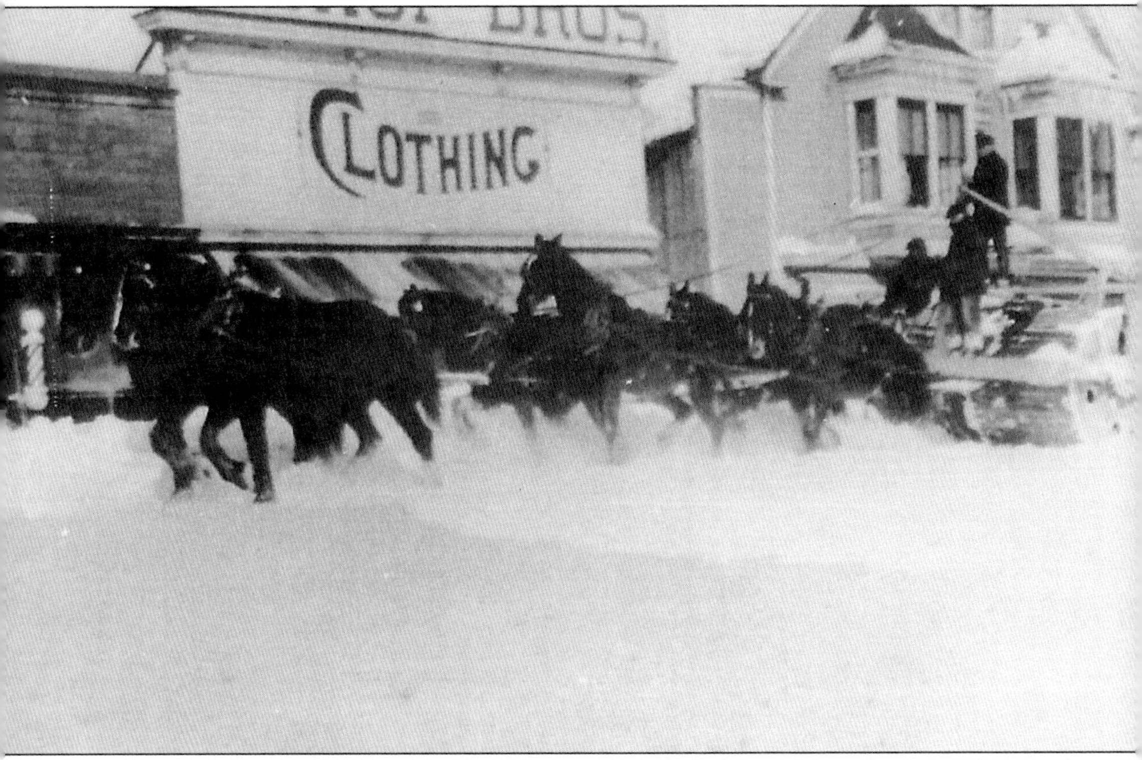

Yes, the winters could be conquered. Back in 1920, with the horse-drawn sleigh and sled popular, they packed down the snow instead of plowing it. The horse-drawn vehicles then ran on top of the hard snow. Note Bishop Bros. clothing store in this Caribou picture.

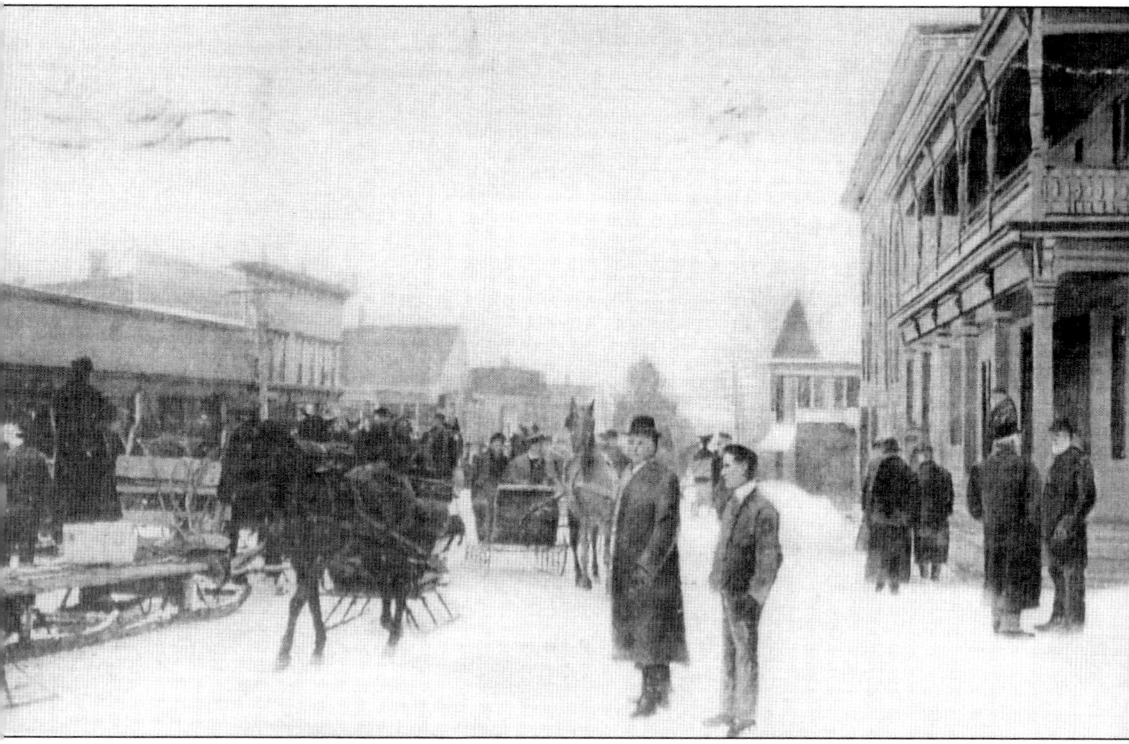

Main Street in Presque Isle about 1910. There are two sleighs with horses. Another sleigh, on the left, doesn't seem to have any horsepower attached. Without a doubt—the winters were long, cold, icy, and full of snow. But people adapted.

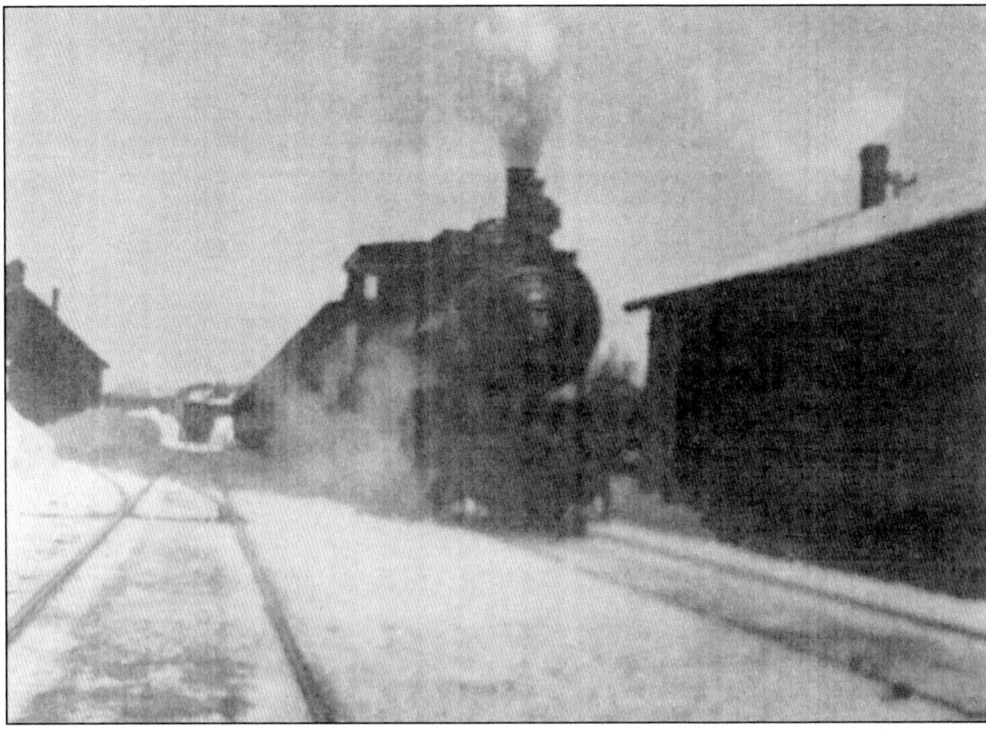

And the railroad came through all that snow. A Bangor and Aroostook train pulls into the Presque Isle station about 1900.

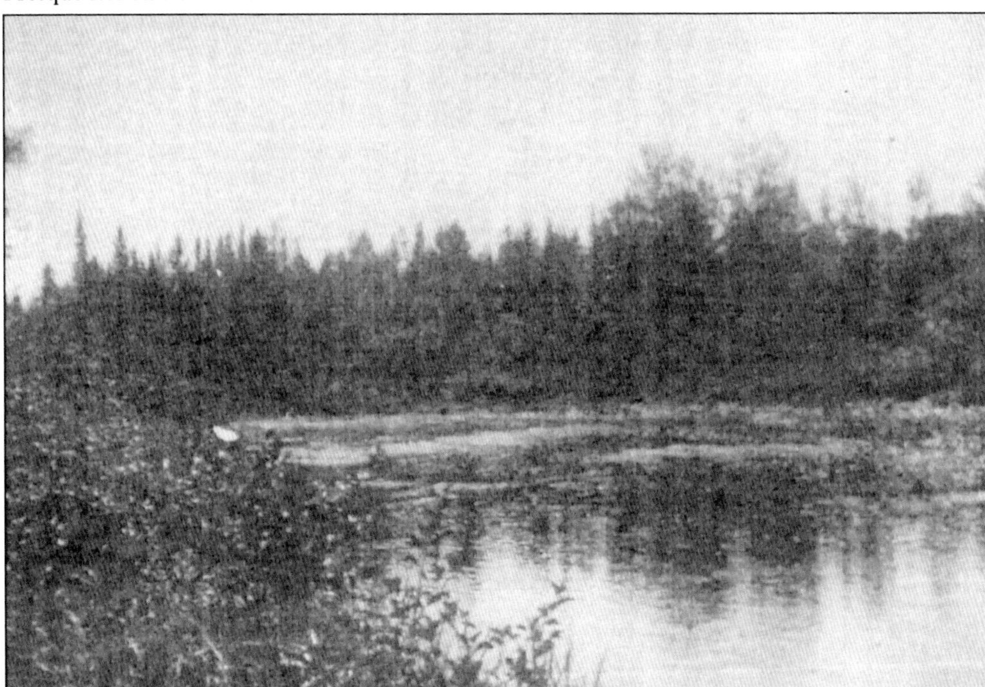

Sometimes, the environment could be both peaceful and beautiful. Presque Isle Stream in Presque Isle was just that about 1900. In flood season, it was a different story.

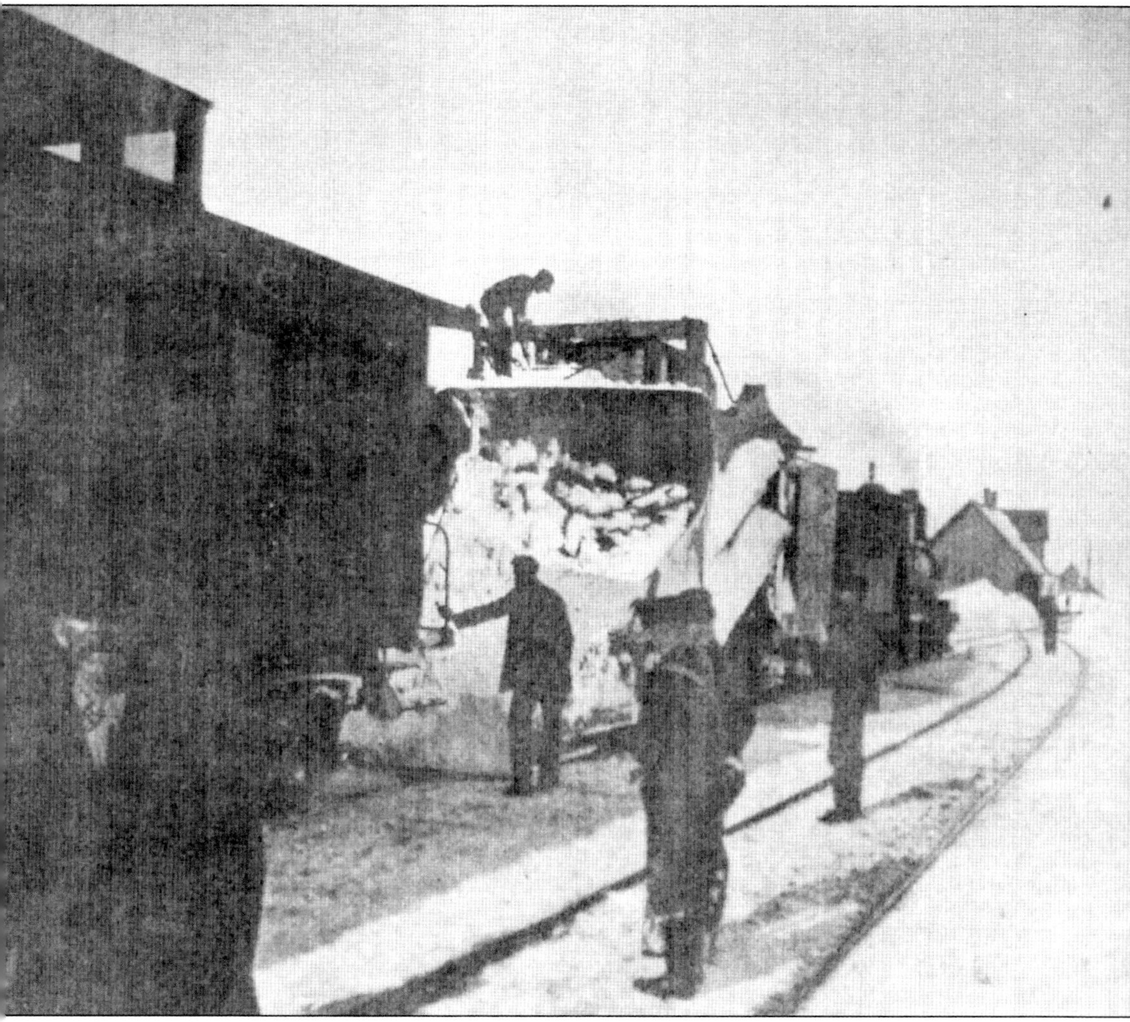

Another way the railroad controlled the snow: the Canadian Pacific Railroad shows off a wing snowplow about 1900 near Academy Street in Presque Isle.

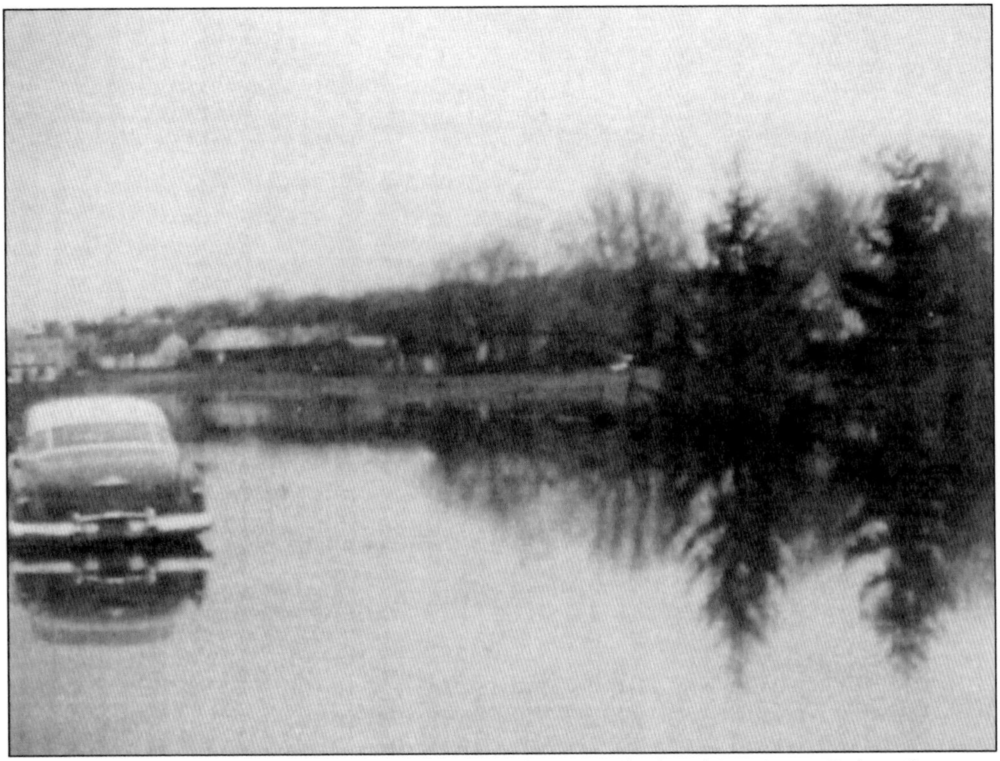

A car belonging to a neighbor of the Smart family sits parked and lonely on Bishop Street in Presque Isle during a 1954 flood.

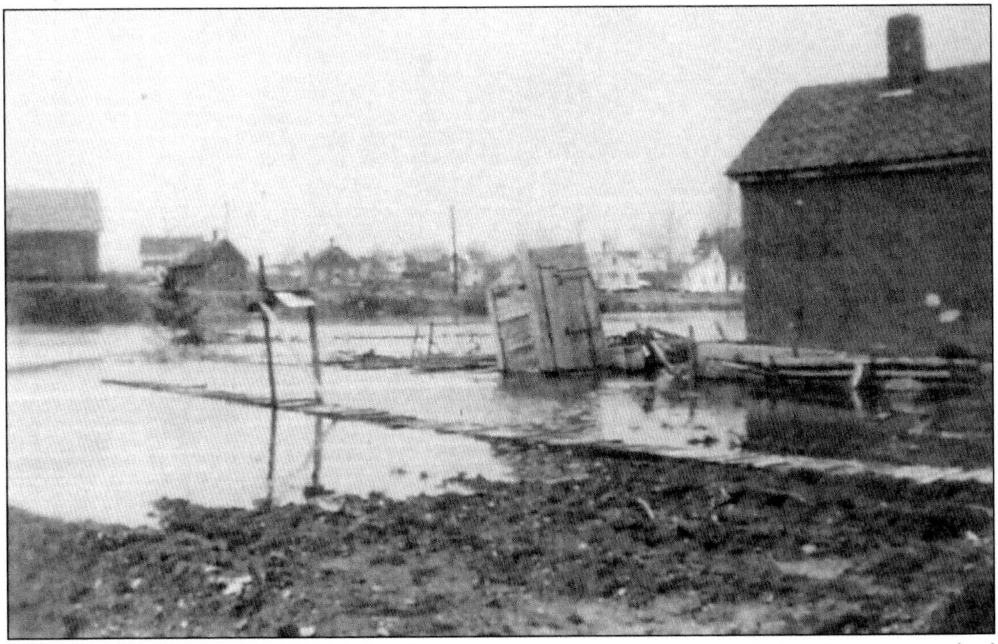

Floods can do strange things. This one-hole outhouse or backhouse on Bishop Street was tilted by a 1950s flood. It continued in use after the flood subsided although the tilt remained. Its owner was Clifford L'Italian.

Three

Fun and Recreation

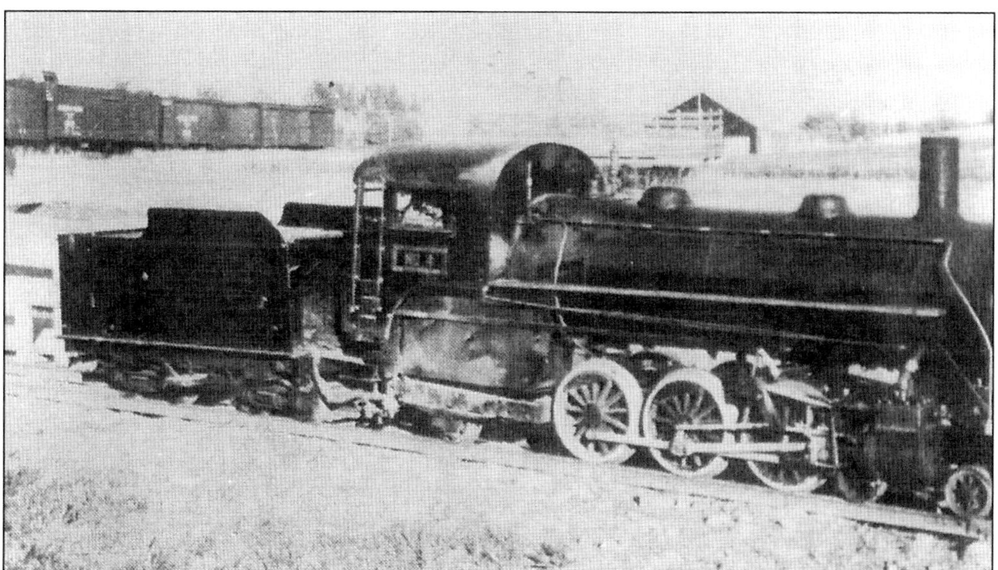

You adapted to the snow. You enjoyed the snow. A miniature locomotive on Sweden Street hauls visitors to the Caribou Winter Carnival, possibly in the 1920s.

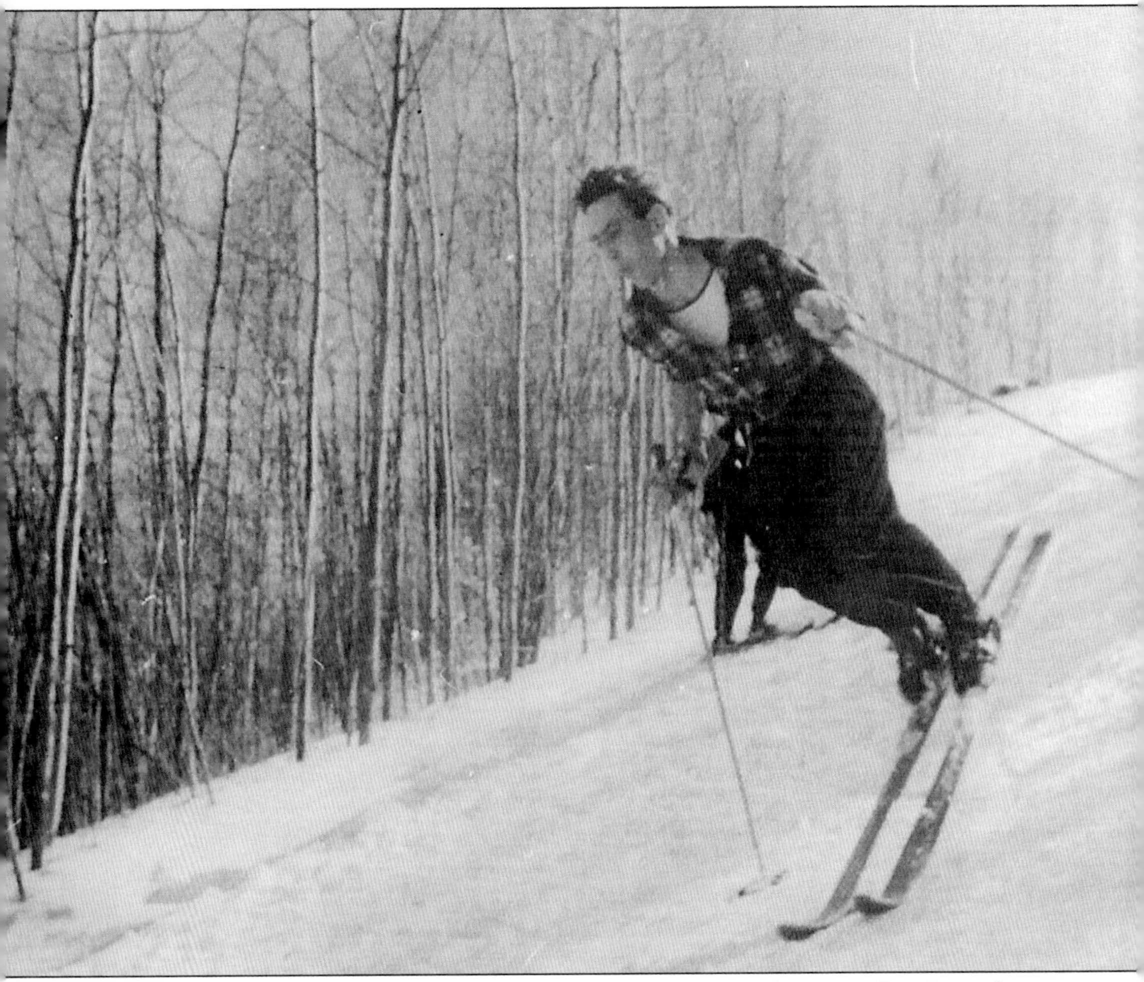

Ah, the skiing! Jim Briggs of Caribou shows how it was done in the 1940s. Ezra James Briggs was for many years one of the leading state legislators and environmentalists in the area. Many of his environmentalist battles were successful, even though his area, with its many farmers, was not in the forefront of Maine's environmental movement.

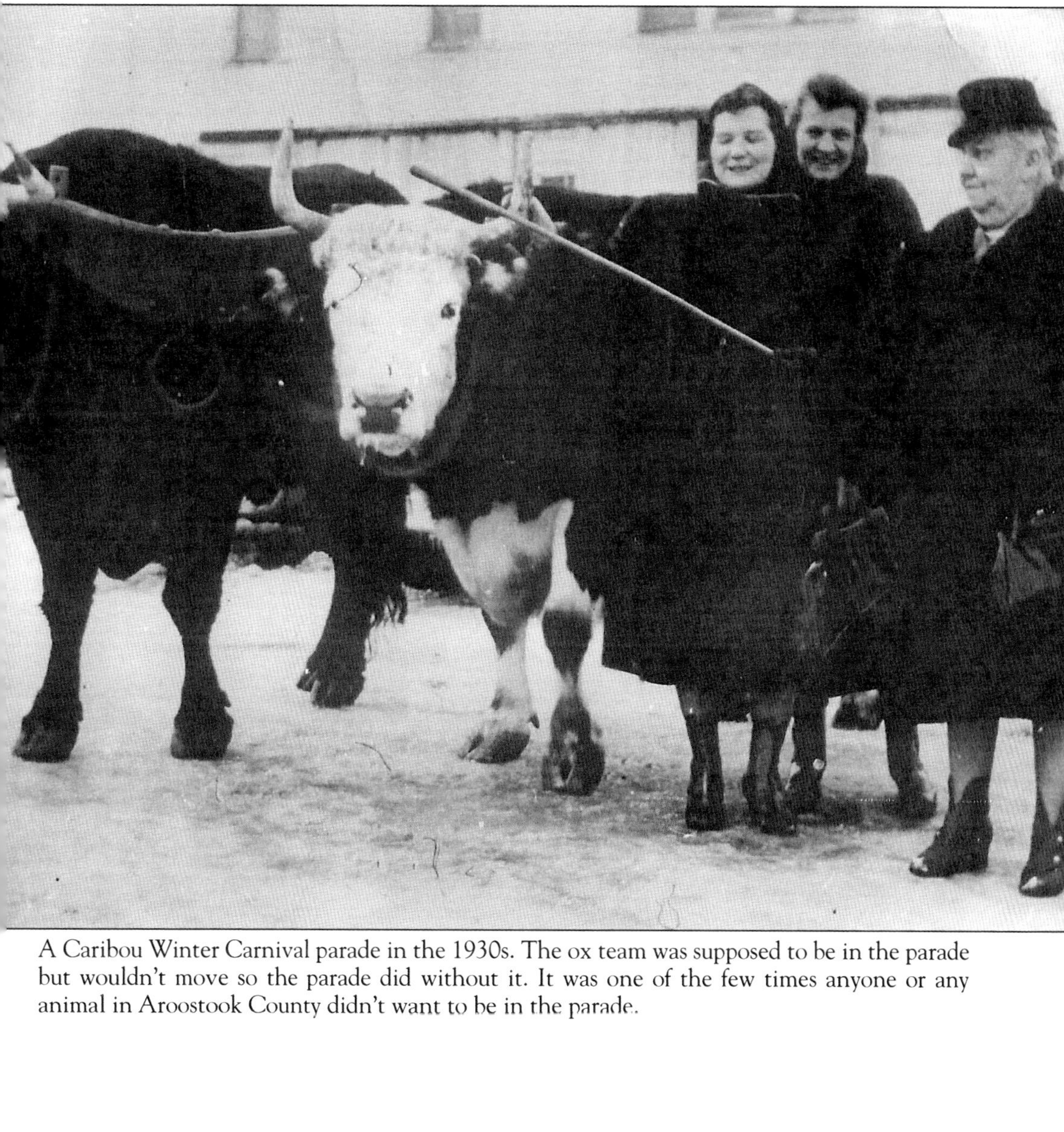

A Caribou Winter Carnival parade in the 1930s. The ox team was supposed to be in the parade but wouldn't move so the parade did without it. It was one of the few times anyone or any animal in Aroostook County didn't want to be in the parade.

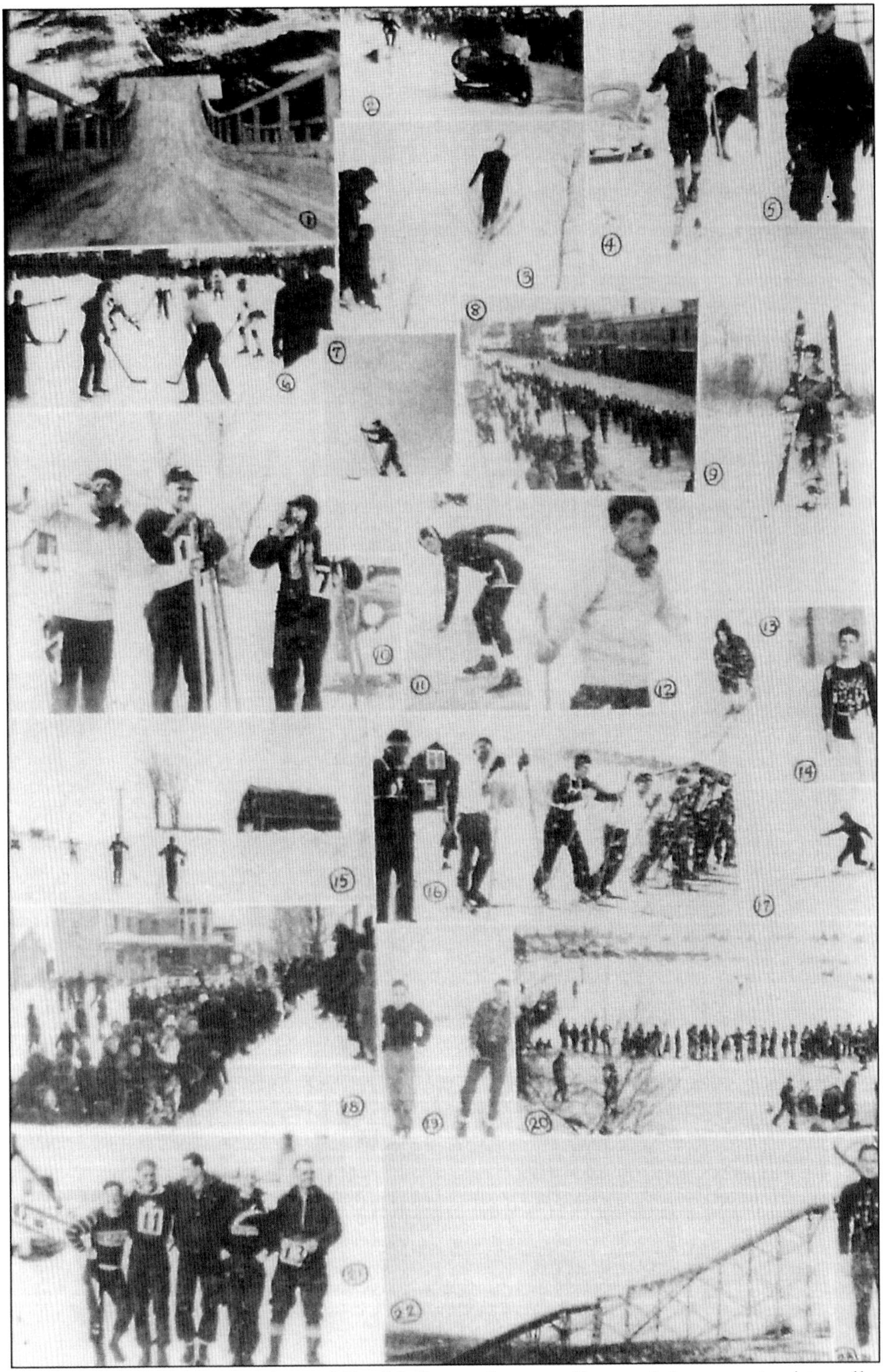

The Caribou Winter Carnival was full of different features. Some of them are in this collage. The diversity of winter sports and events was only exceeded by the Swedes living in the New Sweden-Stockholm-Westmanland section of Aroostook.

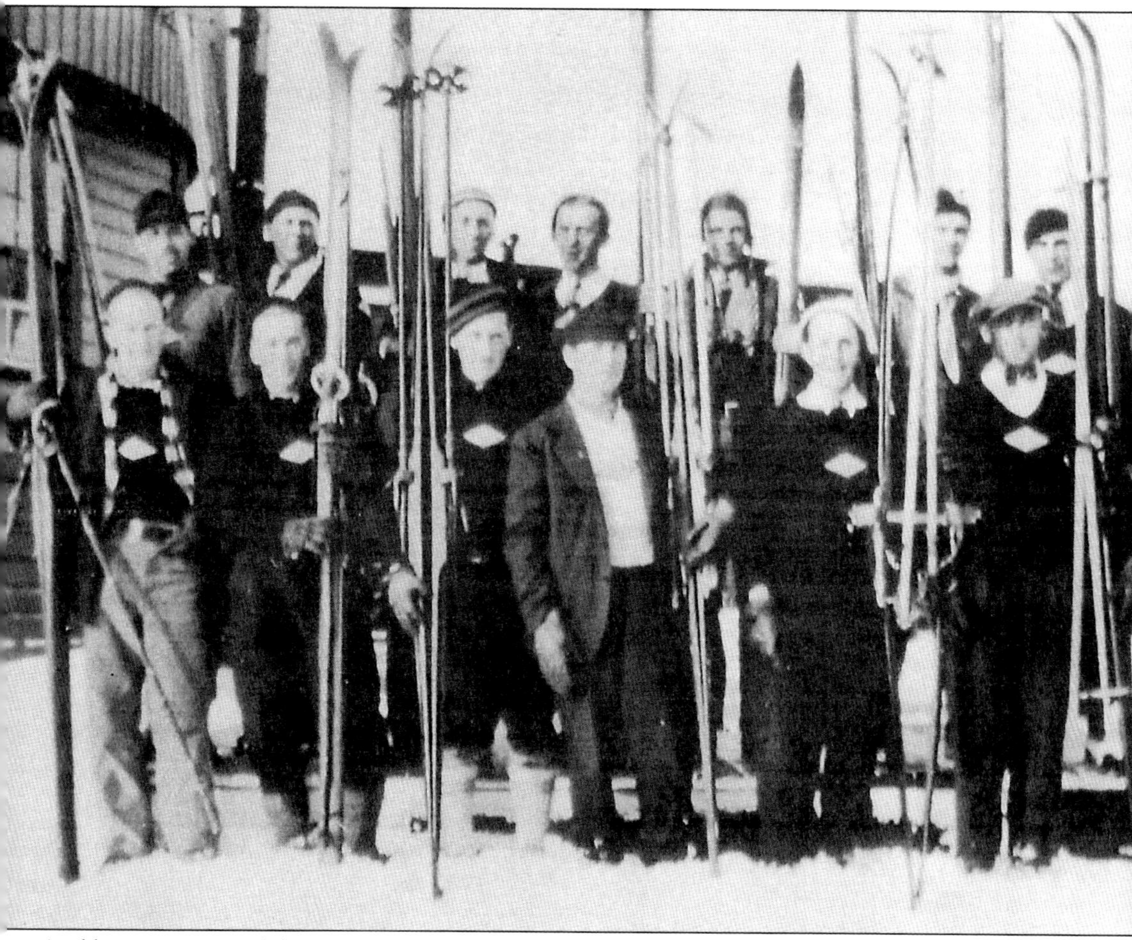

And here are some of those New Sweden skiers. Every February, a group of cross-country skiers from Bangor skied the 175 or more miles to visit the New Sweden group. The New Sweden skiers were, left to right: (front) Ernest Anderson, Ralph Anderson, Egon Espling, Carl Johnson, Bob Johnson, and Arvid Jacobson; (rear) Arne Menton, Henry Anderson, Raymond Peterson, George Anderson, Gustaf Ekman, Allen Kampe, Sr., and Evald Anderson.

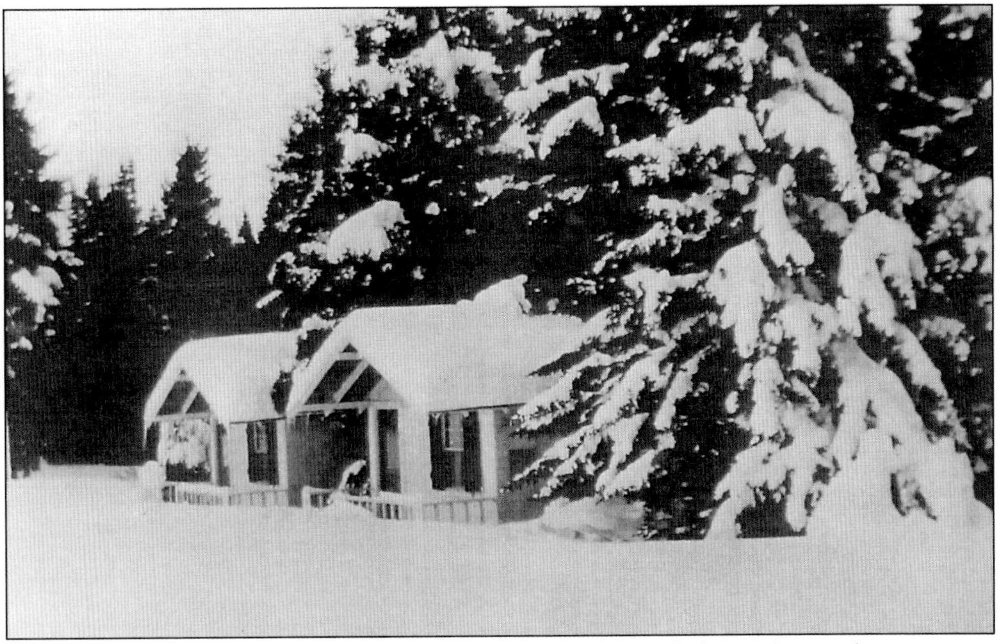

Harry Anderson's cabins in New Sweden housed some of those skiers who came up from Bangor.

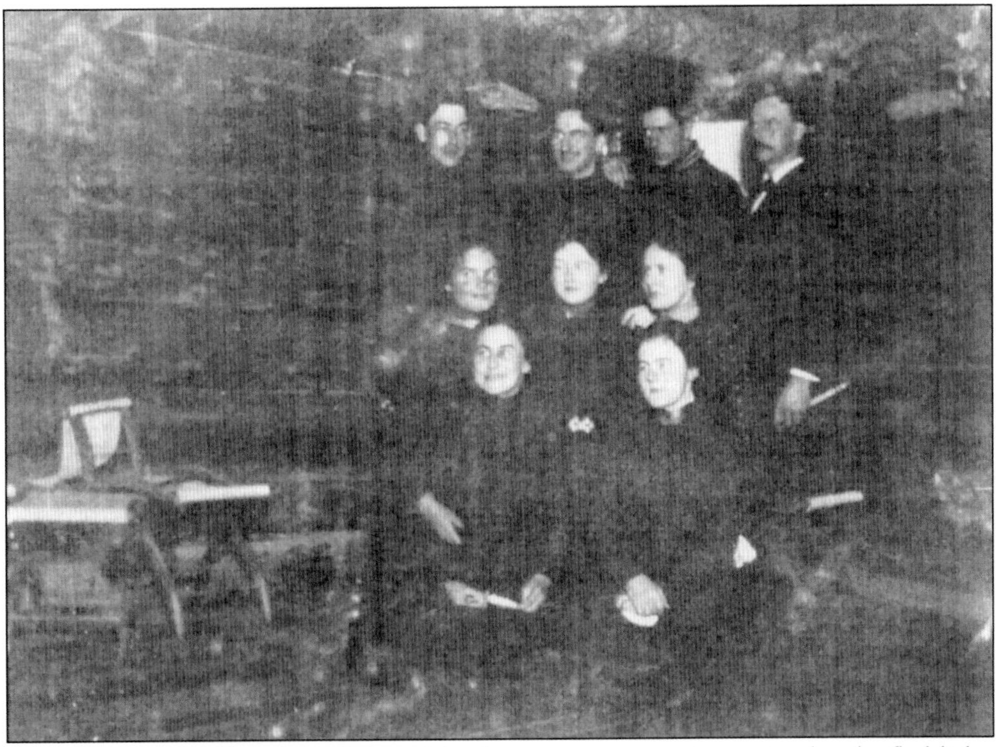

At another camp, Hayden's in Presque Isle, faces peer out as a picture is taken by flashlight. There are nine in the group in this c. 1900 photograph. We know Charlotte Collins in the second row (left) and Mabel Barker next to her.

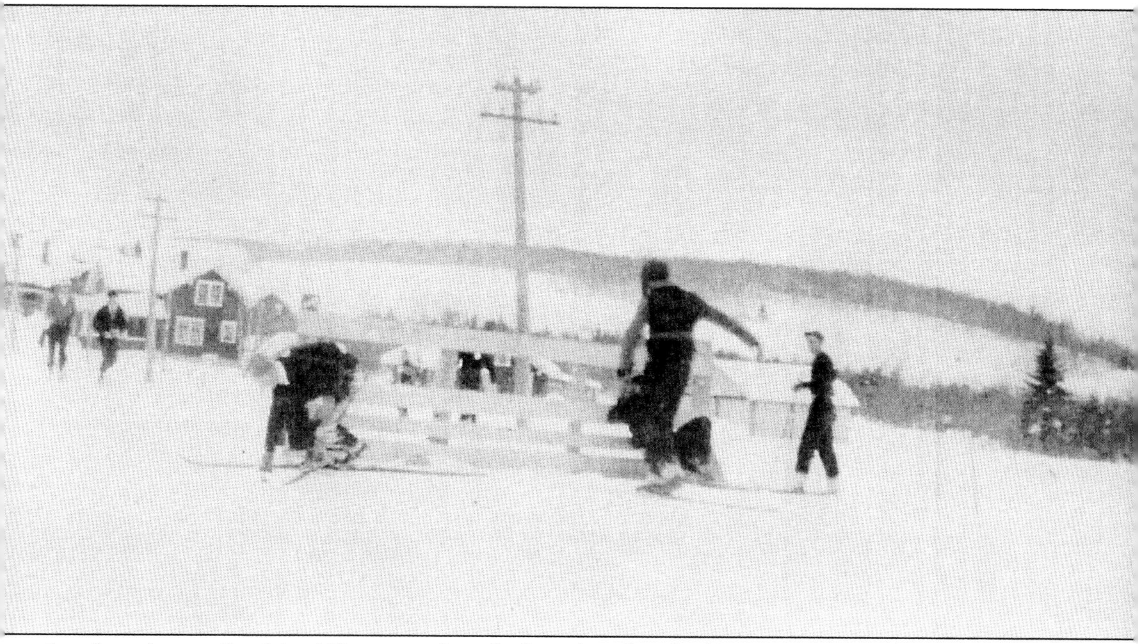

An obstacle race for skiers? I've never heard of one but they had 'em in New Sweden. This was opposite Johnson's Garage, probably sometime in the 1930s. You crawled through the obstacles, jumped over them, or just did the best you could. This is one example of the diversity of winter sports that came to Aroostook County and Maine with the Swedes. Maine hasn't yet capitalized on all of them.

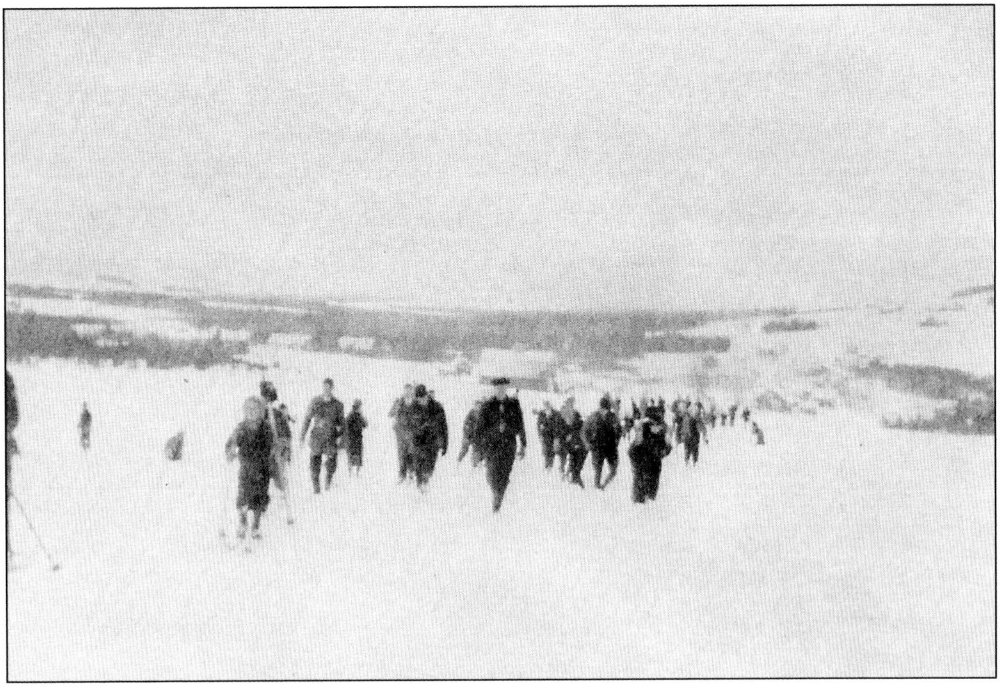

Are the ski jumpers coming or going from Ringdahl Hill in New Sweden in this 1920s or 1930s photograph? Who can tell? Compare this with the next picture. Swedes, of course, are probably the world's leading ski jumpers.

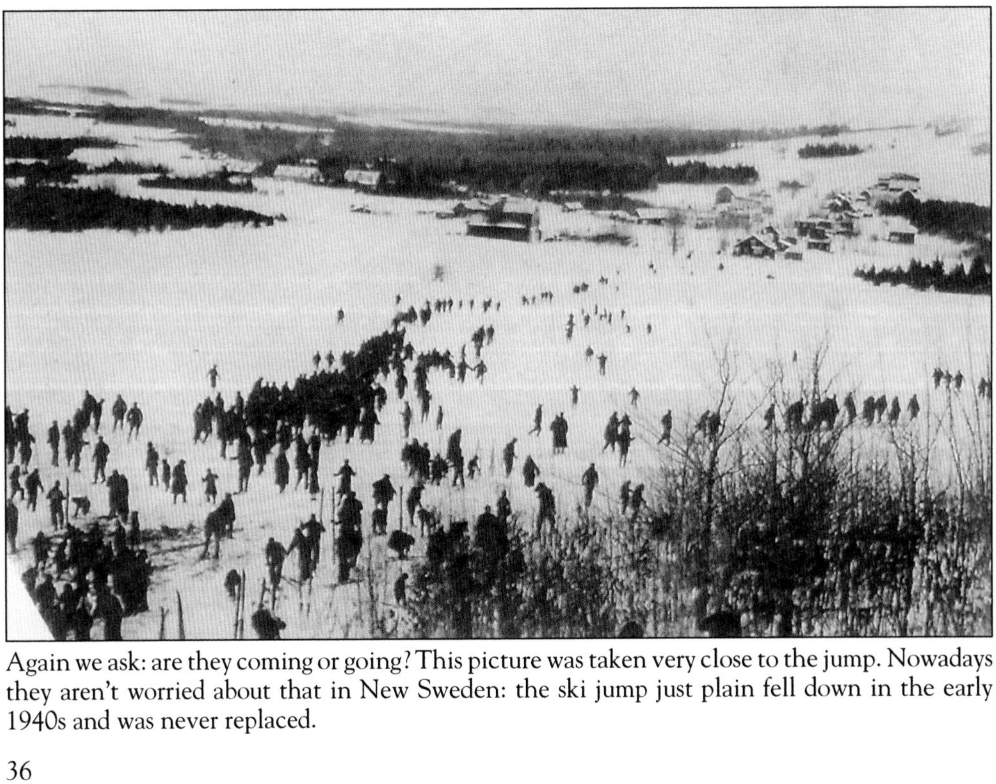

Again we ask: are they coming or going? This picture was taken very close to the jump. Nowadays they aren't worried about that in New Sweden: the ski jump just plain fell down in the early 1940s and was never replaced.

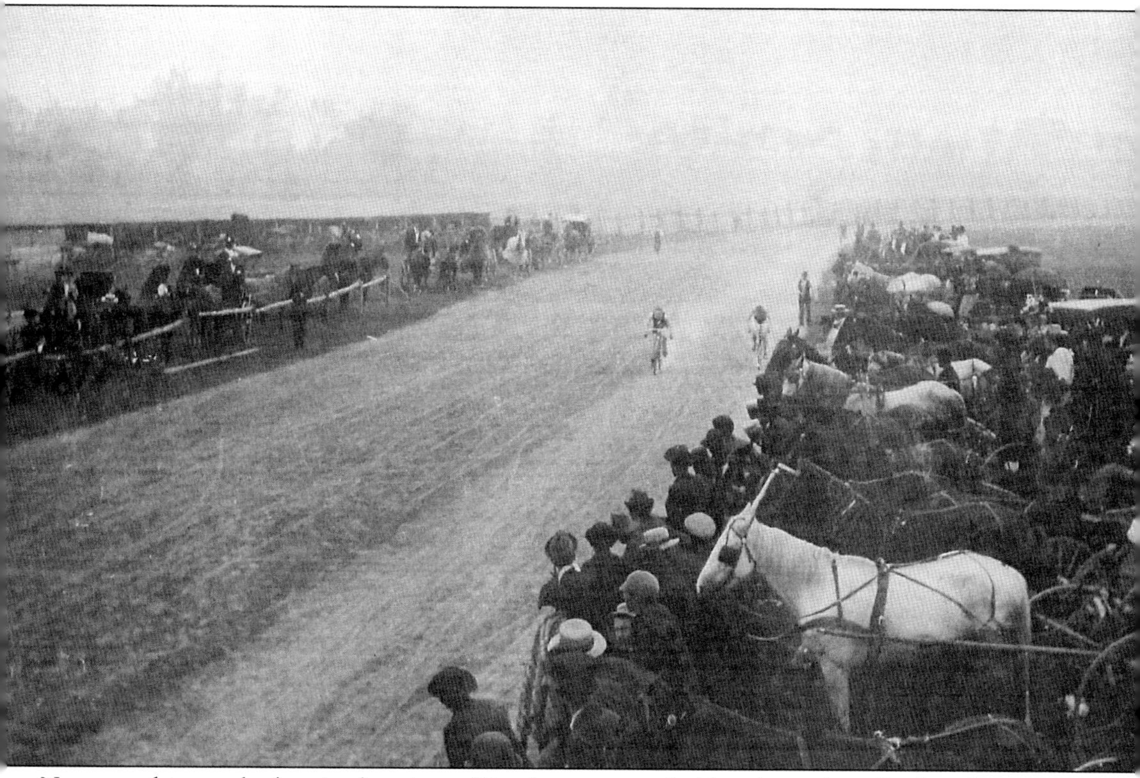

Not everything took place in the winter. Bicycle races were held at the park in Caribou during the 1890s. This photograph was taken in the dead of summer. Unfortunately, the bicycle races didn't survive. They petered out just as the six-day, twelve-day, and other races did in this country's cities in the late 1930s. But there's still plenty of bike riding in the area and in Aroostook County, and even a bit of racing.

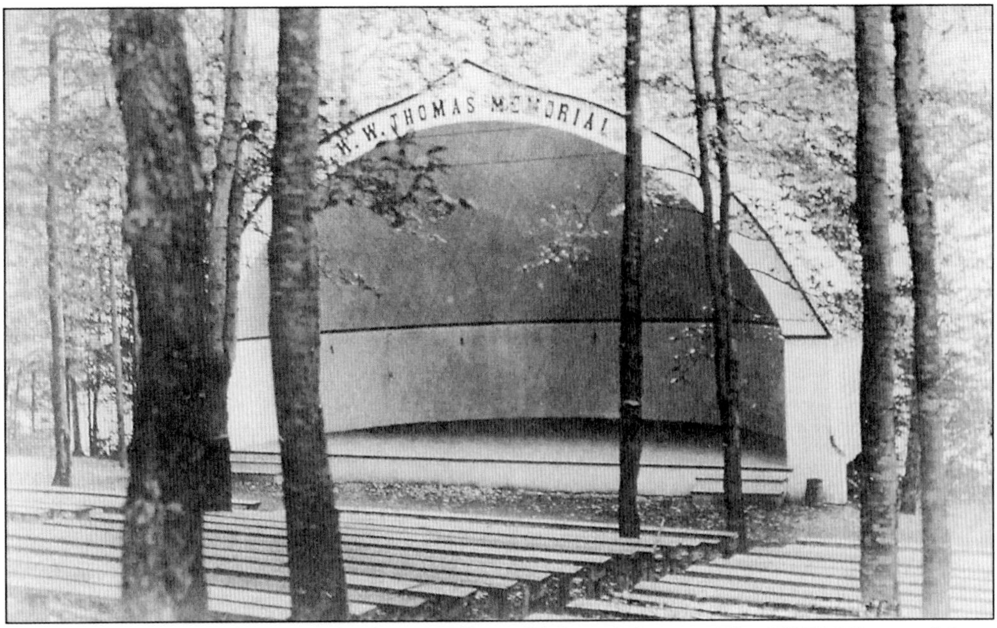

New Sweden received many gifts from William Widgery Thomas. The W.W. Thomas Music Bowl was erected in 1937. It is still used and has some of the best acoustics around.

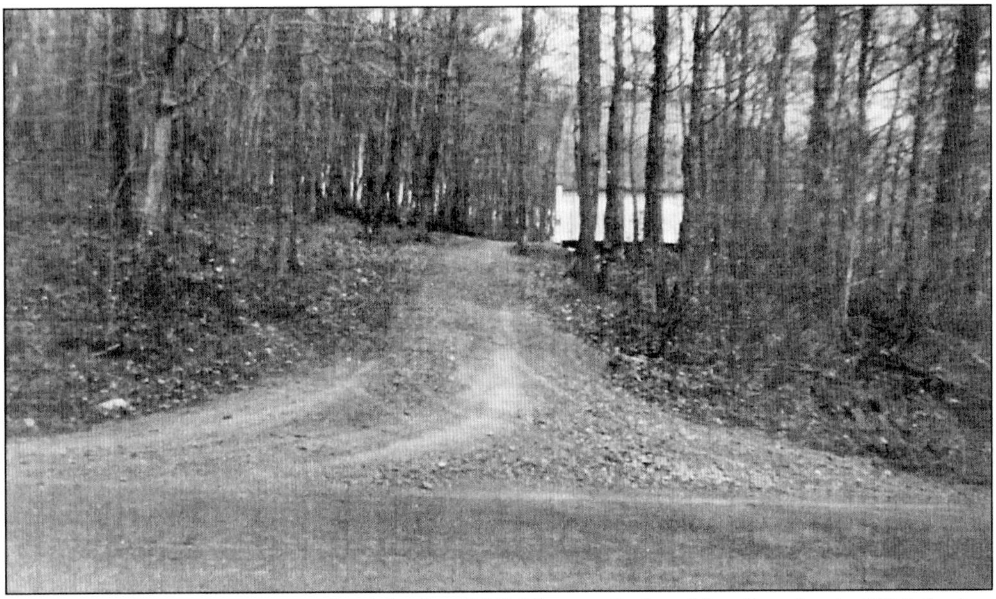

William Widgery Thomas gave land for the W.W. Thomas Park in New Sweden in 1920. It also, of course, is still in use.

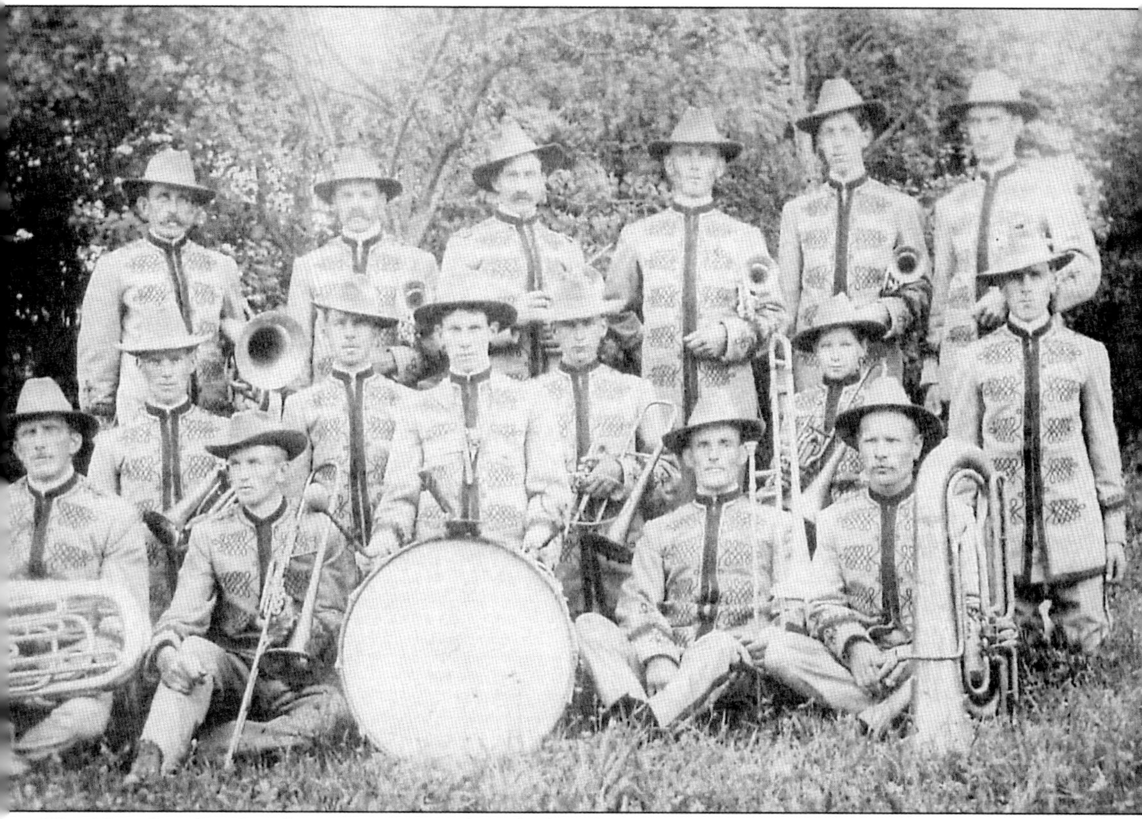

The New Sweden Band was in existence long before the W.W. Thomas Music Bowl was built but has played there ever since 1937. In this picture are, from the left: (standing) Andrew Nelson, Edward Anderson, Leader Alfred Strobeck, Arthur Anderson, Walter Hedman, and Joseph Pearson; (sitting) Peter Viberg, Isiah Stadig, Axel Trone, Henning Trone, Drummer Harry Rogers, Albert Sealander, Gustaf Stadig, Herbert Uppling, John Uppling, and Nels Lundin.

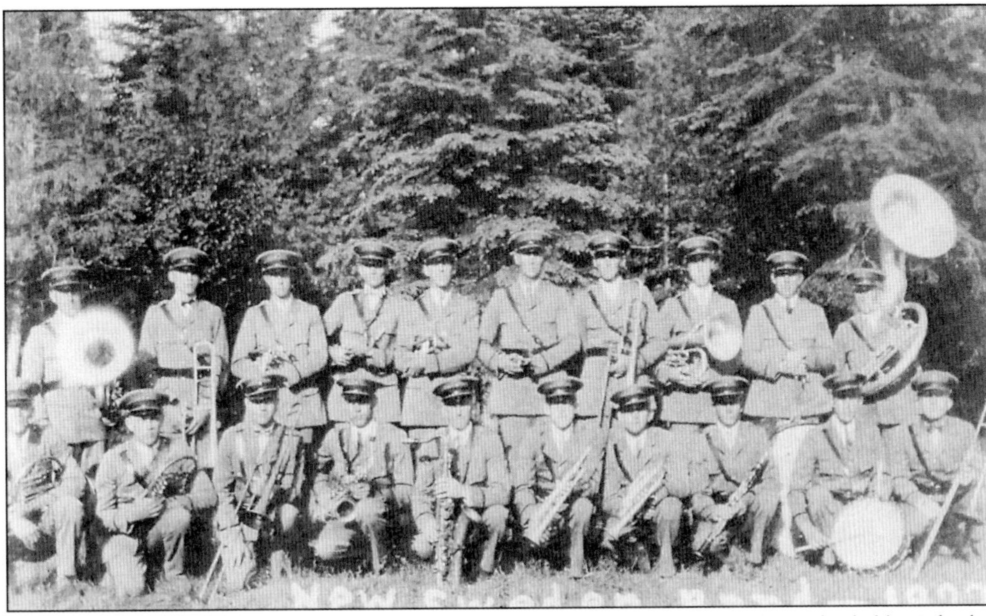

And here is the 1927 New Sweden Band. It included: (first row, fourth from the left) Malcolm Peterson, and (four more over) Melvin Anderson; (second row, starting behind Malcolm) George Lindsten, Walter Hedman, Henry Anderson, Evald Anderson, Clifford Anderson, unknown, and Olaf Stenson.

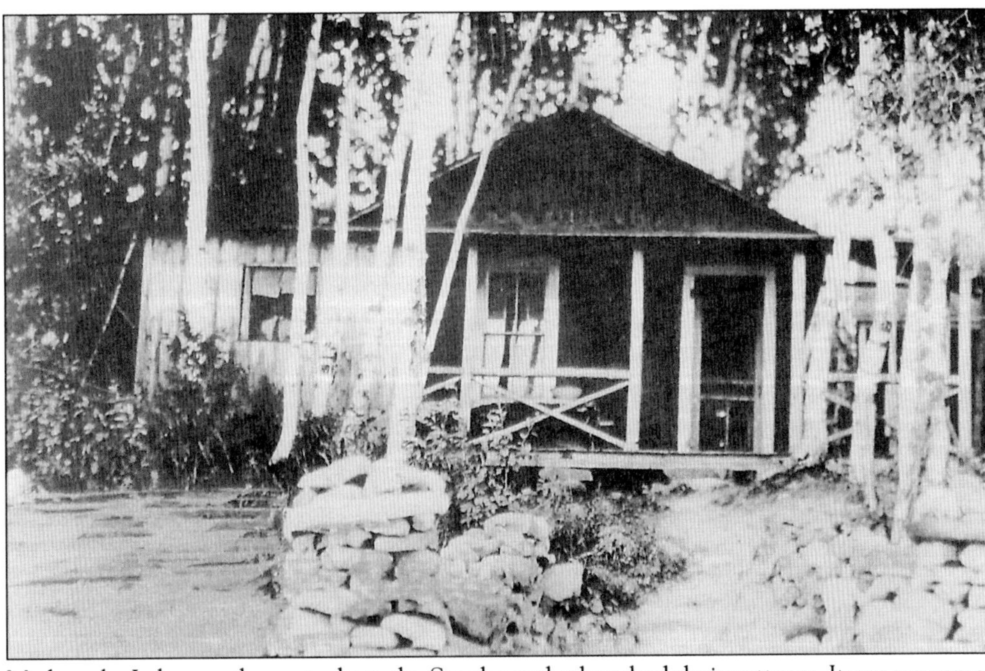

Madawaska Lake was the spot where the Swedes and others had their cottages. It was a summer resort. This is a typical cottage.

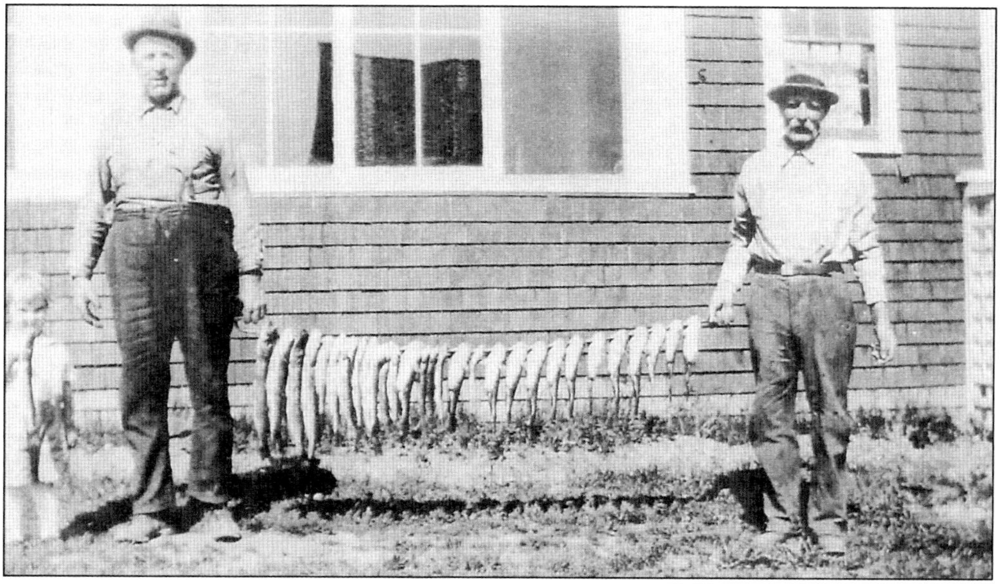

A big catch from Madawaska Lake, probably in the 1920s.

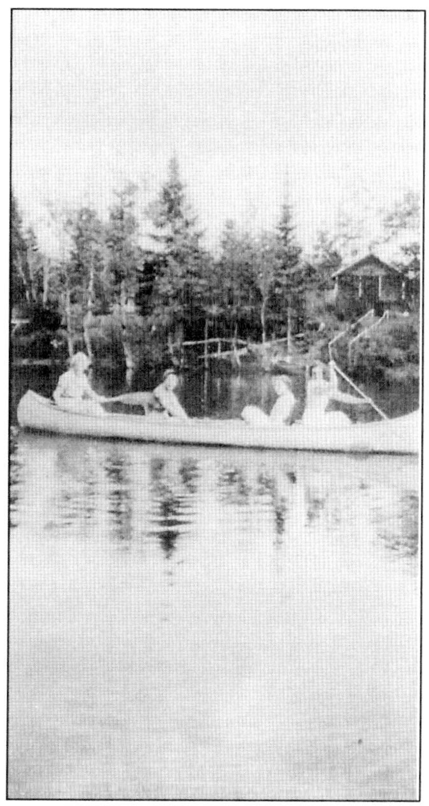

Canoeing on Madawaska Lake.

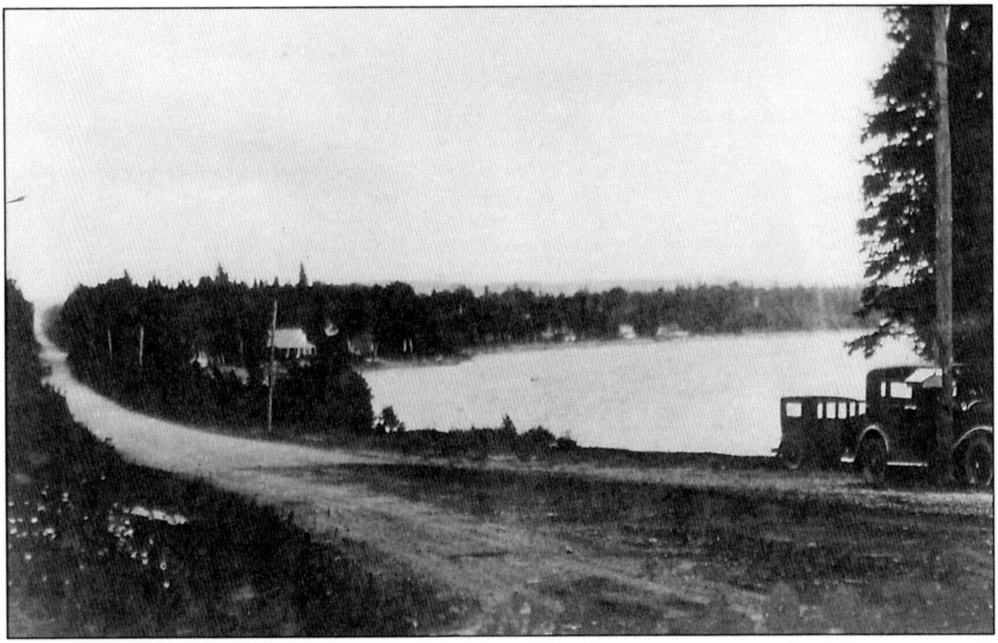

An old view of Madawaska Lake. Stan's Store, used by almost everyone at the lake, now stands at this location.

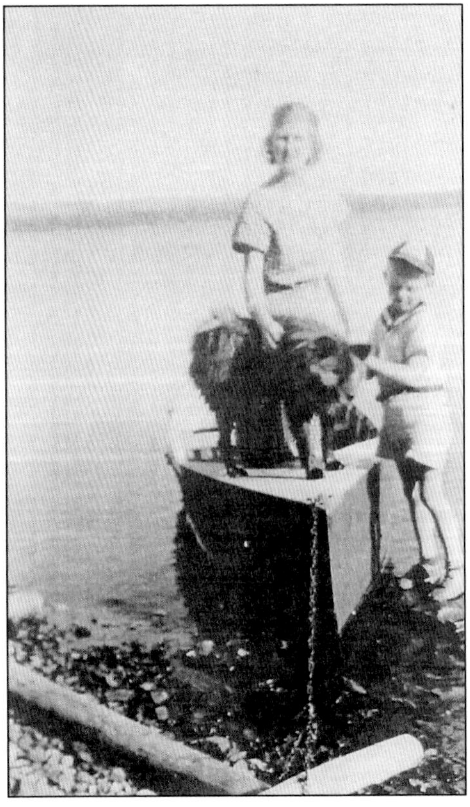

A family boating at Madawaska Lake.

Off to a picnic in the woods at Presque Isle about 1900. Note the picnic basket.

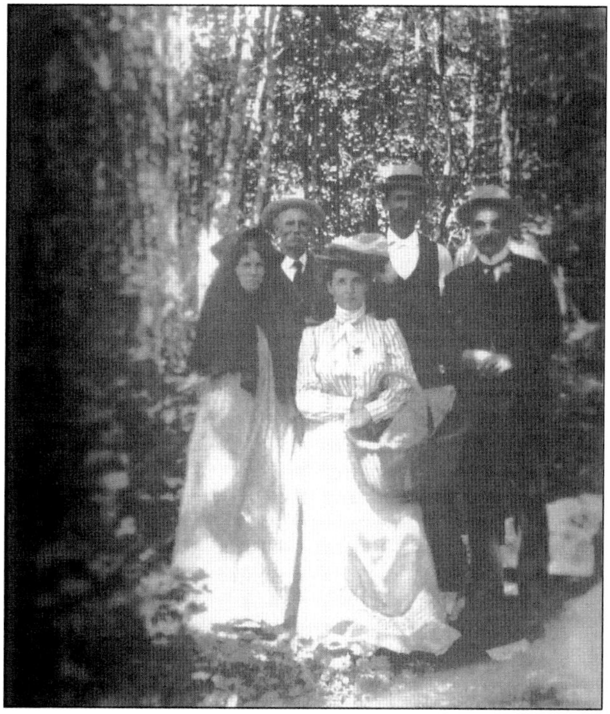

A playful group in Presque Isle about 1900. The man in the rear wears a ladies' hat while the girl on the left in the second row has on a man's derby. Did the two swap chapeaux? The two children in front are also hamming it up.

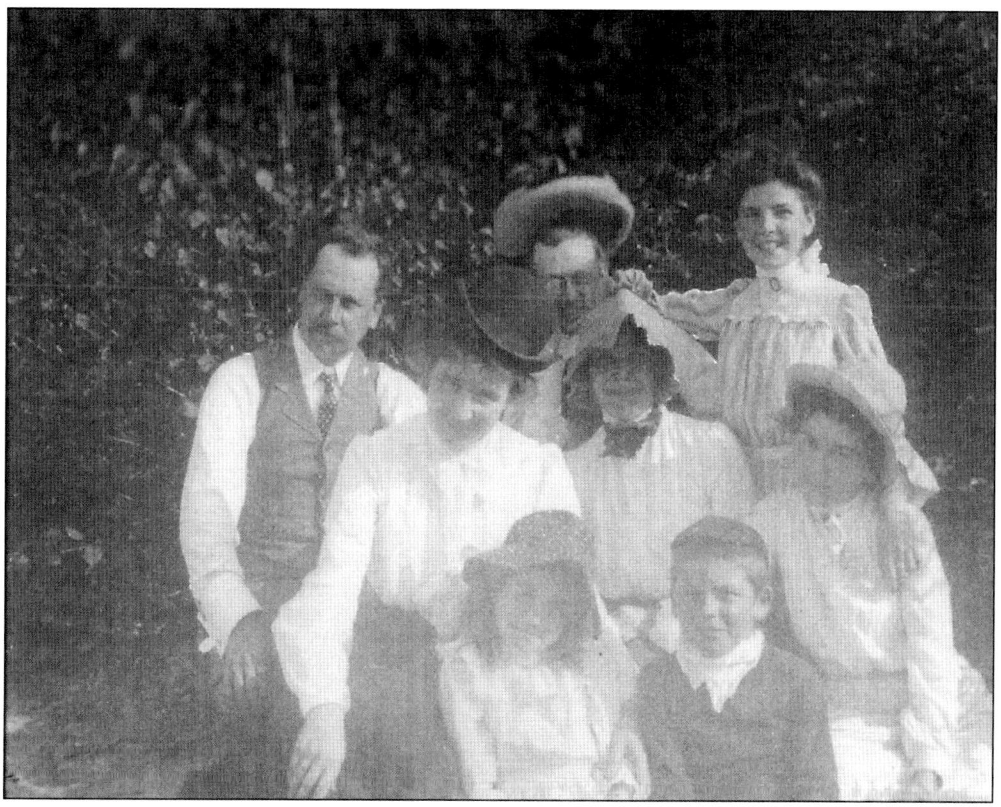

JOHN R. BRADEN
MARCH SONG

By BYRON VERGE

The Maine Shipyard Song Writer

To be Sung to the tune of

"BOOM OUR STATE"

March Song

By BYRON VERGE

Dedicated to the "Mooseleuk Club," promoters of clean sport

There's a song of triumph ringing clear with a chorus full and strong,
You can hear it ring to the very skies with an echo loud and long,
There's a mighty band from "Aroostook land" with heart and hand so true
They are with you to stay and they're backing you today---
John R. Braden! Aroostook is with you.

CHORUS

So you'll "take the pole" today in your nifty little way,
While Aroostook County cheers you "to a man."
With John Willard on the seat, shake your light and dainty feet
O, you can do it boy! Right well we know you can
Let each horse that steps with you then see the glitter of your shoe, when
You have set the pace they follow in your dust
John R. Braden you're a winner just as sure as I'm a sinner
And in horse and driver lays our trust.

John R. Braden, lad, you've made us glad, in the days now gone before;
May your fleet winged-feet beat the music sweet of a well won race once more.
You're a noble boy, you're our pride and joy, we love you, yes we do,
You have won every heart, we'll be with you at the start,
At the finish we're waiting to cheer you.---CHORUS.

And then there was John R. Braden, the most famous harness race horse that Presque Isle, Aroostook County, and perhaps even Maine ever knew. John R. throttled the challenges of horses bought by groups of horse lovers in Caribou and Houlton. He did go down to five defeats in his career but not to the hated neighbor horses. John R.'s name is still on Presque Isle's leading movie theater. They actually held a banquet in Presque Isle for John R. where he drank some champagne, and, as we see here, John R. had a march written in his honor. His name and fame are still well remembered, even though he raced years ago.

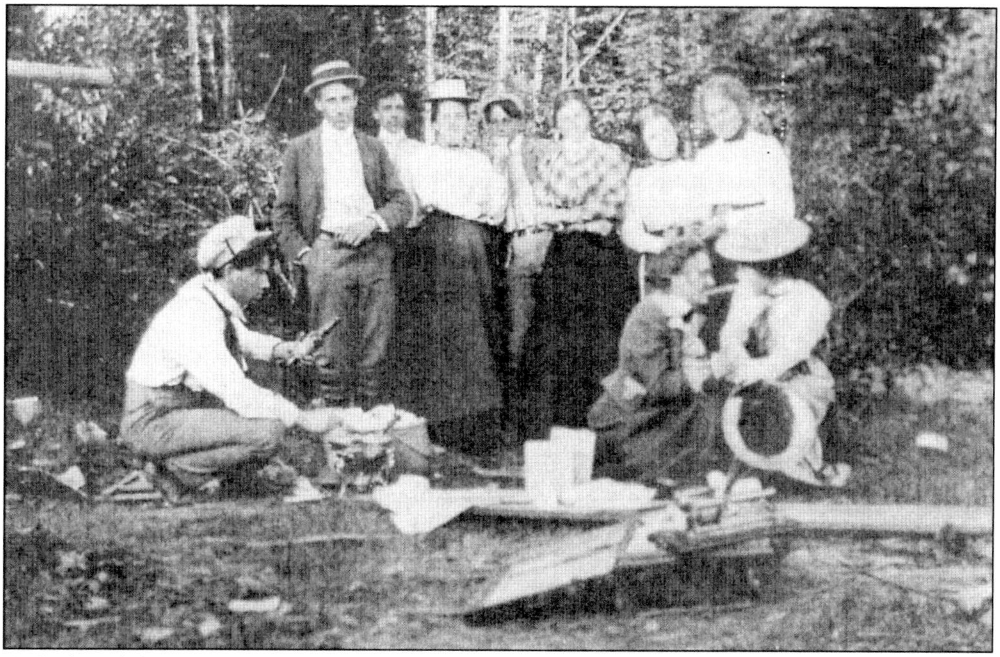

A chafing dish supper in the woods of Presque Isle about 1900. A chafing dish was nothing more than a candle or an alcohol unit underneath a dish to keep food warm. You usually brought your own food to such suppers or parties.

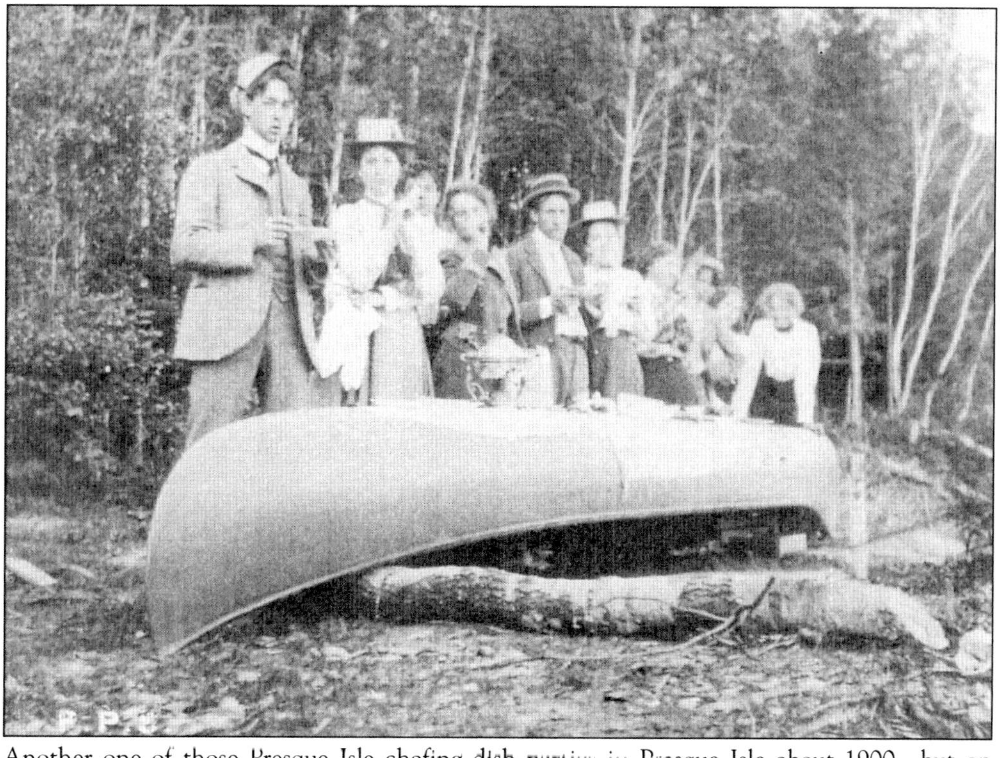

Another one of those Presque Isle chafing dish parties in Presque Isle about 1900—but on a canoe.

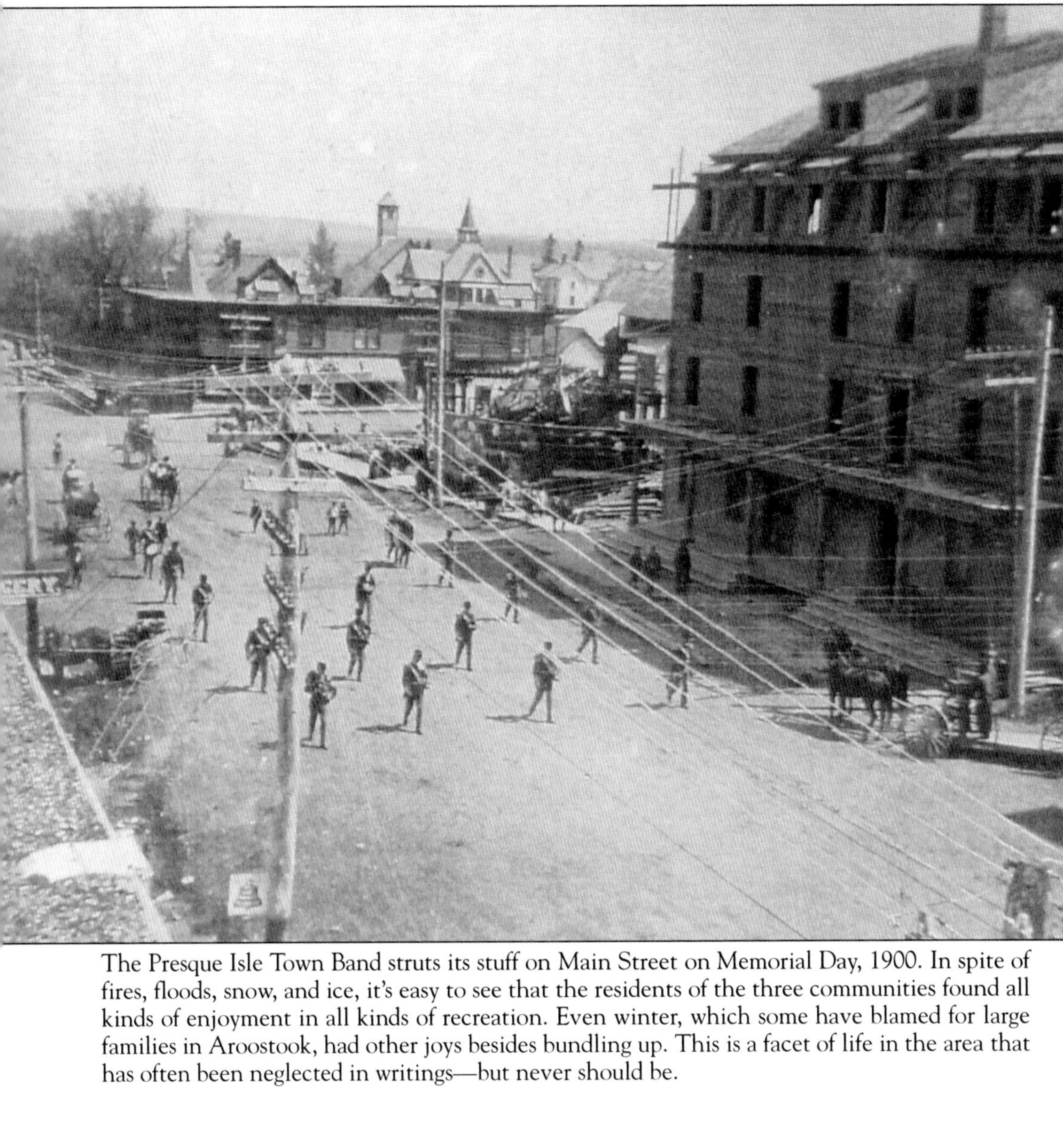

The Presque Isle Town Band struts its stuff on Main Street on Memorial Day, 1900. In spite of fires, floods, snow, and ice, it's easy to see that the residents of the three communities found all kinds of enjoyment in all kinds of recreation. Even winter, which some have blamed for large families in Aroostook, had other joys besides bundling up. This is a facet of life in the area that has often been neglected in writings—but never should be.

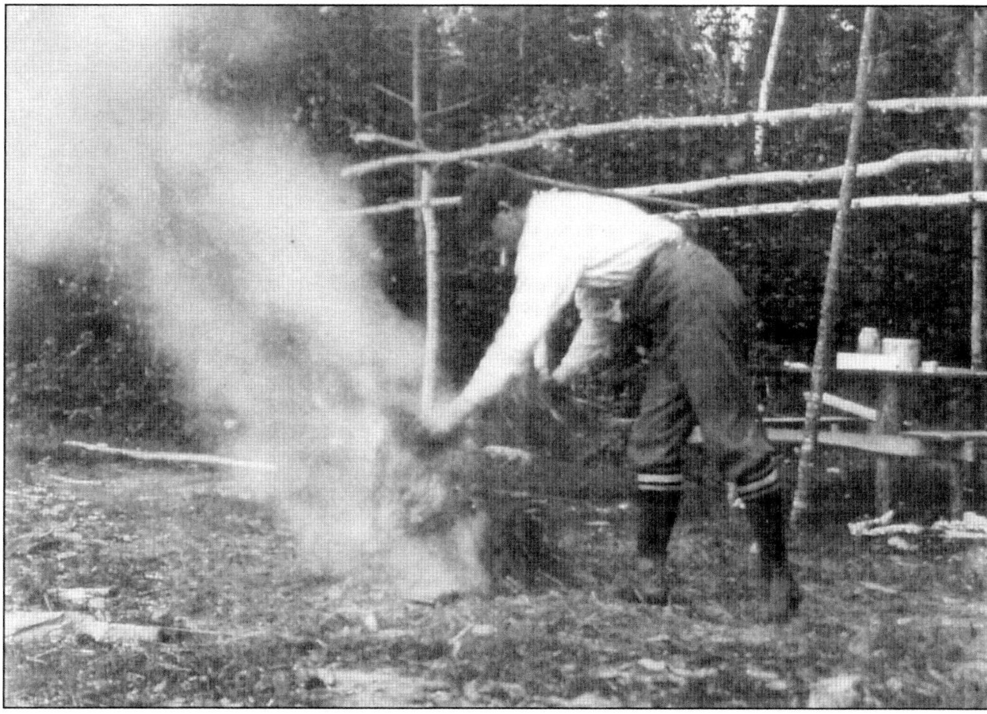

Otis B. Stevens worked for the Arthur C. Perry insurance agency for many years. But Otis was also a wonderful cook and whenever he went on fishing or hunting trips (which was quite often), he used that skill to a high degree.

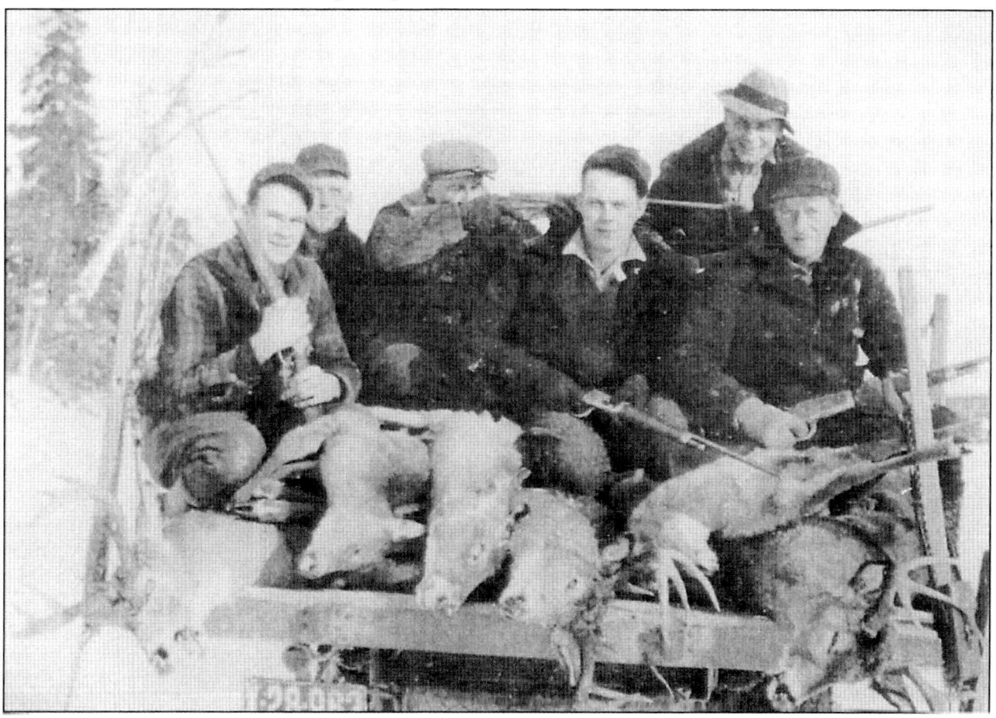

There were hunters as well as skiers in New Sweden. This group obviously did well.

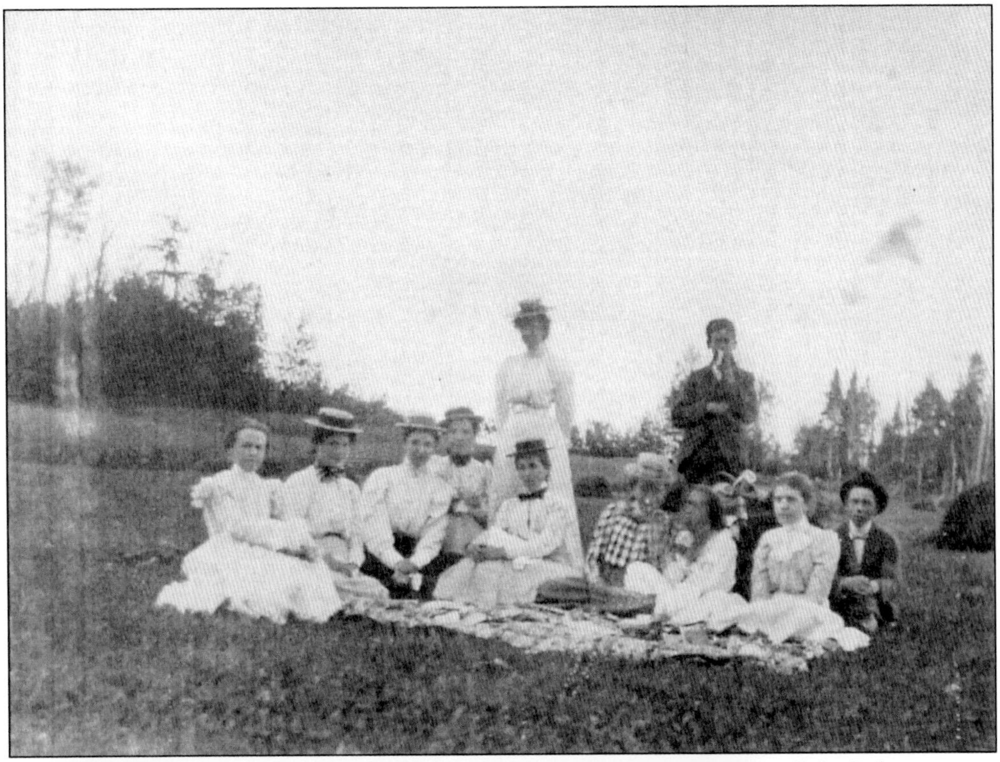

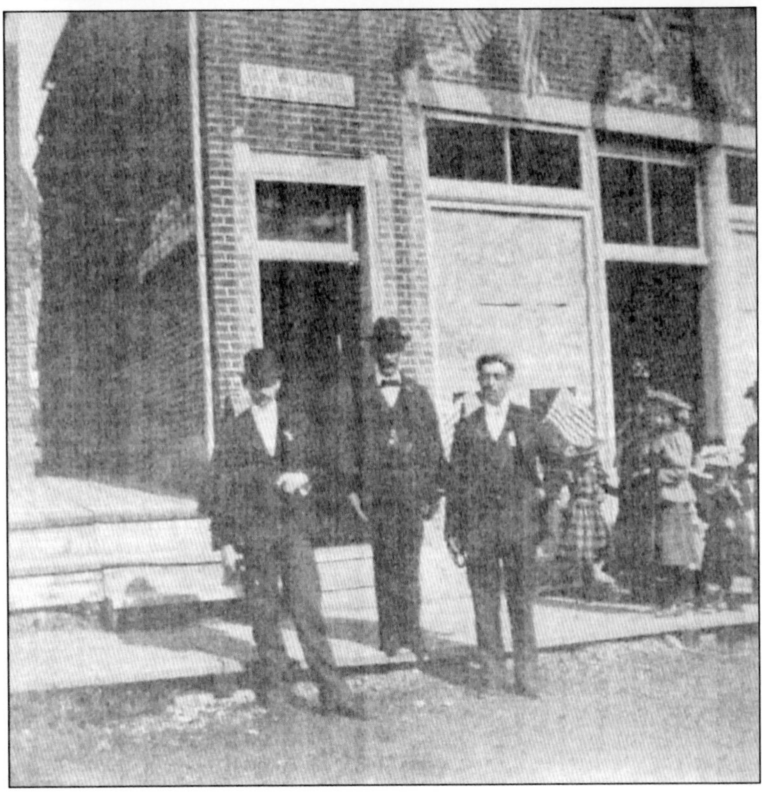

Echo Lake in Presque Isle has always been a popular picnic spot. Here's a picnic about 1900.

Just horsing around is often a form of recreation. These gentlemen in Presque Isle were known as the "umbrella brigade." They came downtown daily dressed fit to kill and carried umbrellas if there seemed to be the slightest chance of rain.

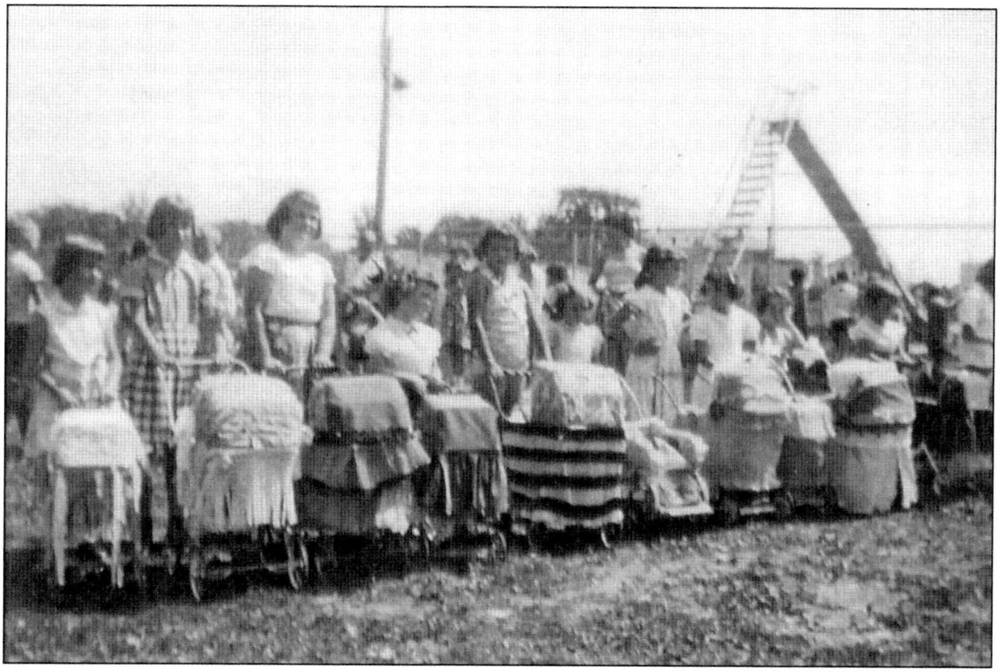

Christie Smart (now Cochran), third from the right, rests her chin on her hand before winning first prize at a doll parade at the Presque Isle Recreation Center in 1949.

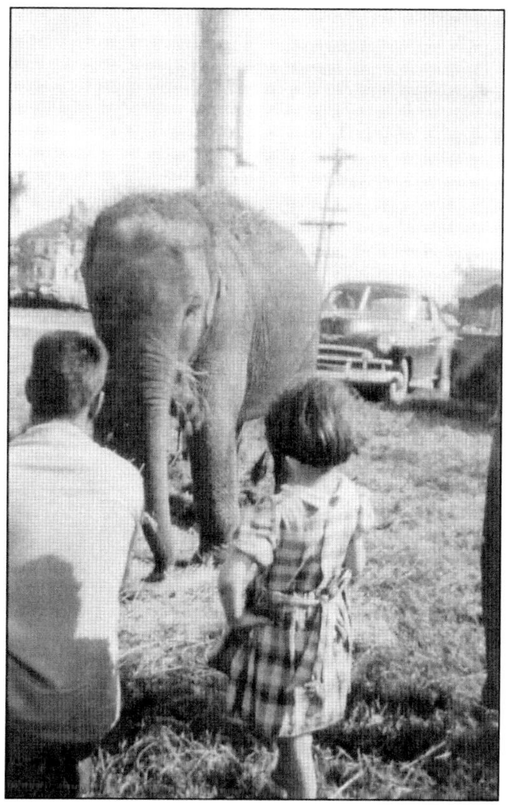

Christie Smart and her uncle, Basil Kierstead, with the elephant at the Presque Isle Fair in 1951. Now, the event is the Northern Maine Fair. It has been around, in one form or another, since 1850.

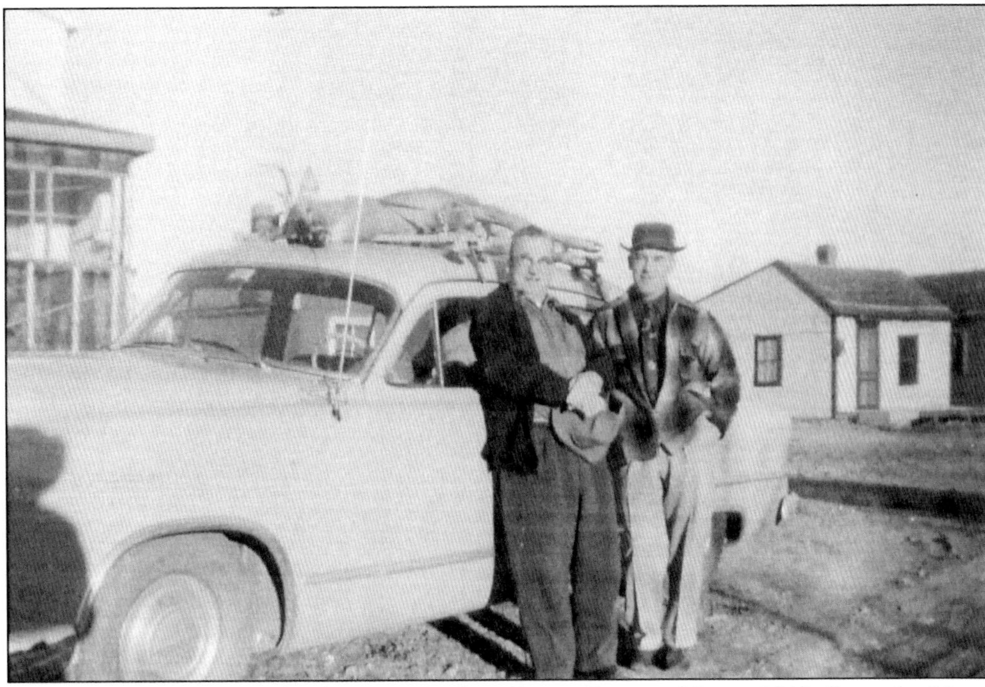

Ernest Smart is shown at his home on Bishop Street, Presque Isle, in 1949. Smart had been hunting with Kenneth Rounds of Massachusetts. He did most of his hunting in the Portage region, north of Presque Isle.

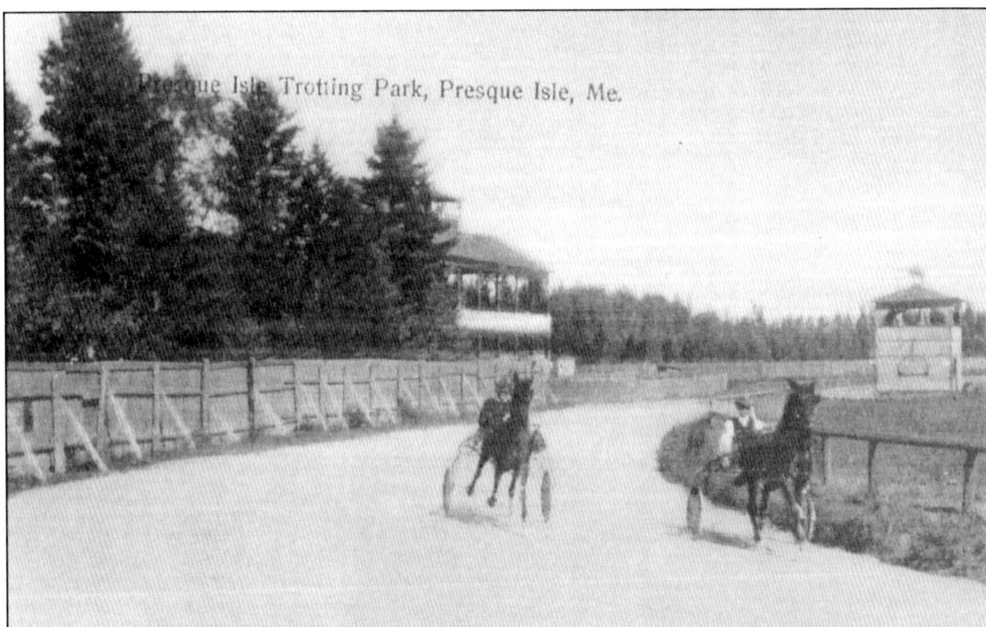

Practice time at the Presque Isle Trotting Park on the Northern Maine Fairgrounds in 1910.

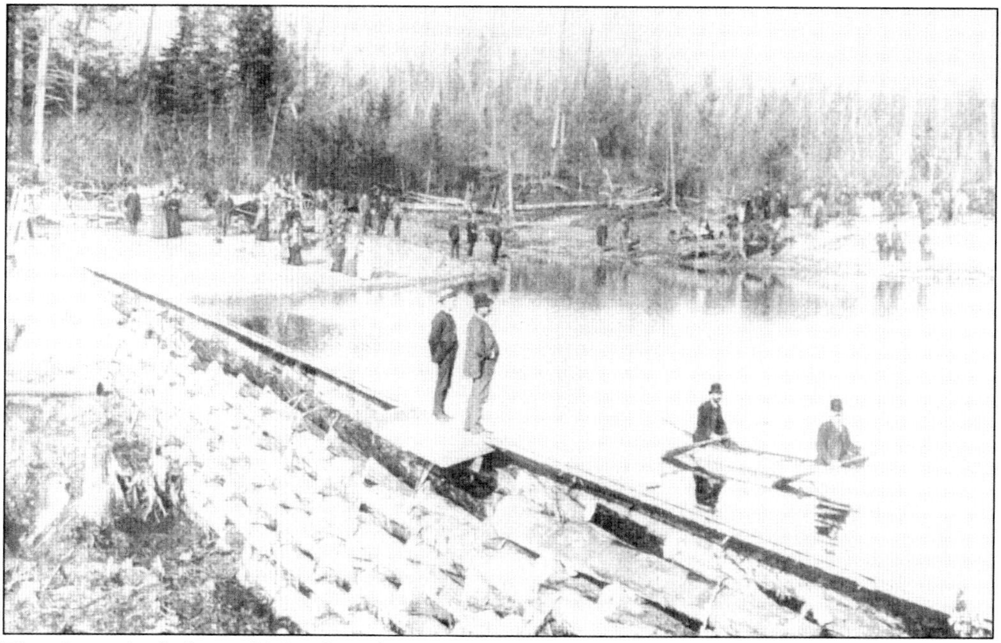

The dam which formed Mantle Lake in Presque Isle was dedicated sometime between 1900 and 1910. There had only been a small stream there before the dam was built. Now, it's another often-used picnic area.

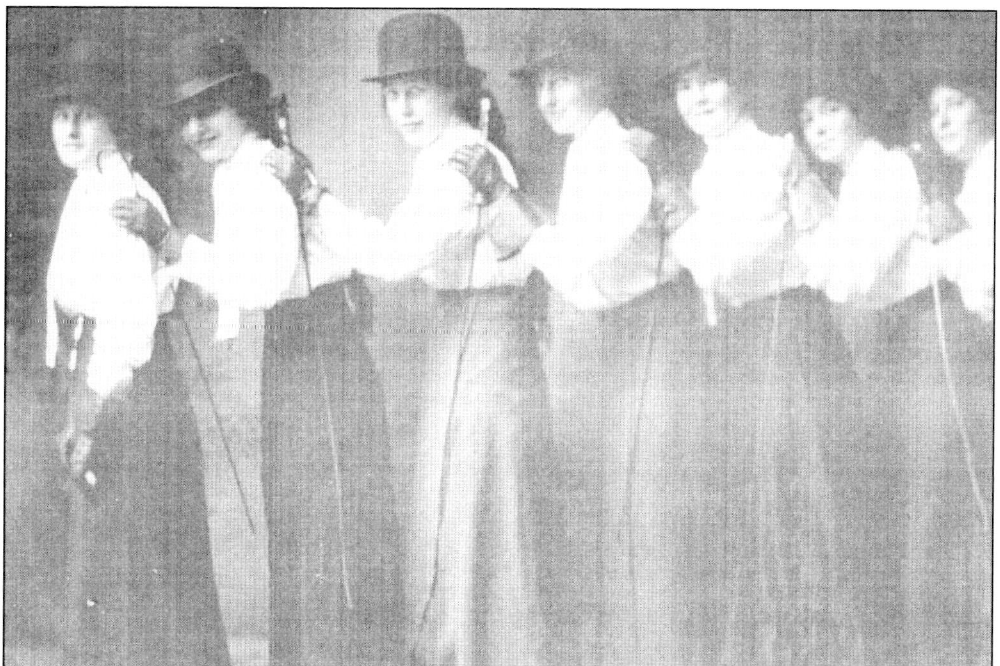

The Presque Isle Follies were very popular, especially during the Roaring Twenties. Shown in this early 1920s edition are, left to right: Jesse Lancaster, Susie Bates Olson, Crystal Pennington, Ruth Stevens Graves, Mildred Graves Watt, Margaret Boone Parsons, and Alicia Hayford Walker.

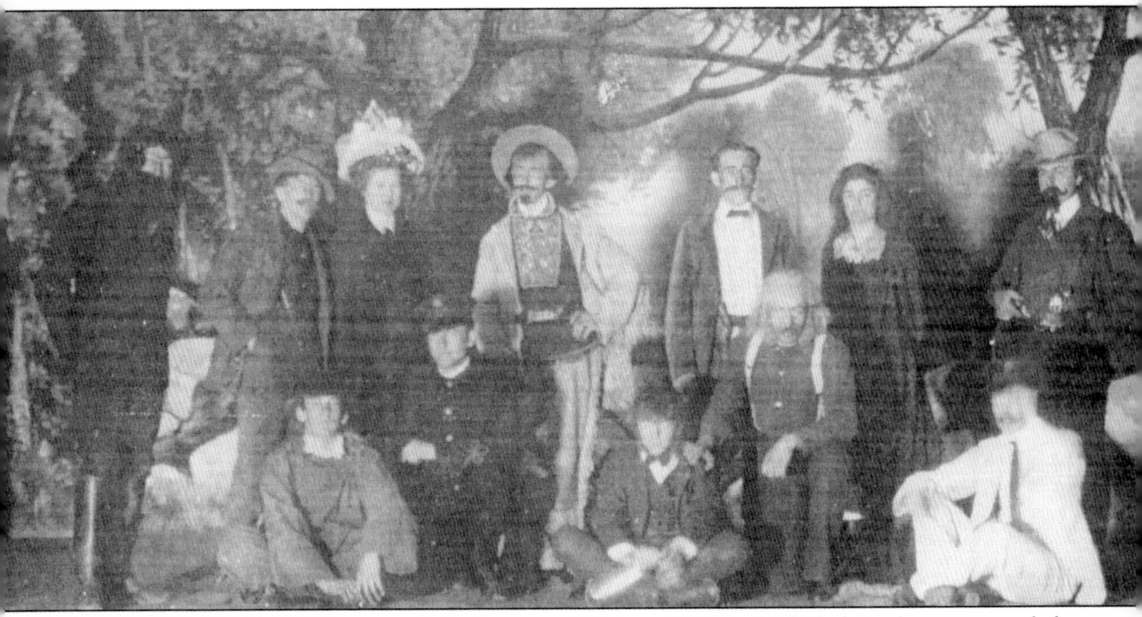

A much earlier Follies, sometime between 1889 and 1900. Included in the cast are, left to right: (front) Harry Whitney, Don McDonald, Fred Stevens, unknown, and unknown; (back) unknown, Louis Gould, Mamie Pipes Franklin, unknown, Fred Smith, Lucy Jacques, unknown, and Eva Hayes.

Four

Potatoes, Farms, and Business

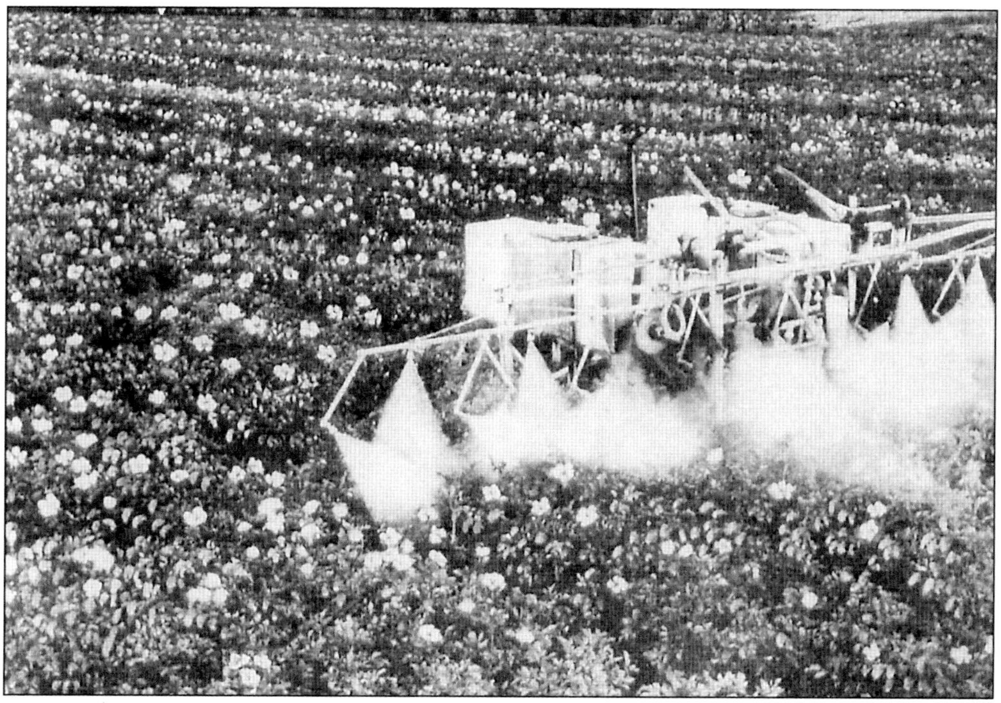

It certainly wasn't all play and coping with the tough environment: it was work, and that meant potatoes. Here, a Caribou potato field in bloom is being sprayed with pesticide.

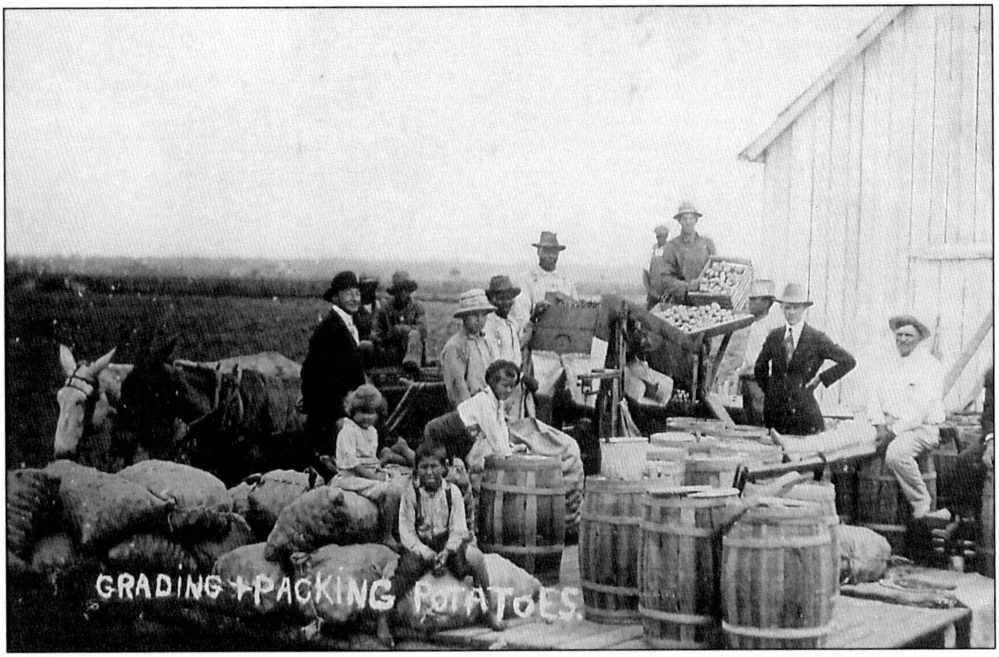

Potatoes are graded and packed in Caribou. This area was even more of a potato-growing area than the area farther south around Houlton.

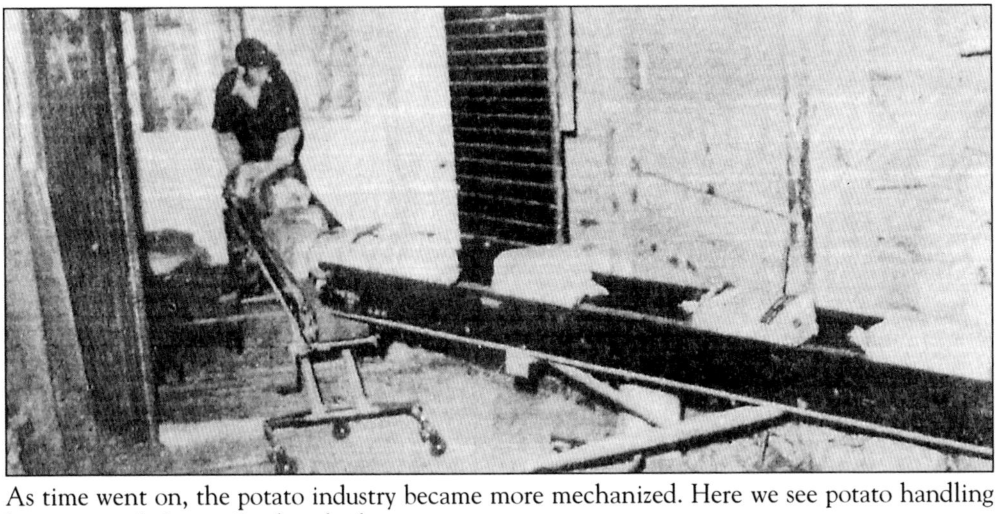

As time went on, the potato industry became more mechanized. Here we see potato handling by a moving belt in a Caribou facility.

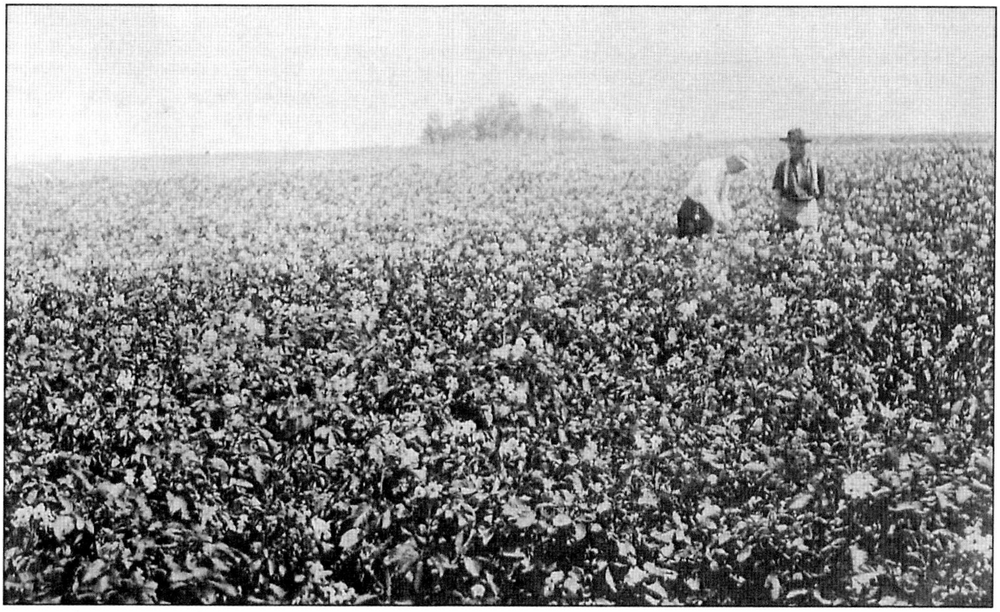

A Caribou potato field in 1910. Potato growing moved this area more rapidly out of the frontier era than any other single cause, except the money the spuds brought here.

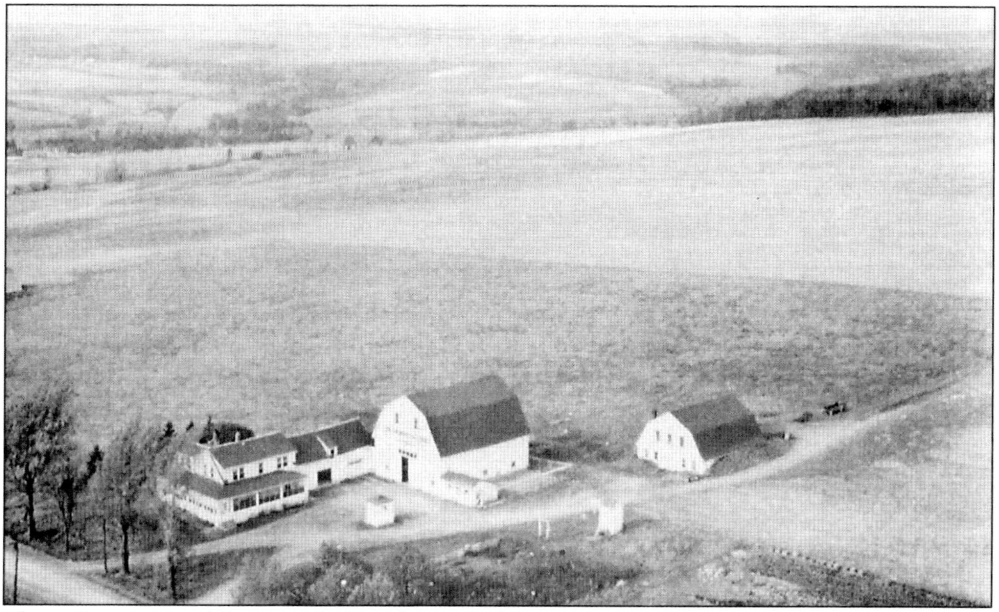

The rolling fields of the area sheltered farm buildings of many varieties. This is the Rasmussen farm in Caribou.

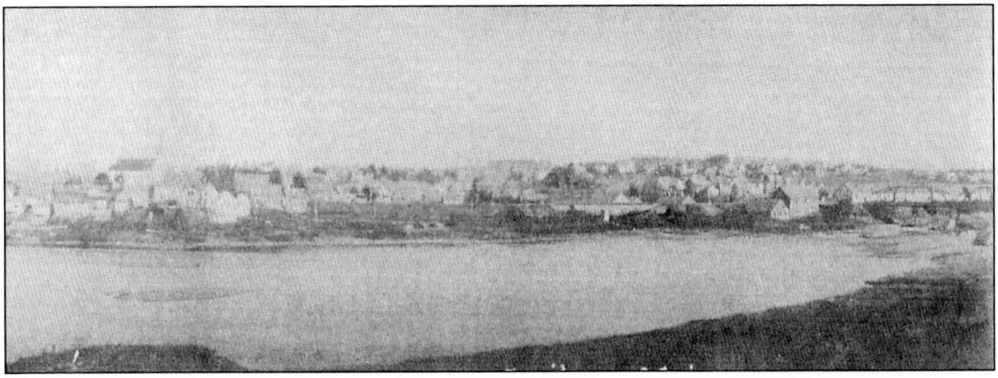

This was taken from behind the old Washburn house in Caribou in 1908. If you look closely, you can see the potato starch factories on the south side of the Aroostook River. The piers are those of the old bridge. The Franco-American section of Caribou is at the left while the old Vaughan house is in the background.

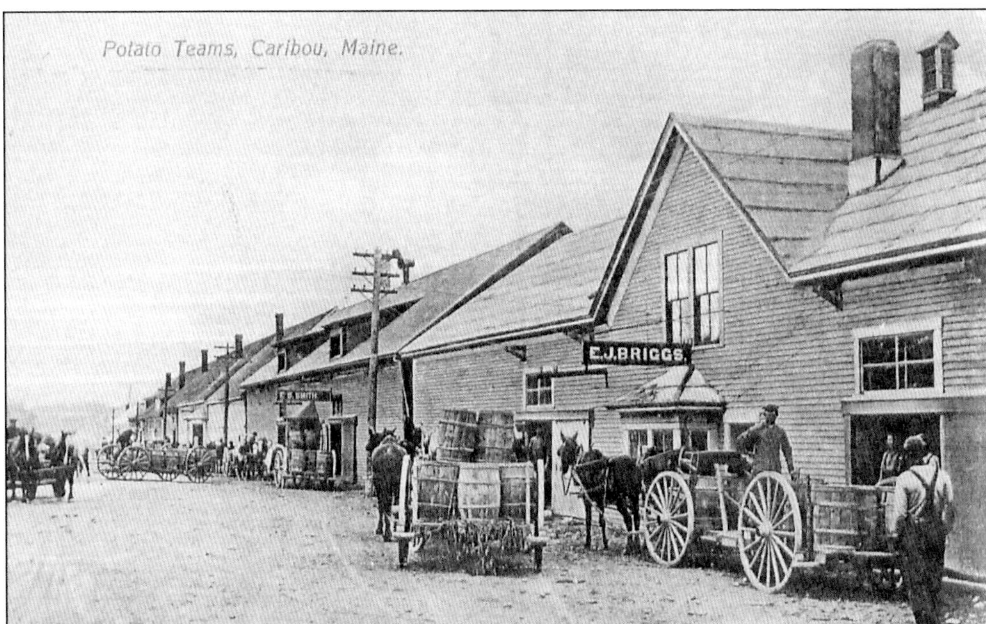

And then there were the teams hauling potatoes in their wagons. Here is a group of them on Limestone Street in Caribou in 1909.

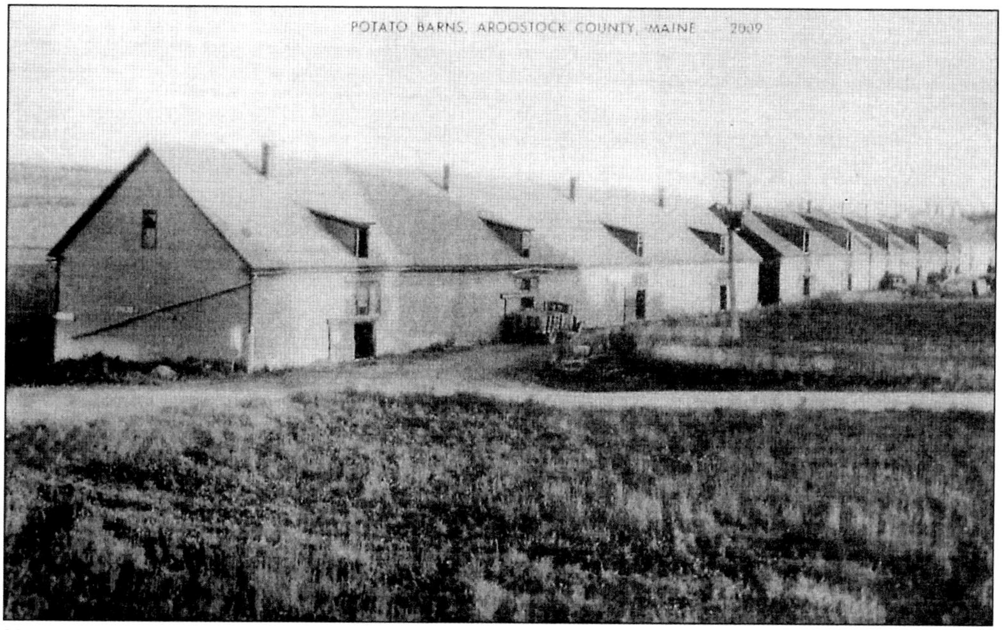

Here are "potato houses" on Limestone Street in the 1920s. The business of potato growing is more complicated than one might think.

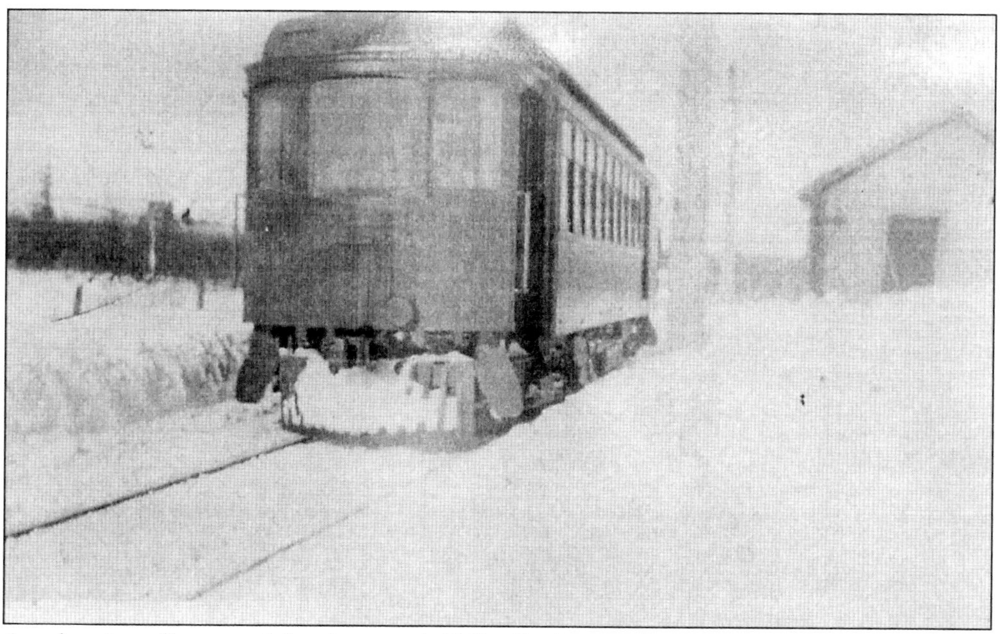

An electric trolley car of the Aroostook Valley Railway makes a nice run in Caribou in the 1930s. The line ran from Presque Isle to Caribou, New Sweden, and Washburn with other stops in between.

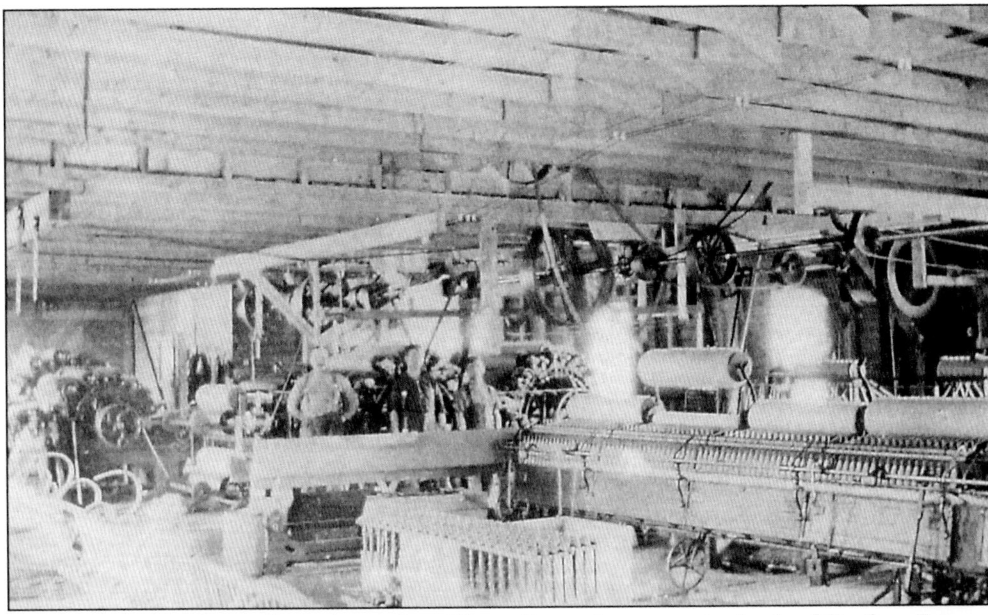

The Caribou Woolen Mill was located on Water Street. It was on the bank of Caribou Stream.

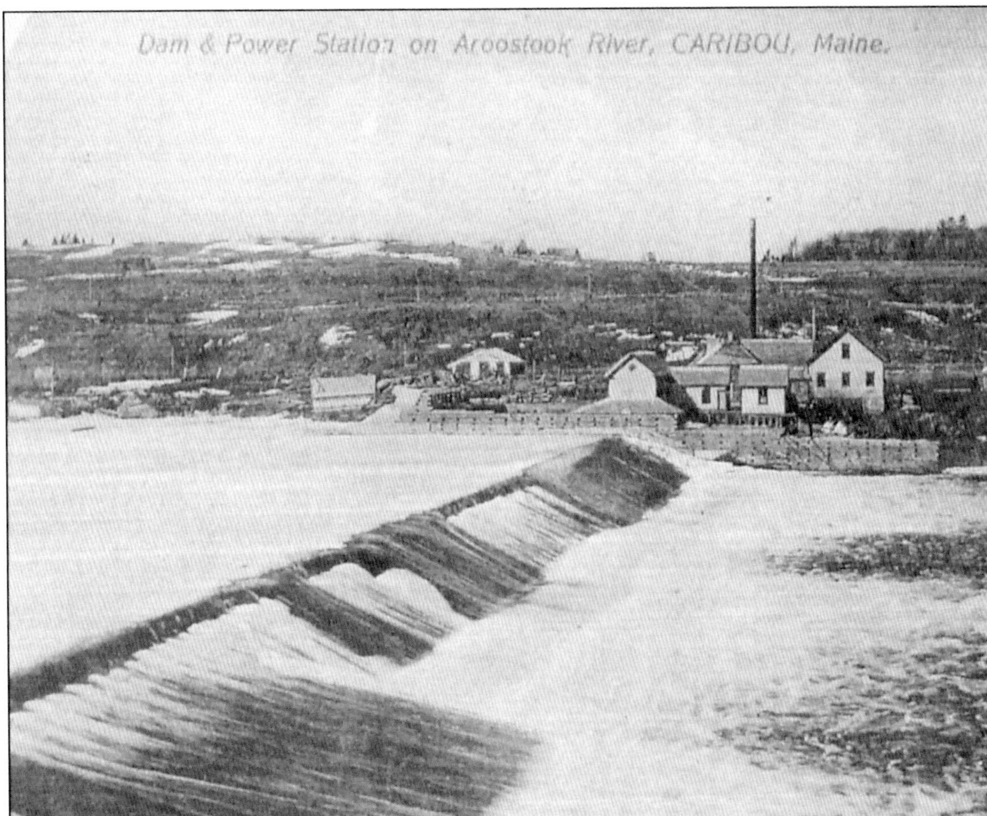

The dam and power station in Caribou was another signal that the frontier era had ended. This postcard had a 1910 postmark on it.

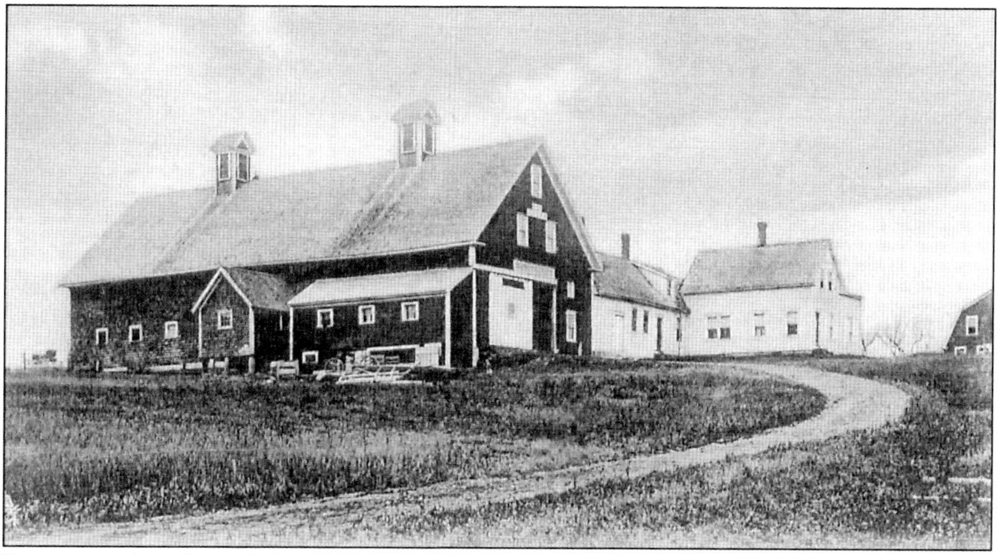

Farming can't and couldn't be forgotten. This is a Caribou barn in 1907.

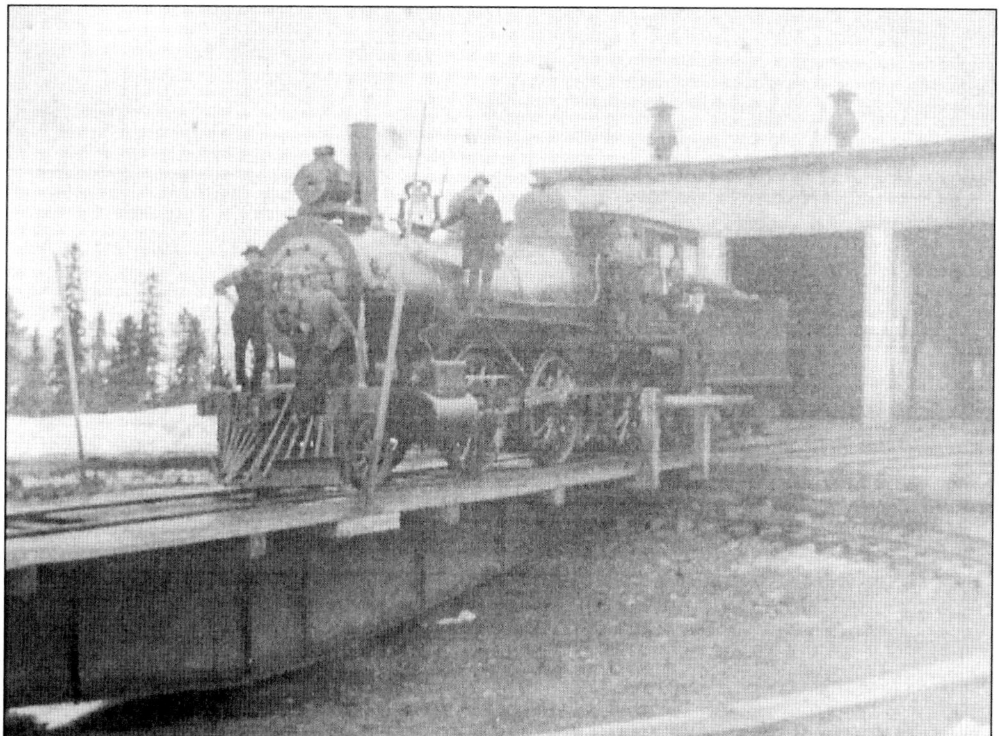

Another sign of the frontier era's death was the Bangor and Aroostook Railroad turntable near Water Street in Caribou. It no longer exists.

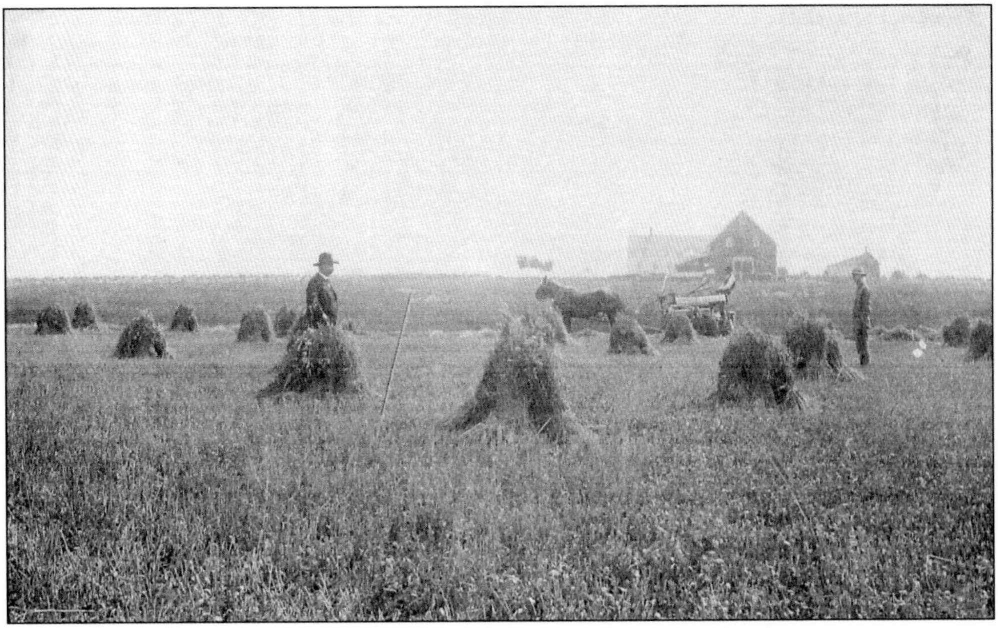

Again, the farms can't be forgotten when one looks at business in the three-community area. It's haying time in this photograph.

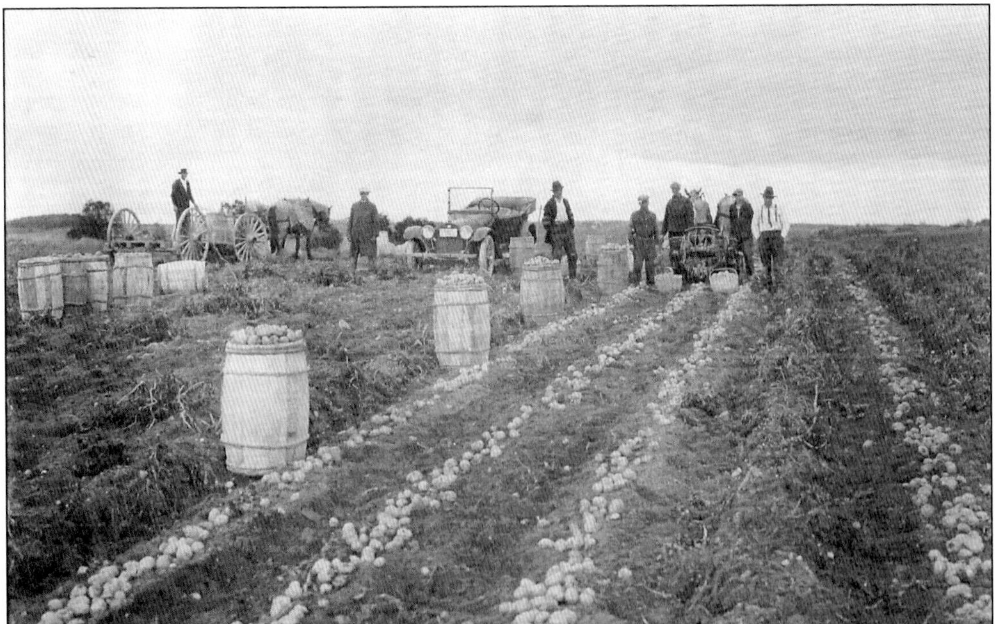

A more modern potato industry picture: potato picking in Caribou in the 1920s. Note the very full barrels. Good picking, no doubt.

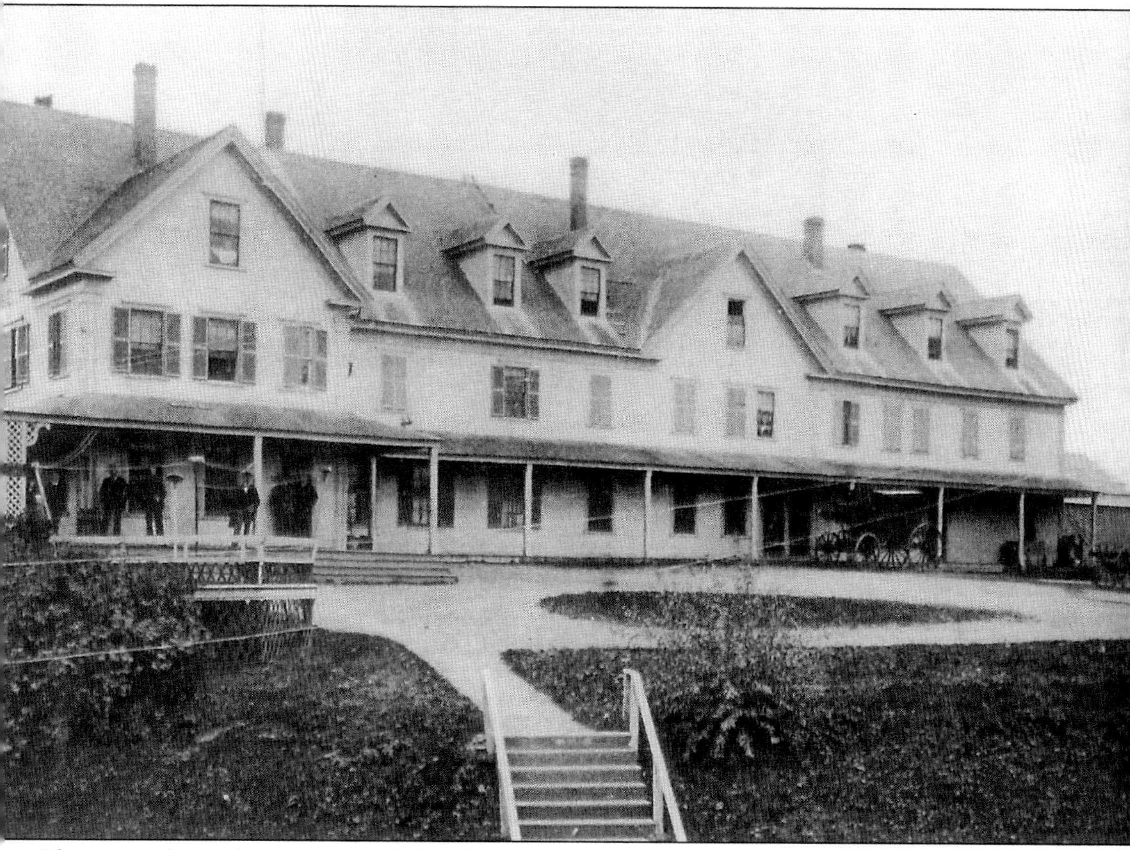

The original Vaughan house, built by Washington Vaughan in the mid-nineteenth century. Vaughan had been in partnership with Samuel W. Collins and the two were among the first settlers of Caribou in the early 1840s. There they ran a sawmill and a lumbering business. In 1857, Vaughan decided to leave the lumber business and the two divided their assets. Vaughan took much of the land south of Caribou Stream and a lot north of the stream. He built the Vaughan house on that lot. It went through several stages with expansions and rebuildings, but this is the original structure.

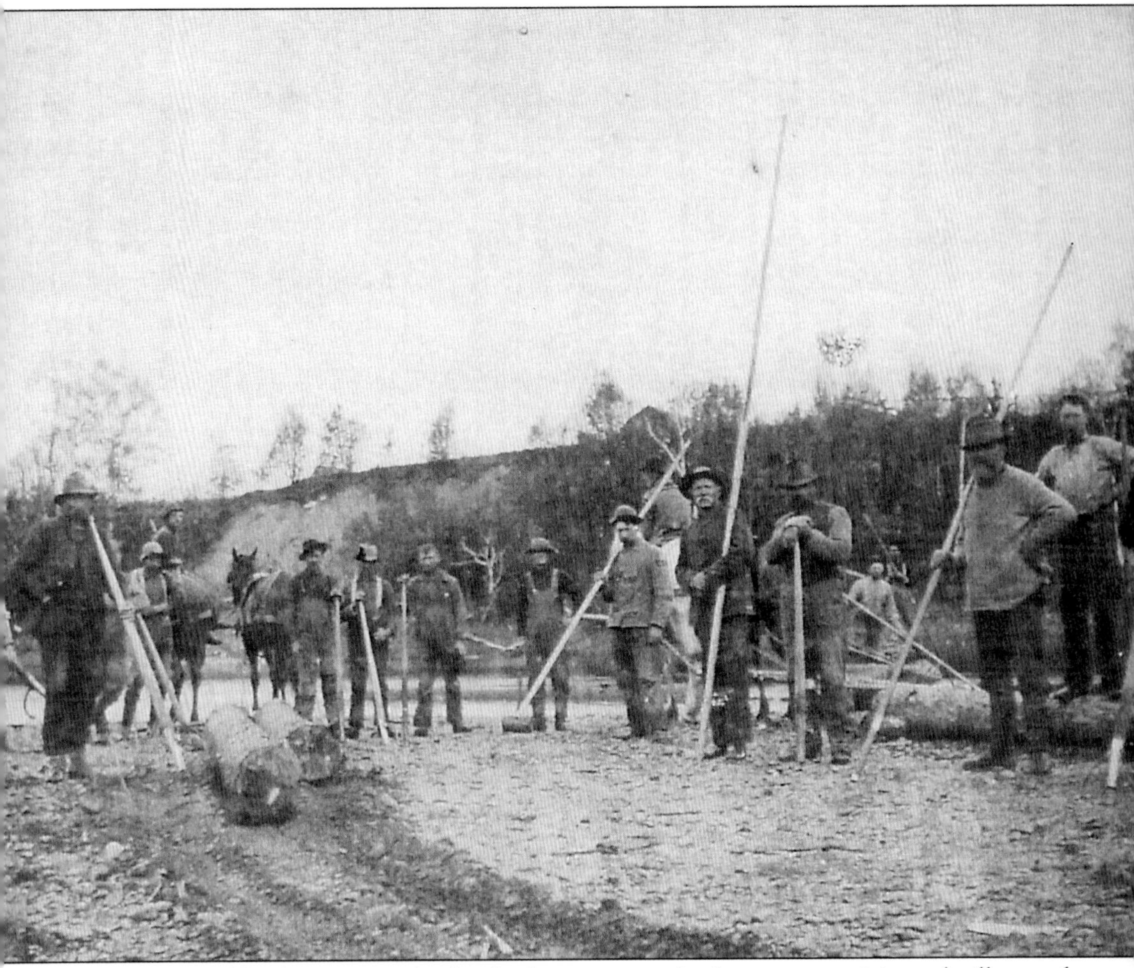

Logging and lumbering were the first big businesses in the three communities and still are today, although now they are tied in with sawmills, paper and pulp mills, and particleboard mills. No longer are the logs sent down the rivers of Aroostook County or any Maine rivers. Here we see loggers ready to pole on the Aroostook River during a logging operation, possibly at the turn of the century.

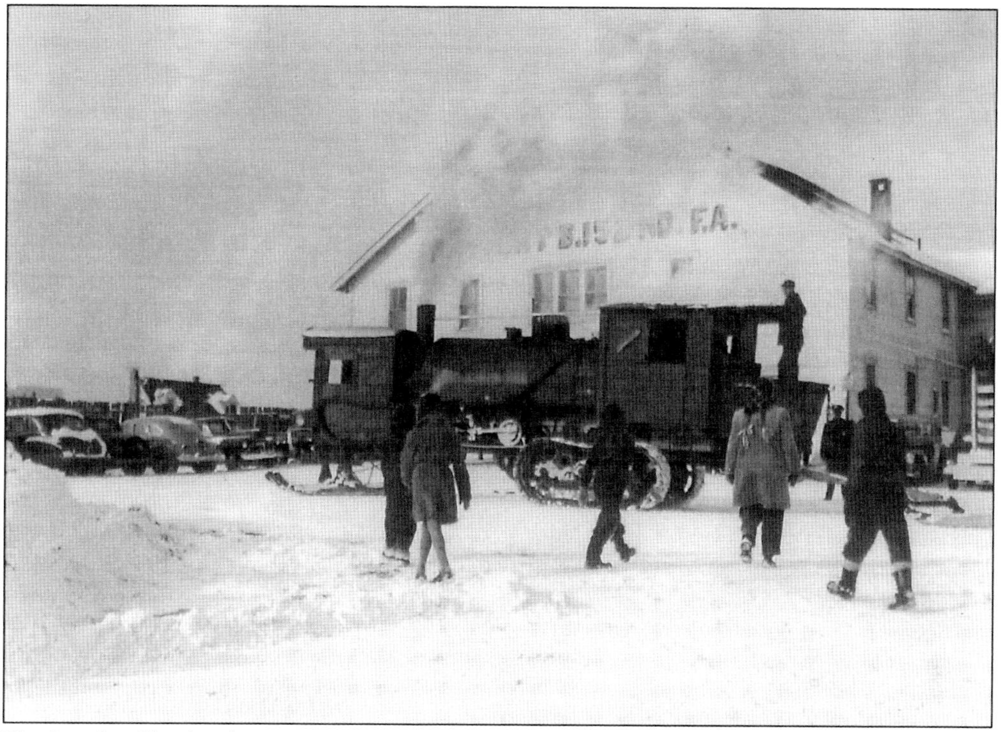

The Lombard log hauler was very popular in the 1920s and '30s. Here we see one in 1936 or 1937 in front of the Caribou building which housed the 152nd Field Artillery Unit.

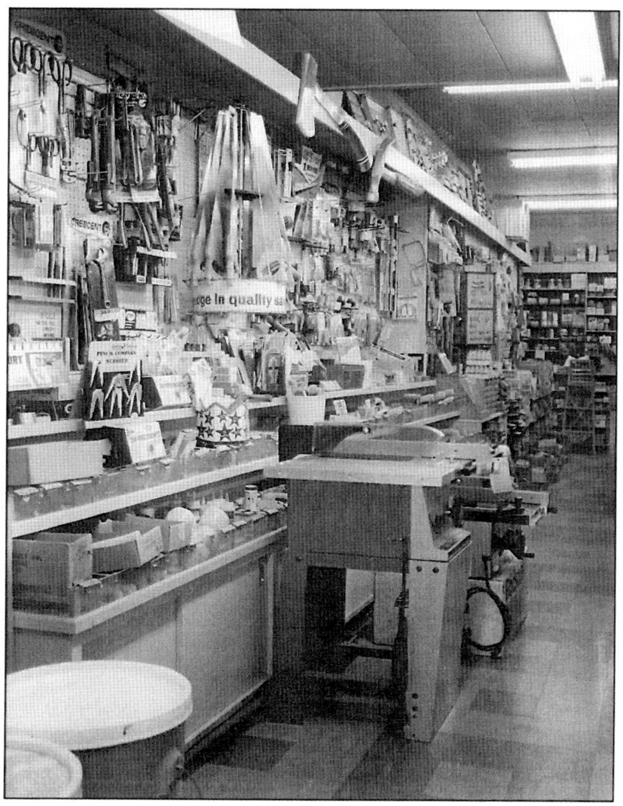

When you speak of the lumbering business in Caribou, you must speak of the Collins family. This is the Collins hardware store. The family has at various times expanded into more businesses than just lumber.

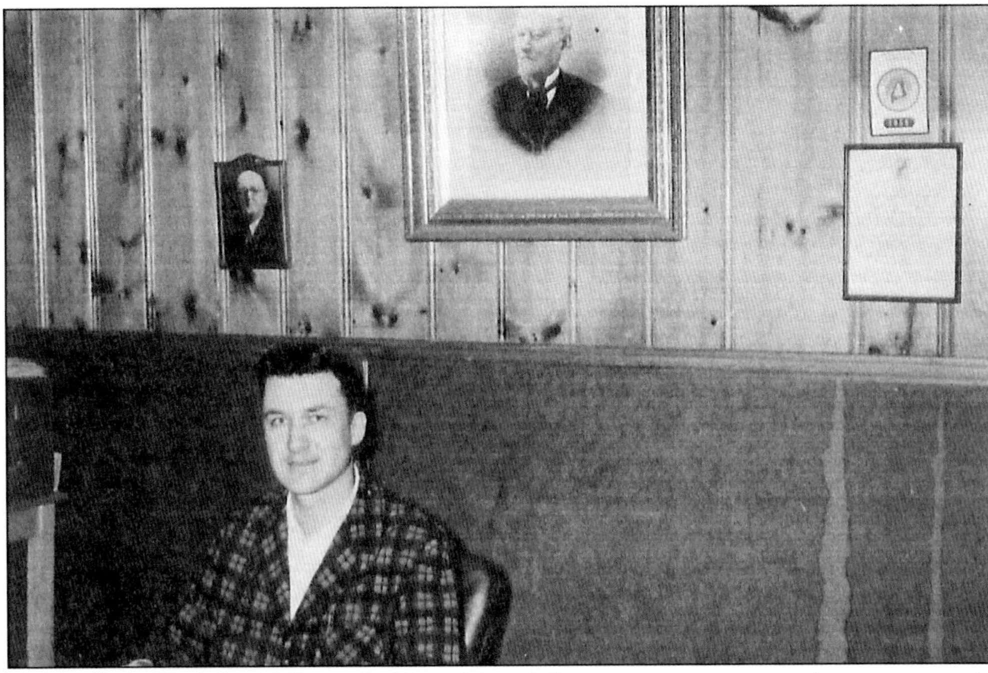

Don Collins, the father of Susan Collins—Maine's first woman ever to run for governor—sits under pictures of his grandfather, Herschel Collins, and great-grandfather, Samuel W. Collins.

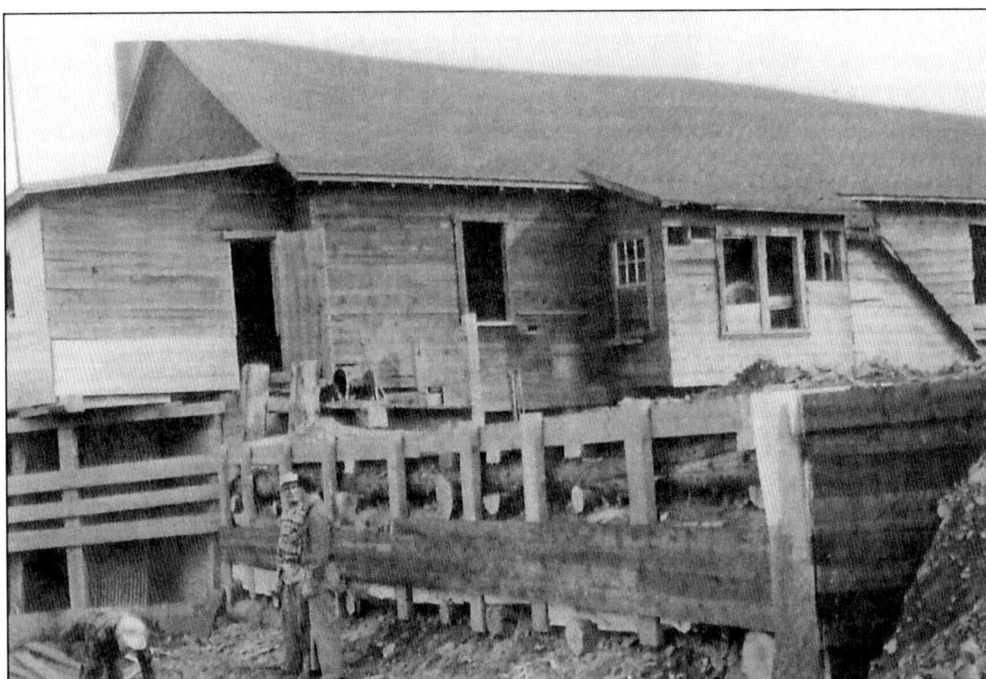

The old Collins sawmill in Caribou about 1947.

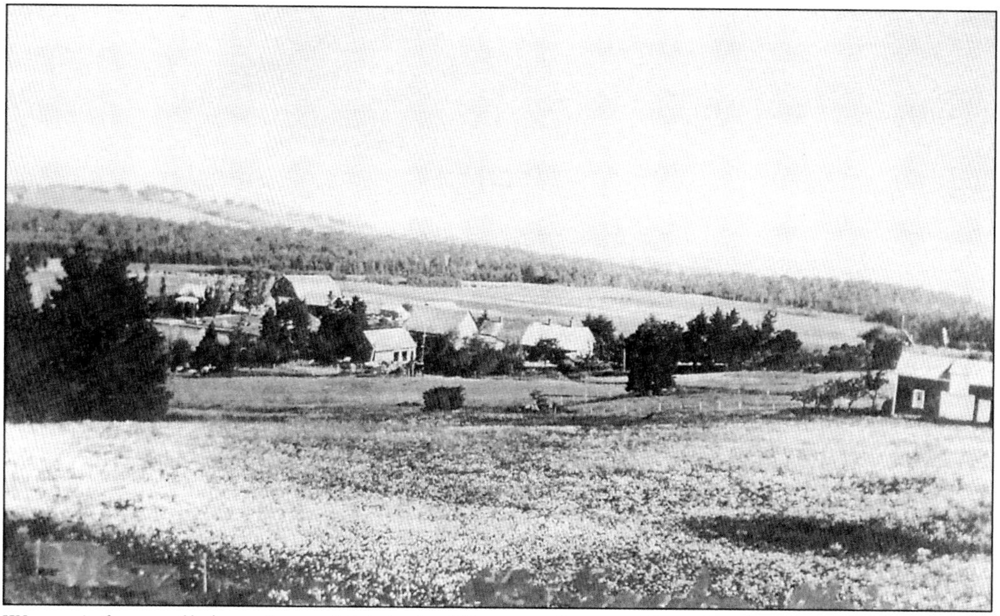

We can't forget all those farms. This is the Westman farm in New Sweden years ago.

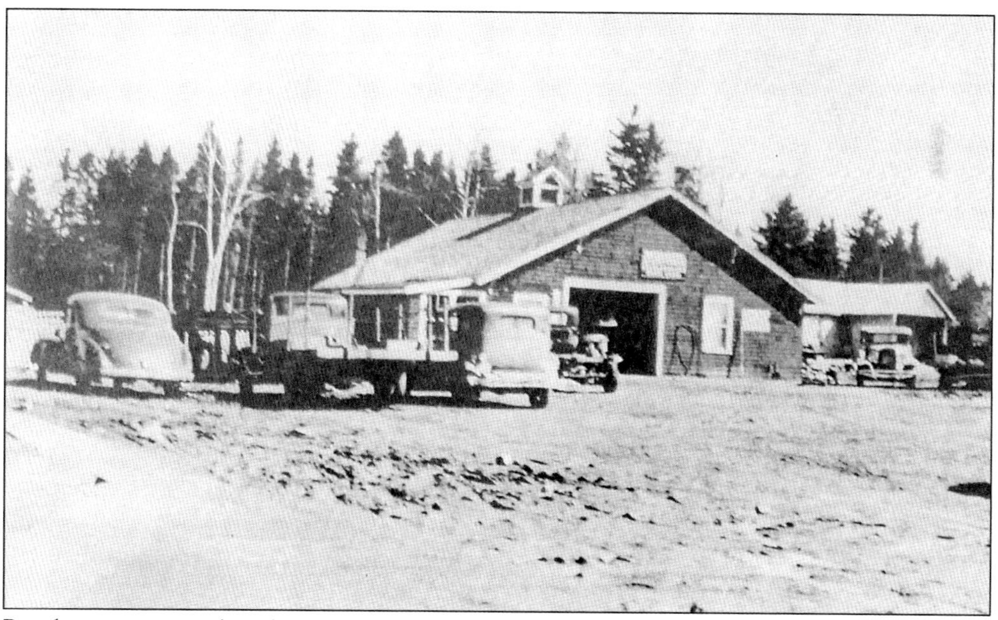

But there was more than farming, business-wise, in New Sweden. John Soderberg, for example, ran a garage in the town.

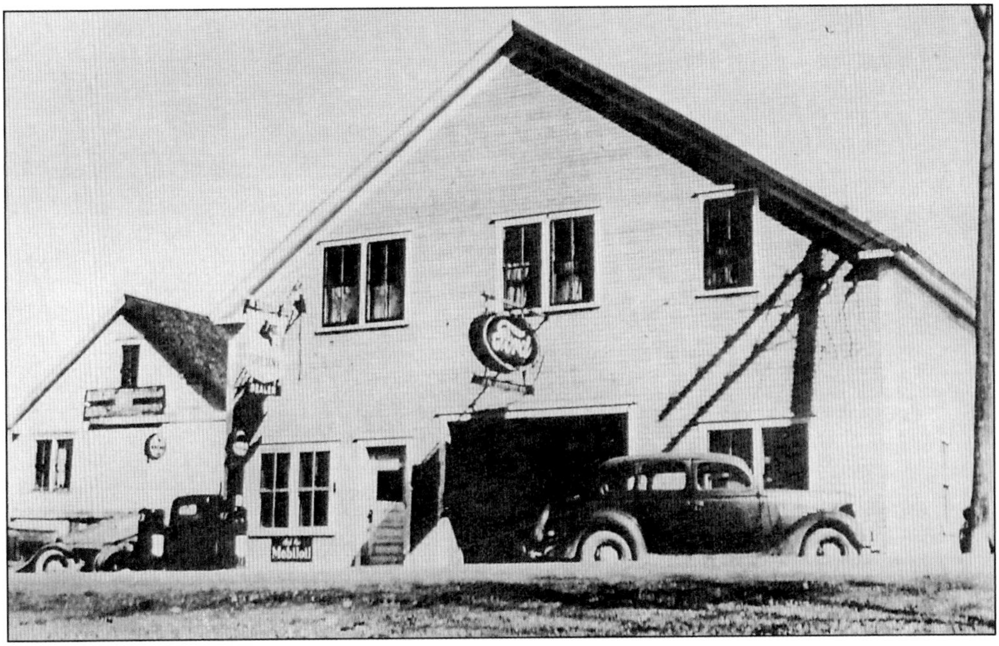

And J.N. Johnson operated this Ford garage in that same community.

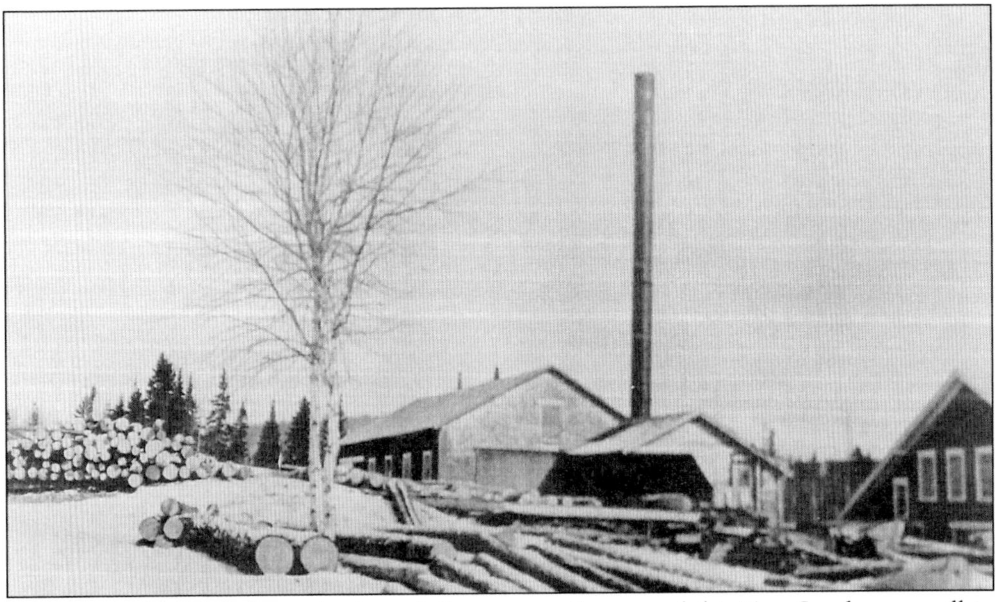

John J. Ringdahl (for whom the skiing hill was named) operated this New Sweden sawmill in the 1930s.

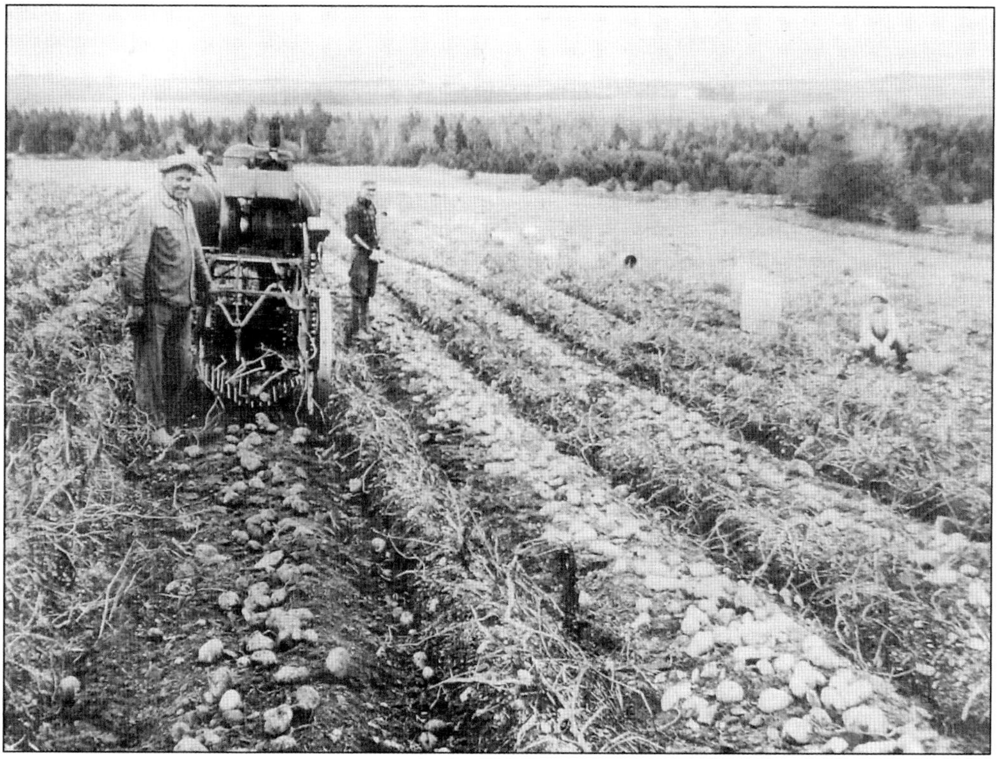

Digging potatoes with a one-row mechanical digger, probably in the 1930s. This is believed to be on the Matt Williams farm in New Sweden.

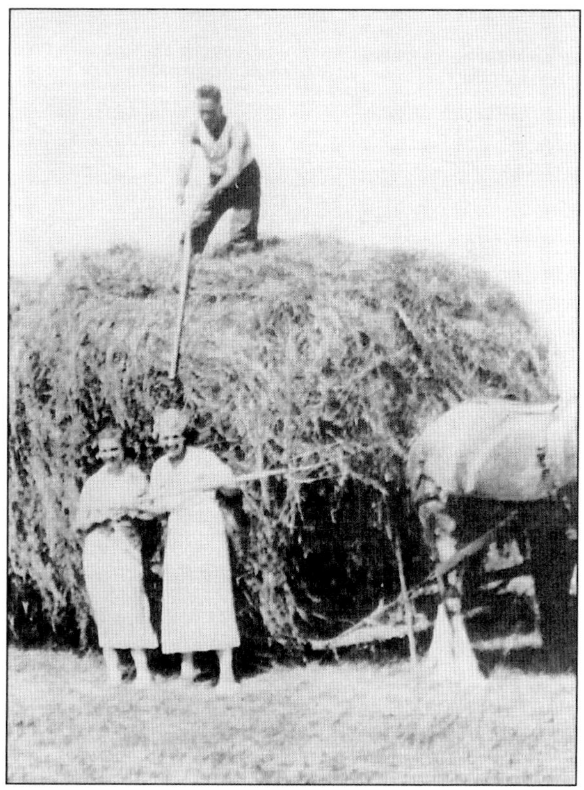

Sylvia Trone is in the front row of this scene on the Trone farm in New Sweden. The Swedes, of course, were excellent farmers.

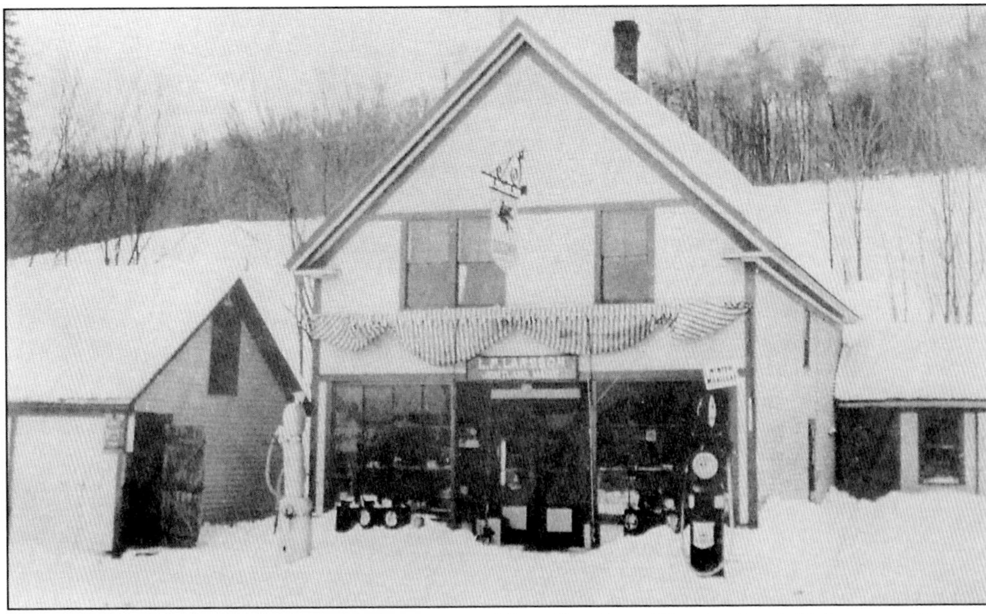

At one time, there were six general stores in New Sweden. This is the L.P. Larsson General Store—one of the first built in the community—in the 1920s.

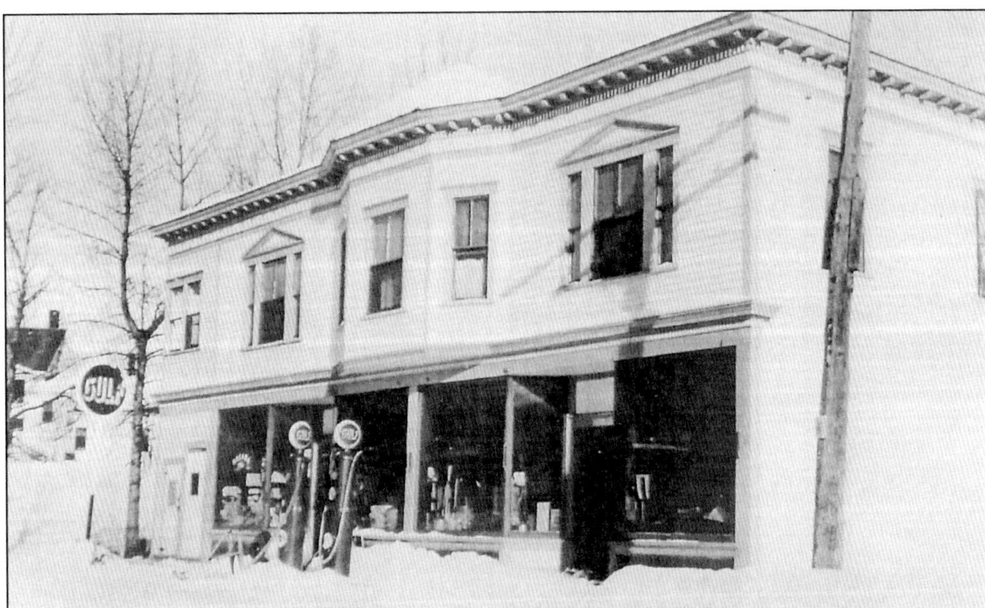

Aaron Anderson's General Store had once been a hotel. There are now two general stores in New Sweden.

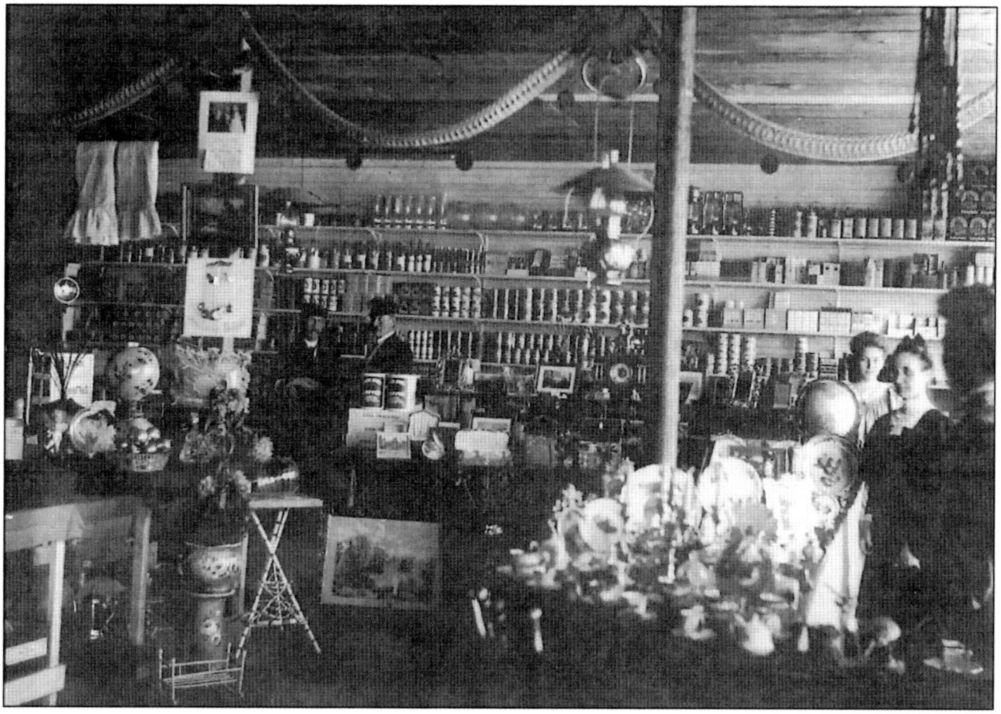

New Sweden had all kinds of retailing. This is the interior of a New Sweden store in the 1910s.

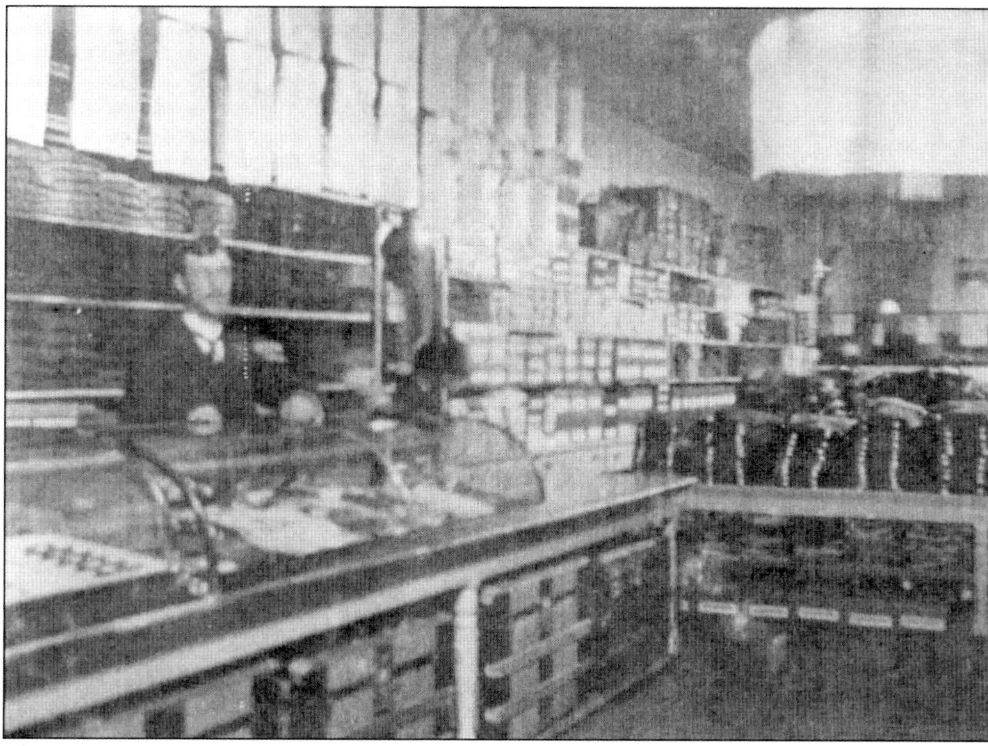

There was also much retailing in Presque Isle. The D.A. Stevens Store had a wide variety of clothing. It still operates as the Fred Stevens Store.

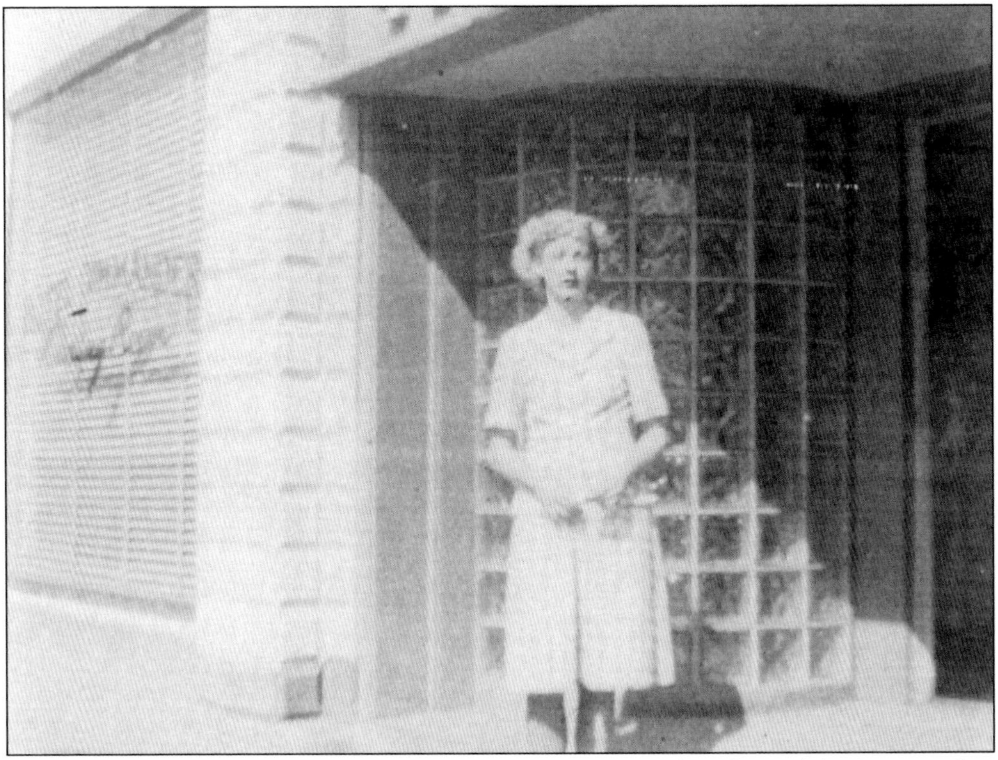

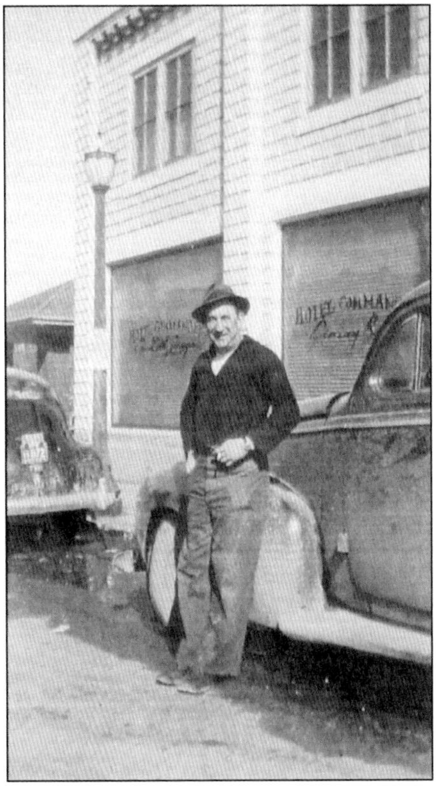

Mildred Smart stands in front of the Commander Hotel in Presque Isle about 1939. She was a cashier and typist at the hotel and her husband, Ernest, operated Smart's Taxi out of the hotel building.

Ernest Smart and two of his cabs in front of the Commander Hotel in Presque Isle. The Smart's Taxi office was on the left.

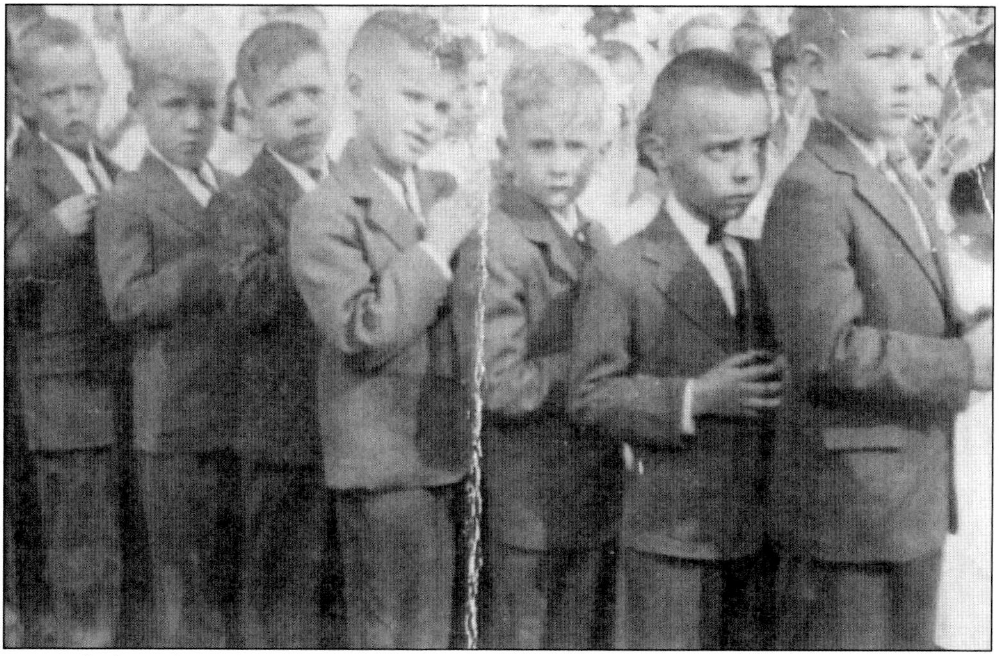

Pictured after taking their first communion at St. Mary's Church in Presque Isle in 1957 are, left to right: Fred Bishop, Dalton Madore, Barry Madore, Gilman Gauvin, Larry Allen, Peter Voisine, and Donald Cyr. Some went on to become successful businessmen.

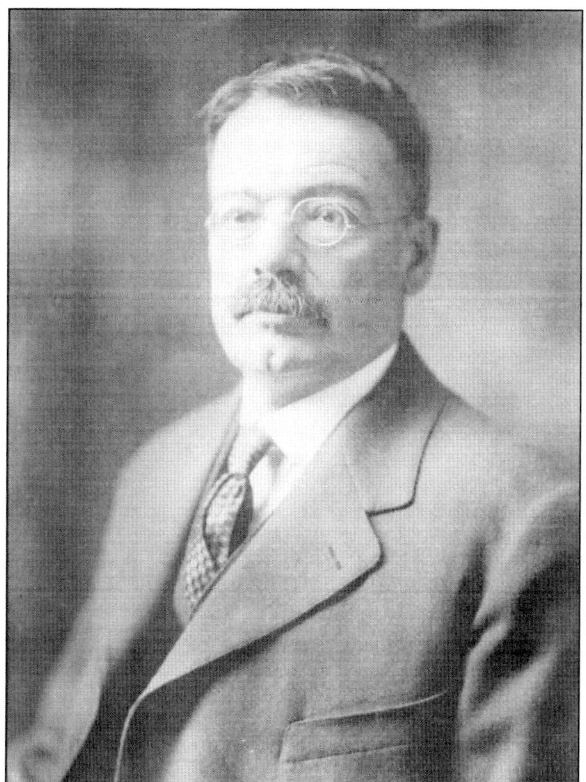

In another aspect of what is sometimes called business, Dr. Sherman W. Boone is shown here in 1925. He was the father of Dr. Storer Boone, who also practiced in Presque Isle.

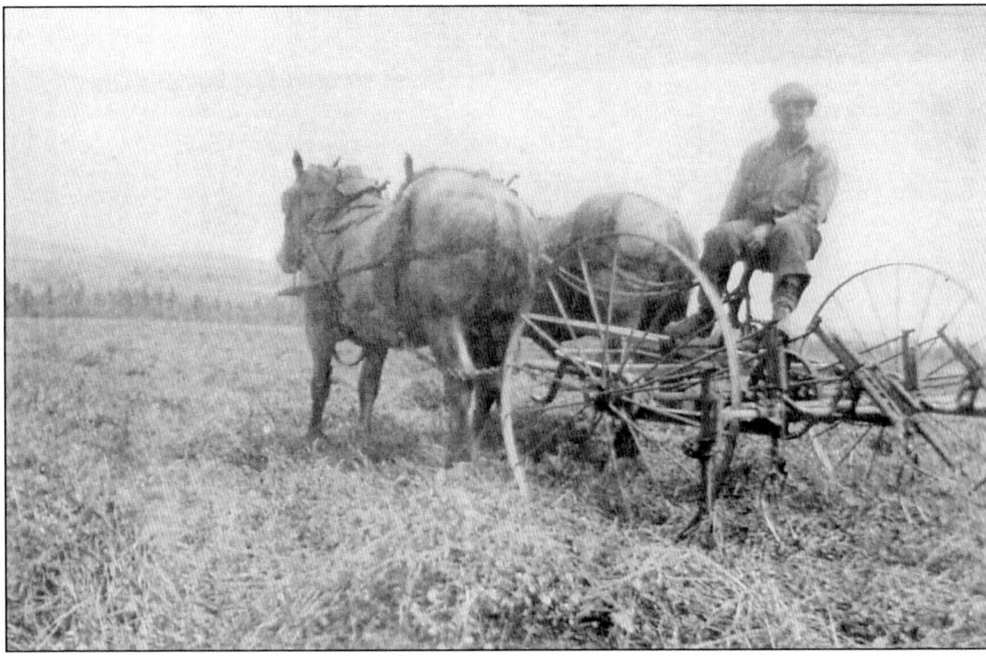

Farming in Presque Isle in 1939: not greatly changed, at least on the surface, from earlier times.

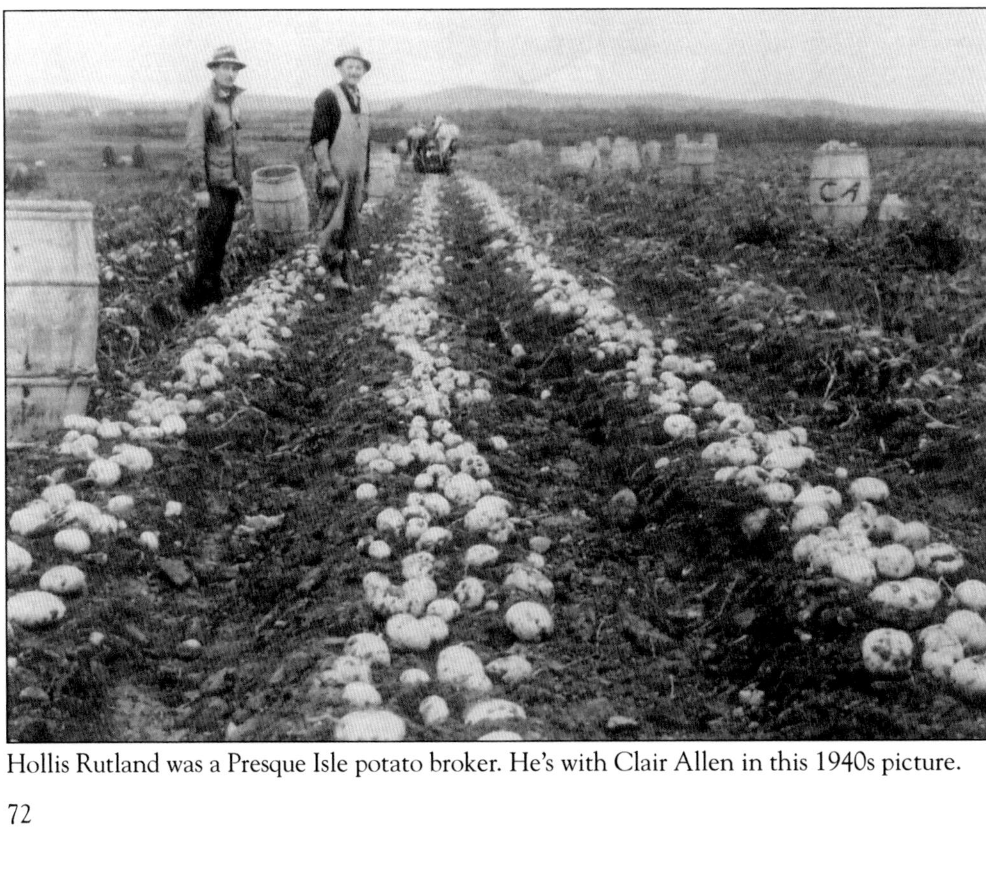

Hollis Rutland was a Presque Isle potato broker. He's with Clair Allen in this 1940s picture.

Five

Defense

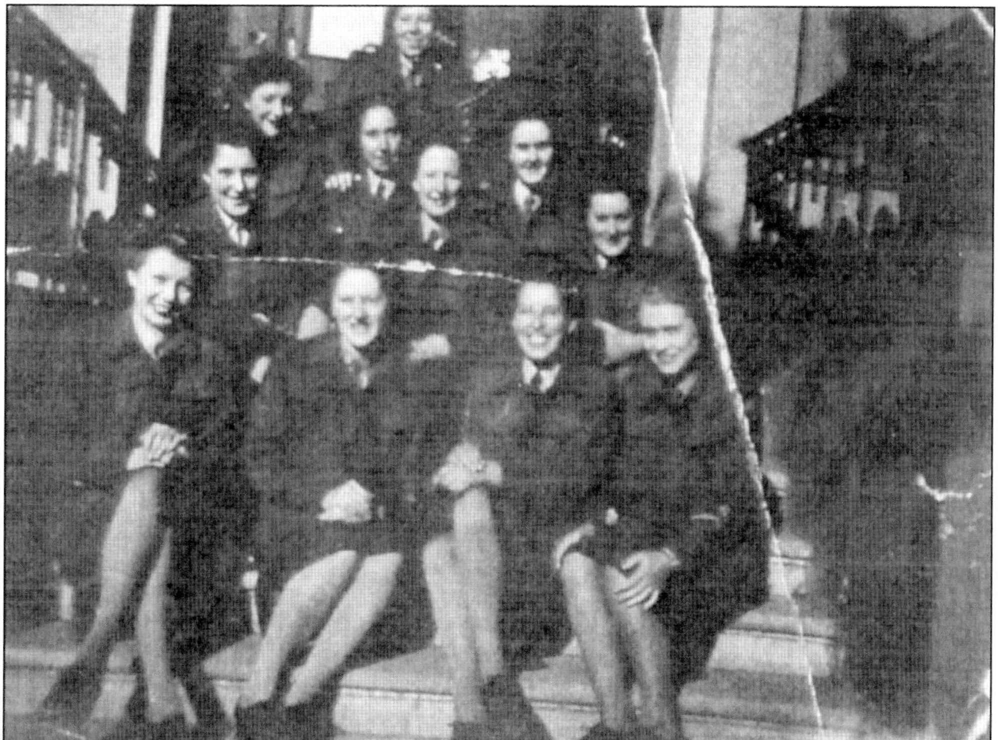

The Presque Isle Air Force Base was crucial during World War II because it was so close to Europe. WACS (members of the Women's Army Corps) were stationed at the base in 1943.

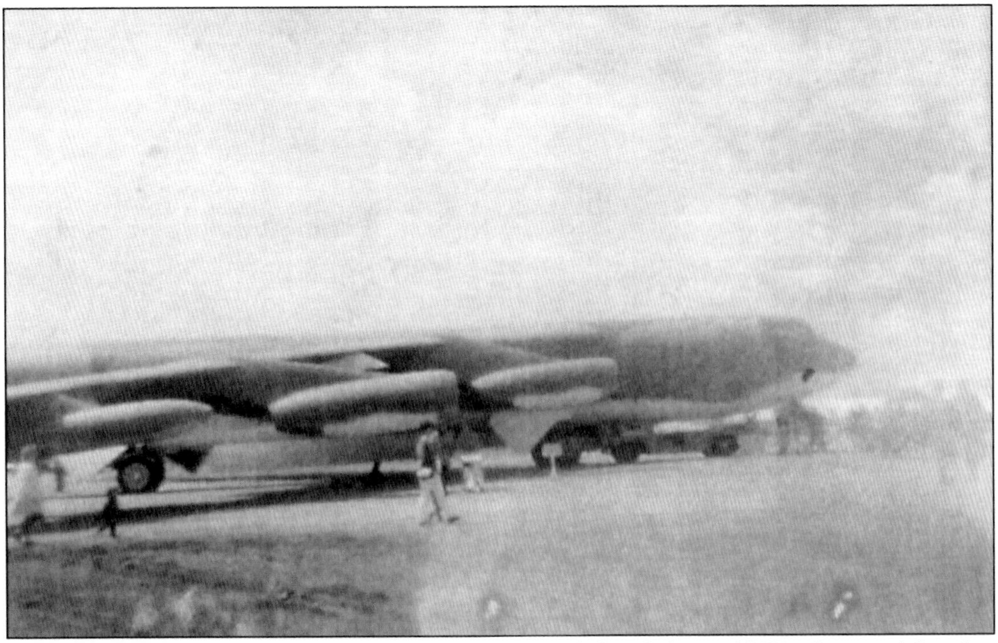

Activity continued at the base after World War II ended and the Cold War began. A bomber stands ready at the Presque Isle Air Force Base in 1956.

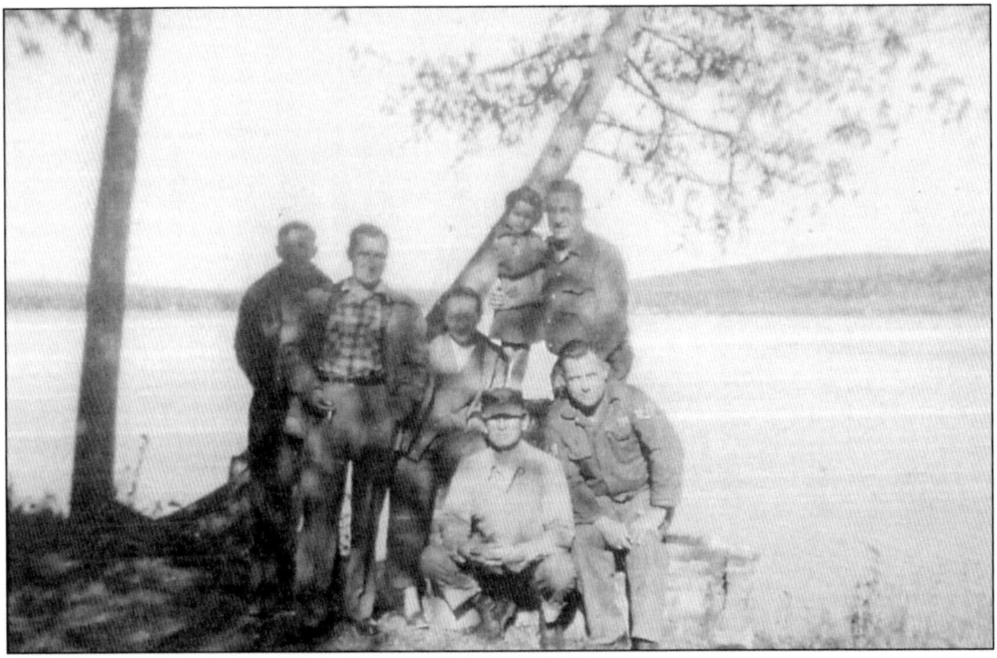

The ground crew of which Ernest Smart of Presque Isle was master sergeant is at the Air Force Base in 1949. Smart is in the rear. Smart, according to his daughter, Mrs Christie Cochran, was in the air force after World War II, after serving in World War I with the US Army and in World War II with the US Navy. During the Korean War, he was a US Air Force advisor.

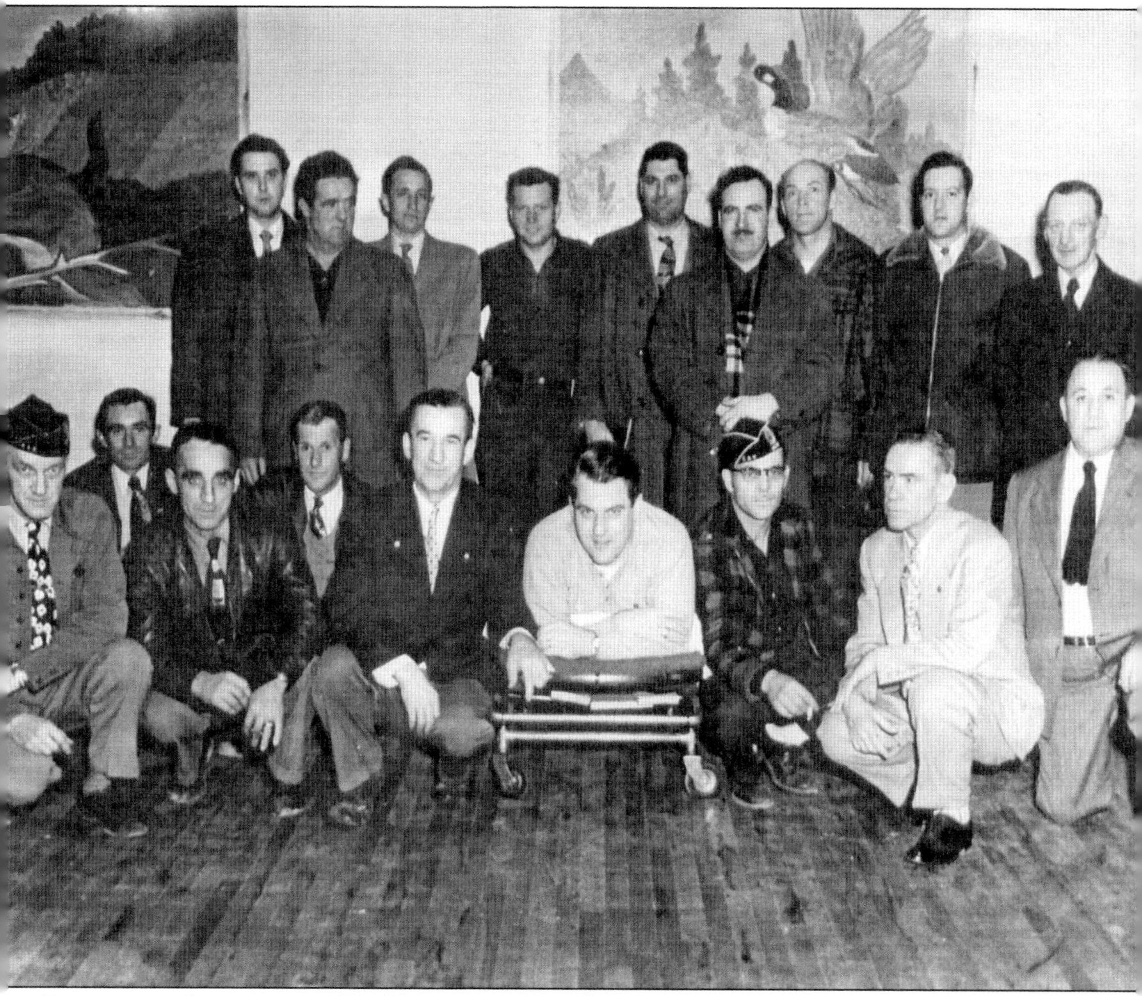

Everyone in this scene is a World War II veteran from Presque Isle. All took part in the D-Day invasion of Europe and all were on the beaches of Normandy. The picture was taken in 1950 at what was then the Northern National Bank Building in Presque Isle. The three communities here, like the rest of Aroostook County, had wonderful records in World War I and World War II.

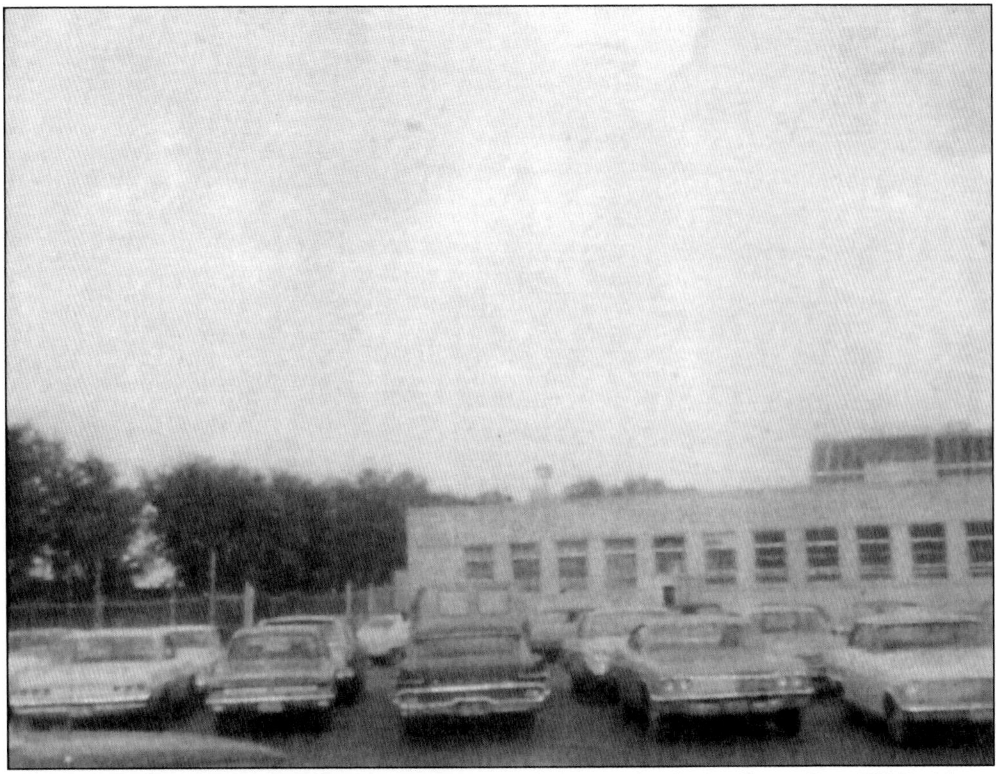

The Presque Isle Air Force Base BX Building in 1956.

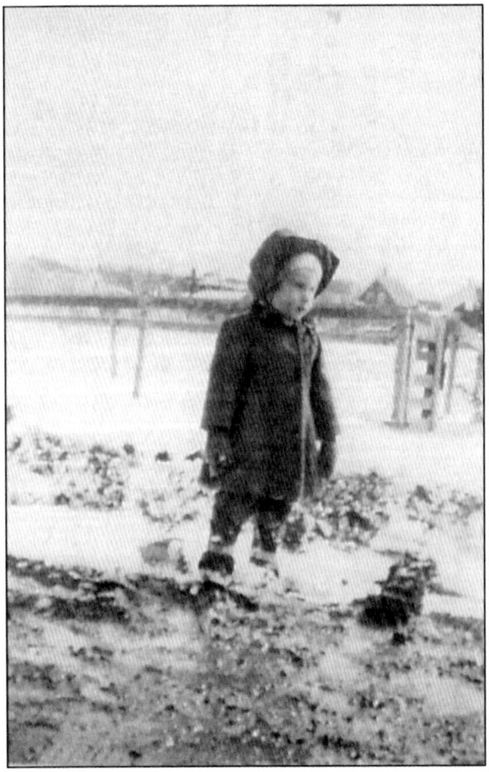

Patsy Smart, who went through high school in Presque Isle and now lives in Connecticut, stands on State Street near the Presque Isle Air Force Base in 1944.

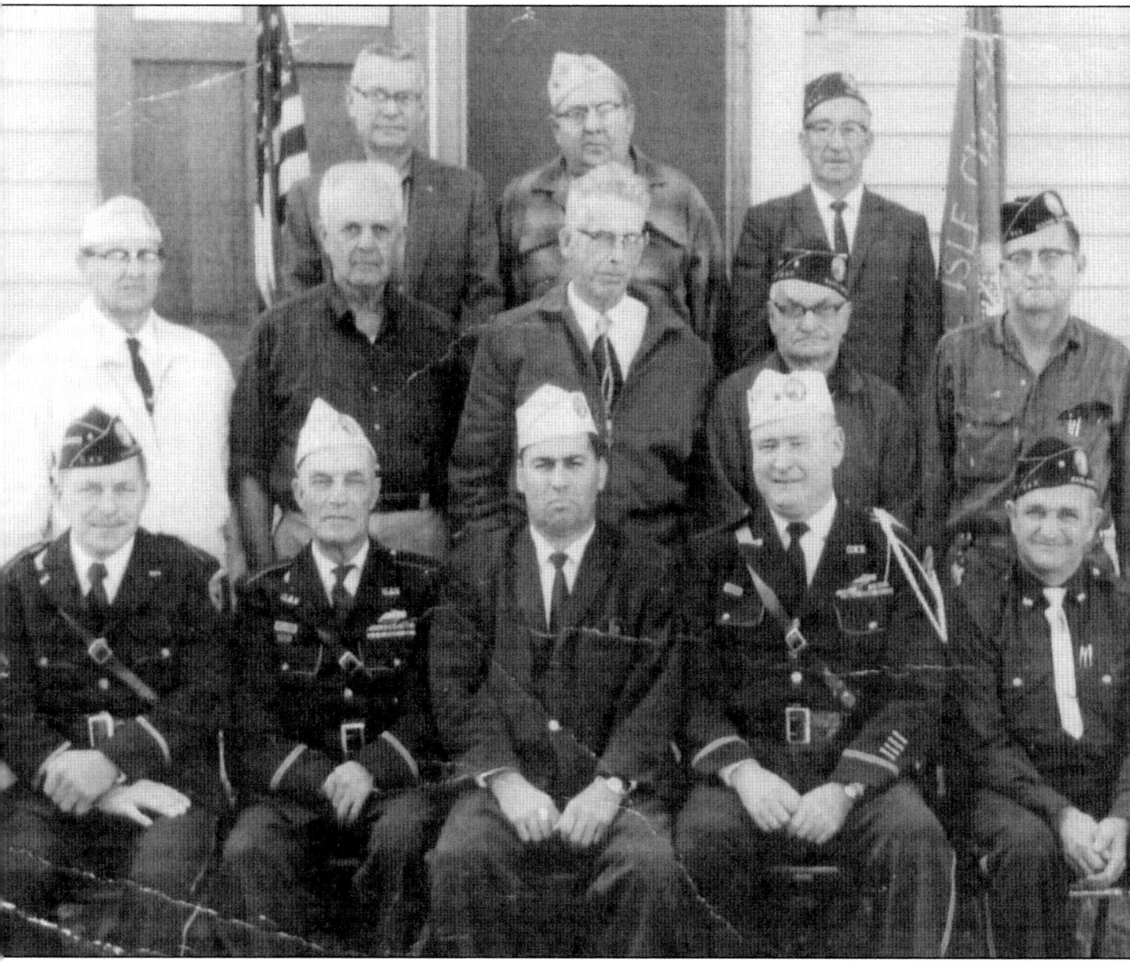

Members of Smart-Ricker Post, Disabled American Veterans, including the two men the post was named after, are shown in Presque Isle in 1960. In the first row are: (left to right) Earl Turner, Bill Ricker (who lost an arm in Normandy), Norman Bourgoin, Ken Monson, and John Chalifour; (second row) Gordon Bourgoin, Wallace Regis, and Dennis Gardiner; (third row) Enoch Stitham, Earl Britton, and Ernest Smart. This photograph was taken the day the post was founded.

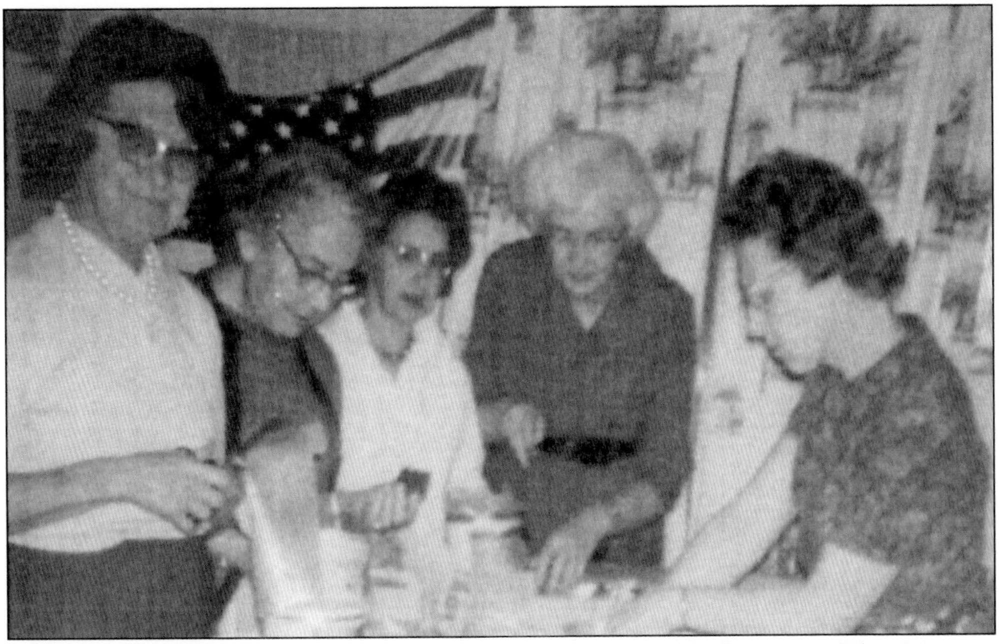

In January 1962, Frances Rizzo, Mary Ricker, Audrey Ryzmeck, Mildred Smart, and Flora Monson, all members of the Disabled American Veterans Auxiliary, prepare for a cake auction.

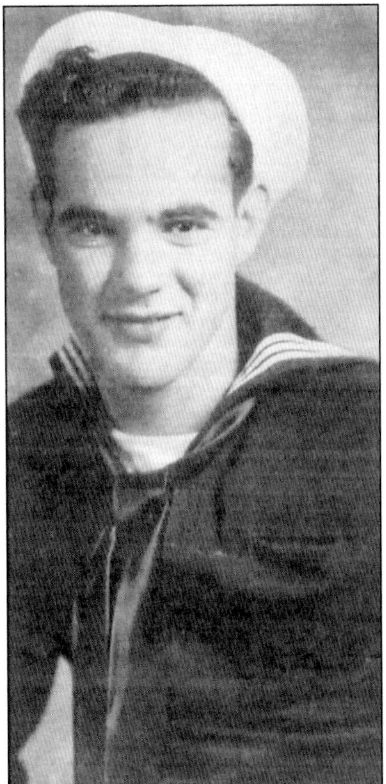

John Henry Kierstead appears in his US Navy uniform in Caribou in 1942. Kierstead, who now lives in Portland, became a surveyor for Cianchette Corp.

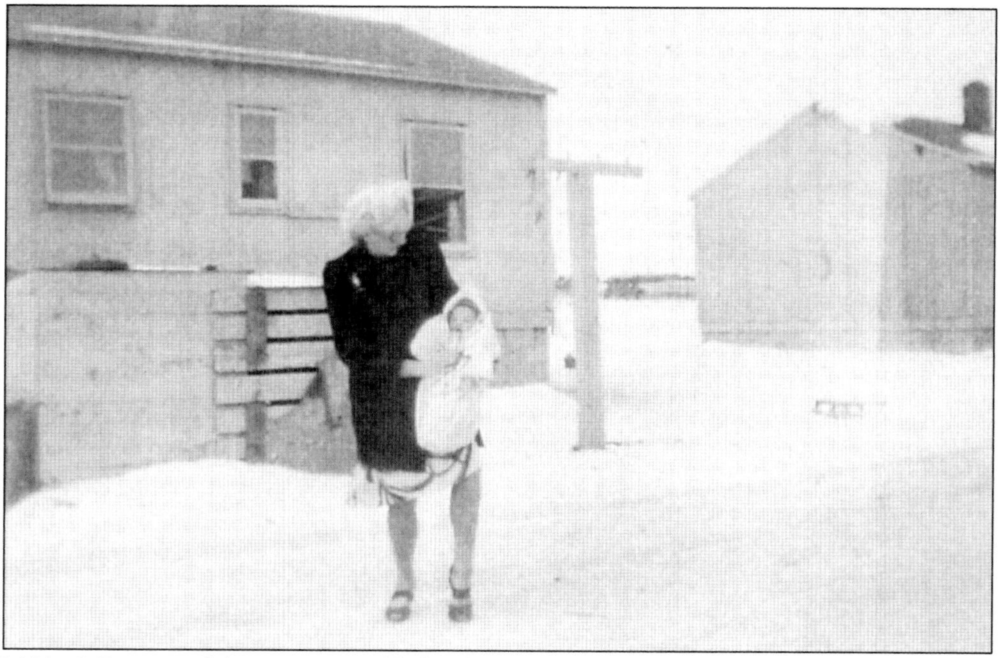

Mildred Smart and her one-year-old daughter, Christie, stand in 1944 at Fairview Acres, housing for the Presque Isle Air Force Base. Ernest Smart, Mildred's husband, was a lieutenant commander in the US Navy at the time and also an inspector. The housing was only available to Navy/Air Force personnel stationed at the base.

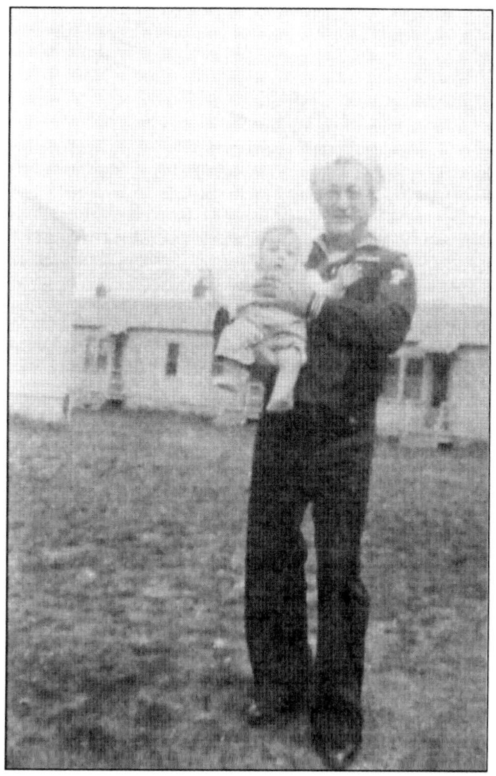

Ernest Smart at Presque Isle Air Force Base housing in 1944. As a Seabee, Smart took bodies off the beaches of Normandy. War can be extremely tough.

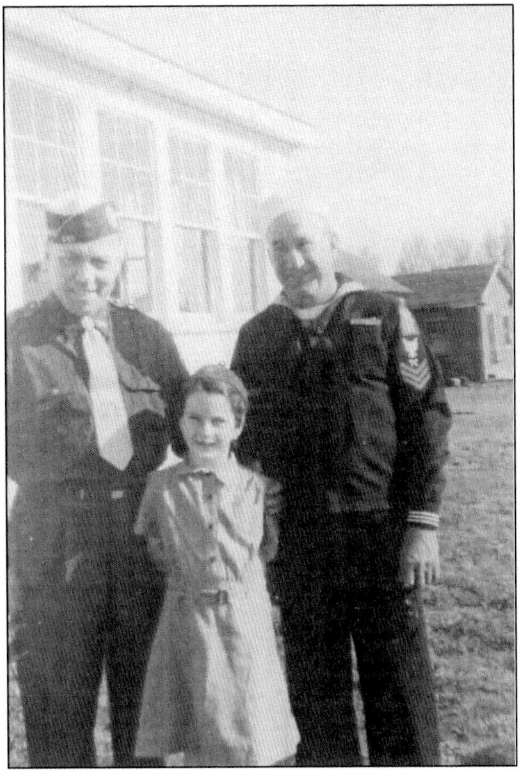

Norman Cormier, then commander of Maine's Disabled Veterans, stands with Ernest and Christie Smart in 1952.

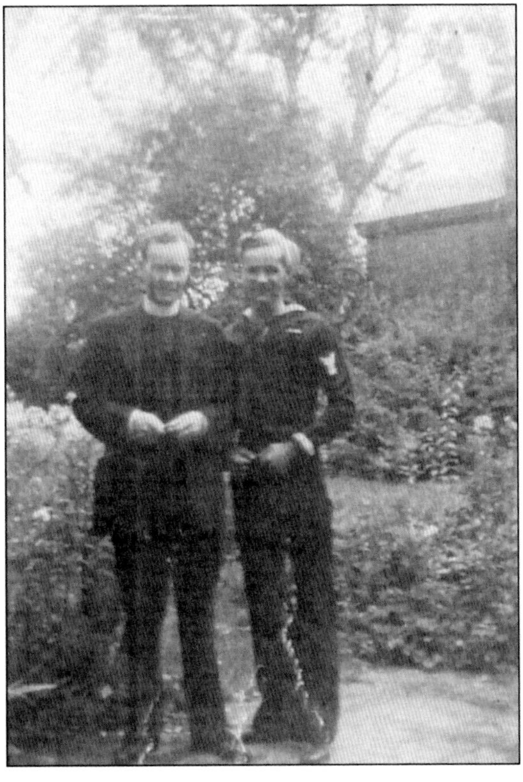

Philip Kierstead, a US Navy chaplain, and John, his brother, were in Caribou in 1941.

Six

Doers and Shakers

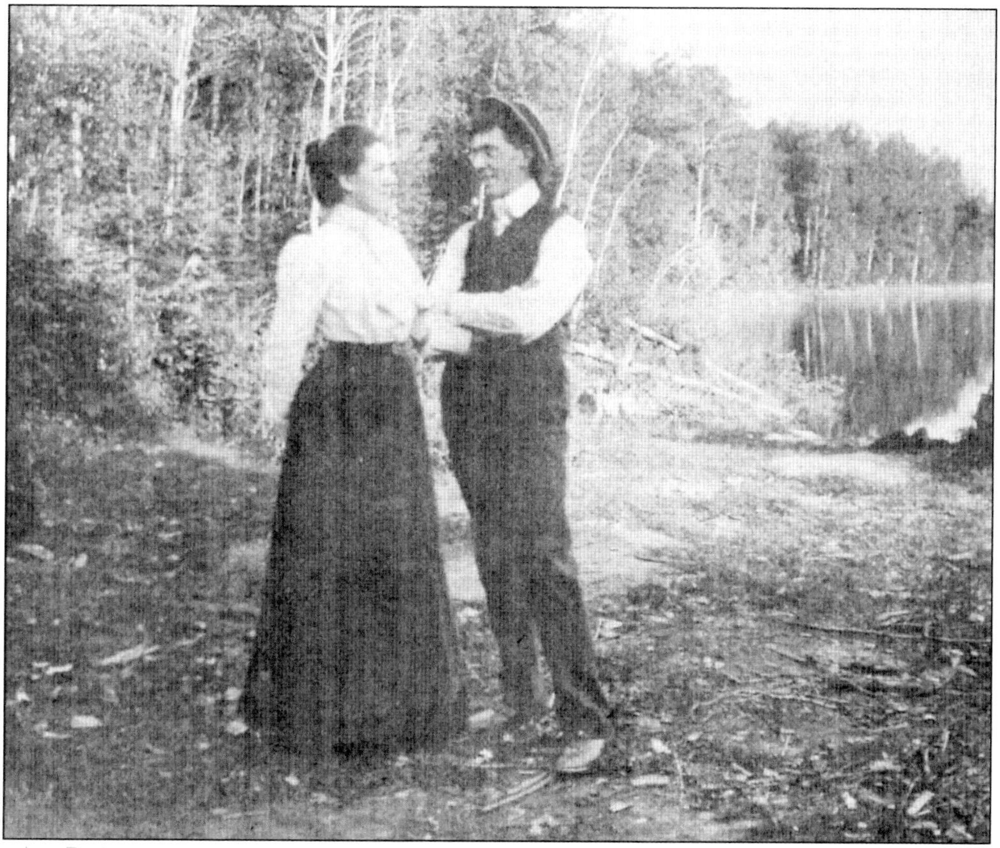

Alice Barker and Fred P. Stevens in Presque Isle about 1900. Stevens went on to become one of the city's leading retailers: the Fred P. Stevens Store is still operating.

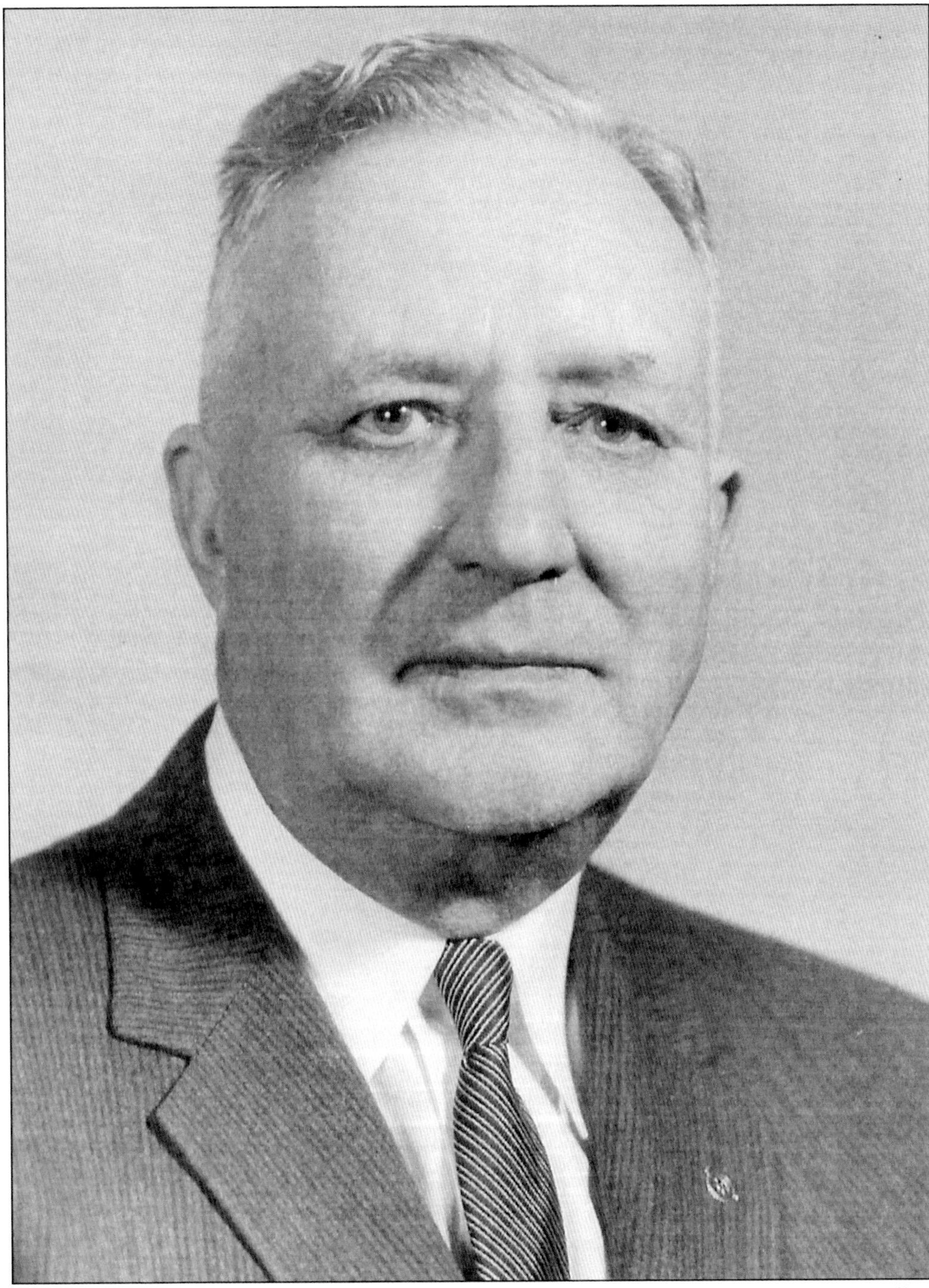

Samuel W. Collins (September 6, 1896–January 7, 1986), one of the bulwarks of the Collins family of Caribou. Sam Collins was a University of Maine graduate and a World War I veteran. He established the Collins Construction Co. in 1951 and set up housing developments on the old Collins farm for the military and civilian personnel at Loring and Presque Isle Air Force Bases. He served two terms in the Maine House of Representatives and four in the Maine State Senate, the last two as chairman of the pivotal Appropriations Committee.

William Widgery Thomas of Portland, the man behind the settlement of New Sweden, stands with the Reverend C.F. Olson at the memorial dedication to him in 1926. Thomas died the following year.

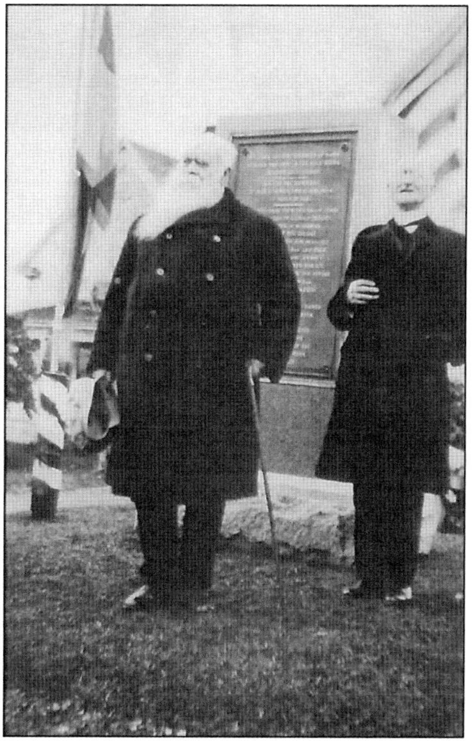

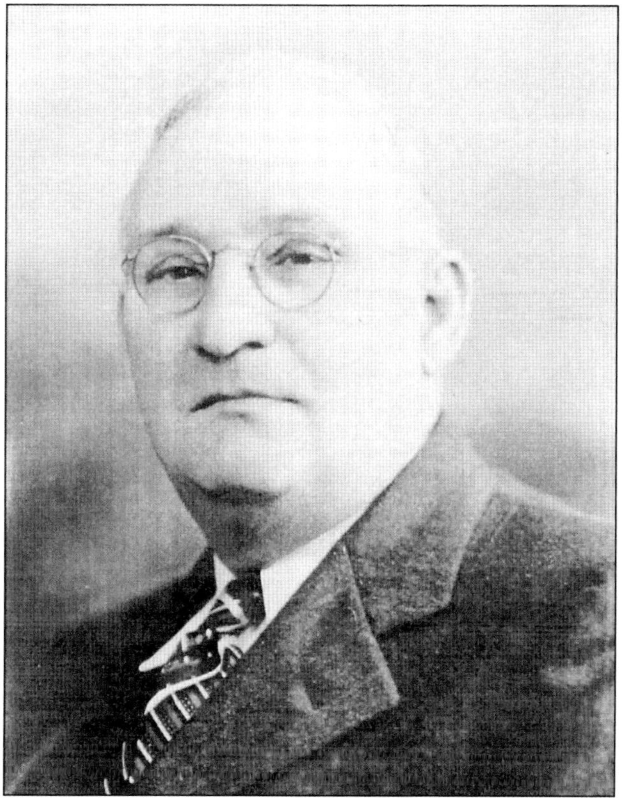

Think there were many Andersons in New Sweden? In 1938, all three of the town's selectmen were named Anderson and none was related to the others. Aaron Anderson was first selectman. One of his sons, Melvin, later became first selectman.

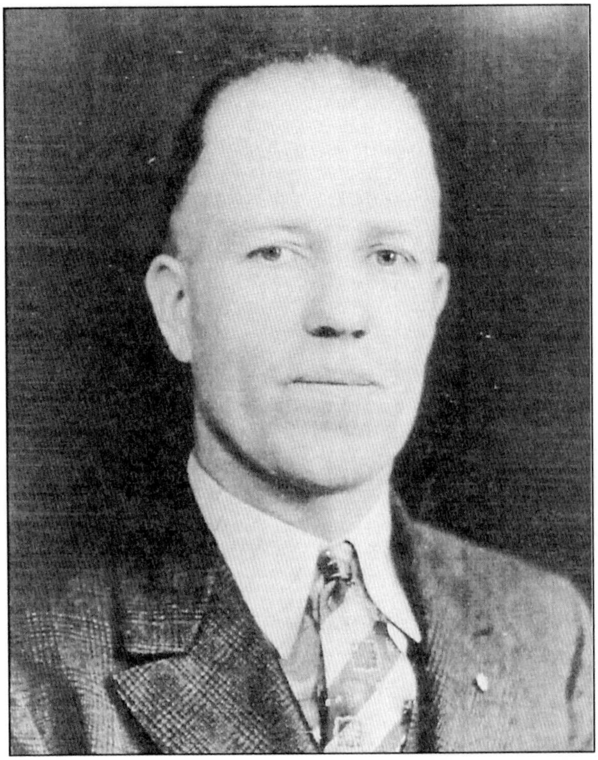

Clifford Anderson was second selectman in 1938. He operated a poultry farm in New Sweden.

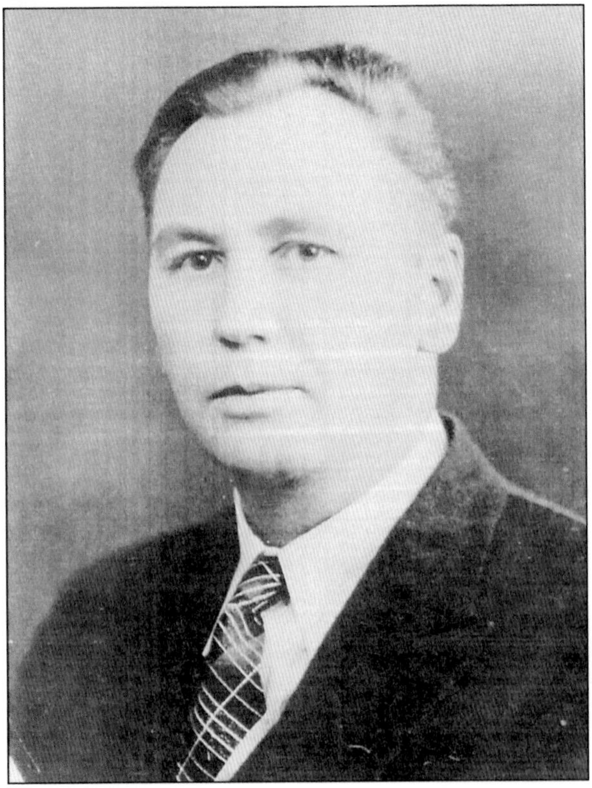

Henry Anderson was third selectman. Henry was a ski maker, operated a filling station, and owned tourist cabins. He later became the leader of the New Sweden Band. His wife operated the Kaffe Steegan coffee shop.

Ernest Smart, a veteran of World War I, World War II, and the Korean War, stands before his taxi company's stand in Presque Isle. The Disabled American Veterans Post in Presque Isle is named after Smart and Bill Ricker.

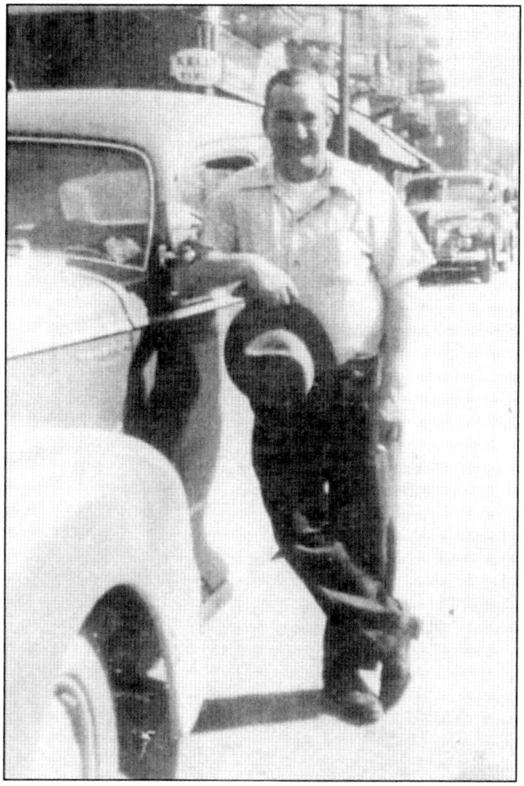

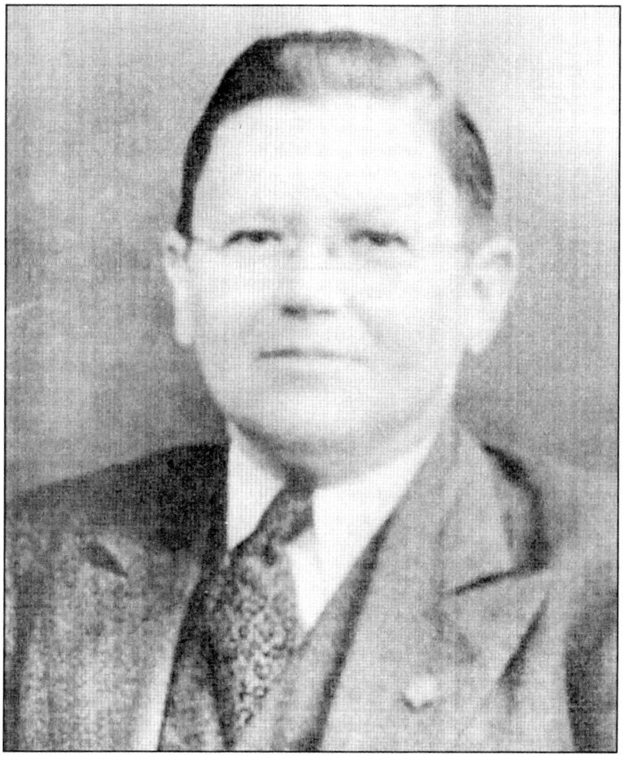

Walter Anderson was New Sweden's postmaster until about 1958, when he was replaced. Anderson's home, however, remained the post office until about 1977.

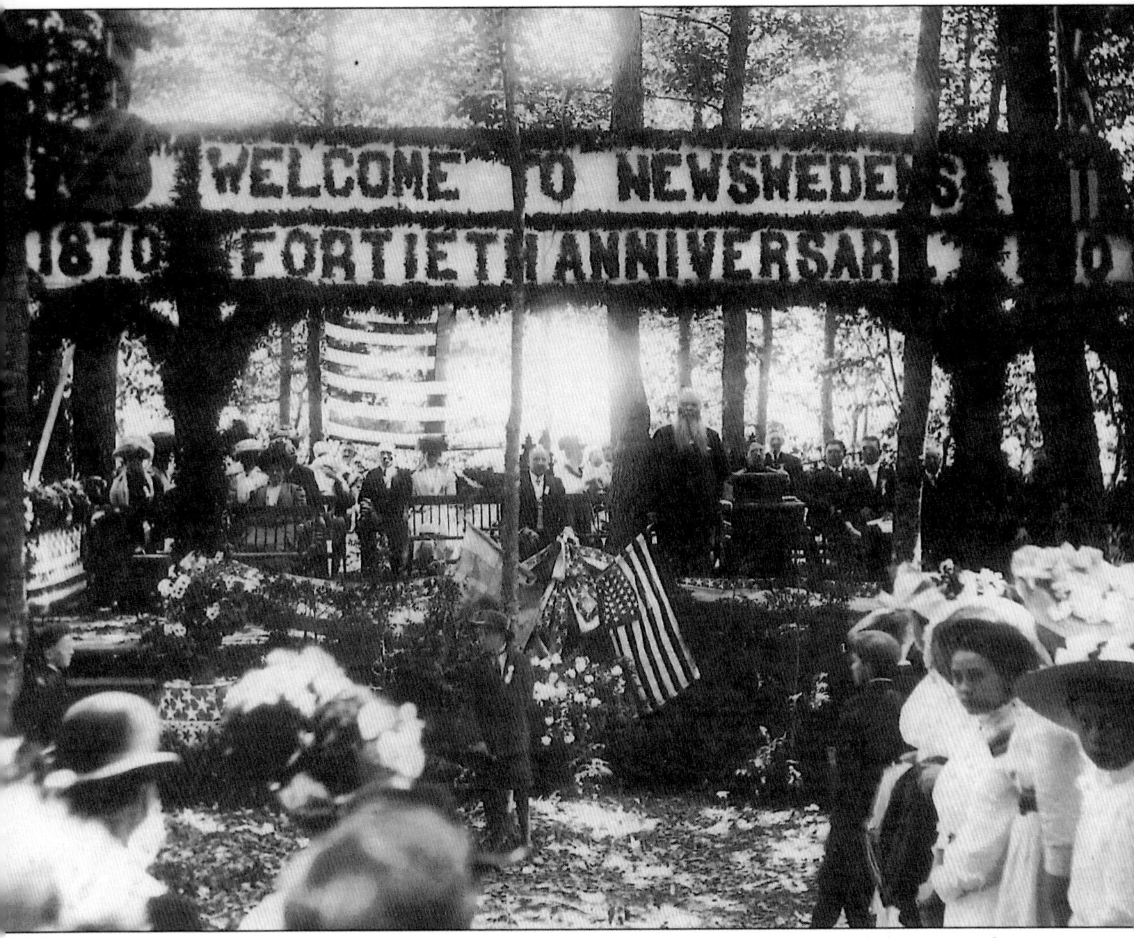

William Widgery Thomas, besides all his skills and talents, was one of the most photogenic people you could ever see. Here he is at the 40th anniversary celebration of the founding of New Sweden in 1910. Several high-ranking Swedish officials attended the ceremony. The settlers always called him "Father Thomas."

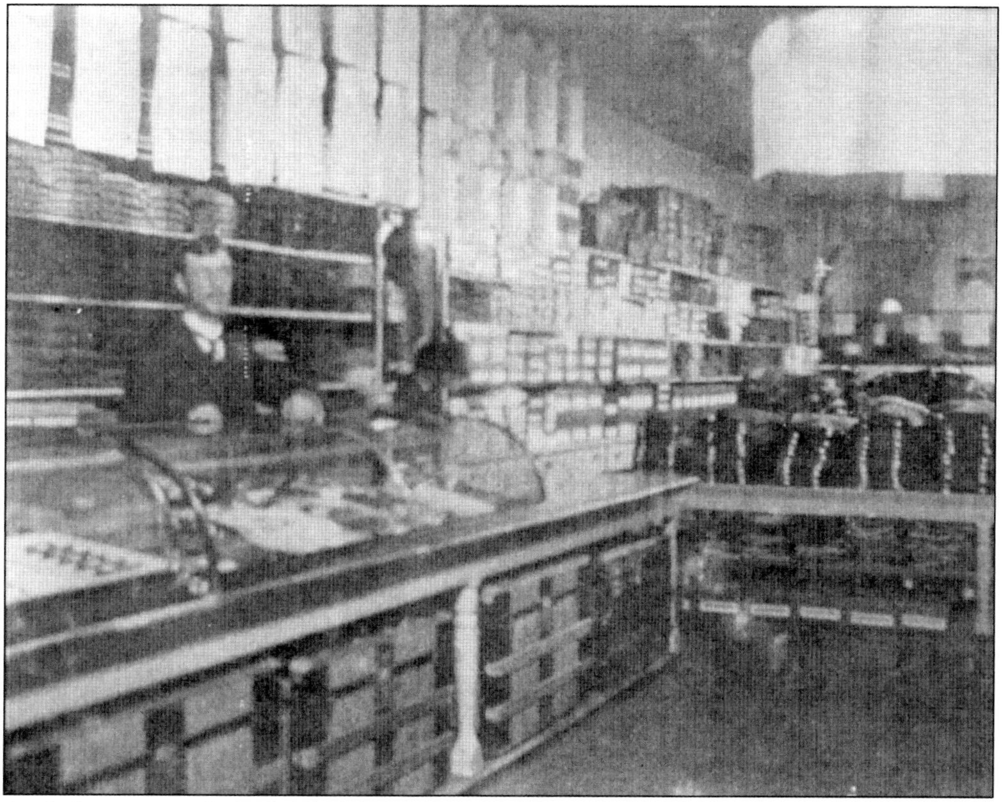

Arc lights were used to take this interior shot of the then-D.A. Stevens Store in Presque Isle. Men's and women's clothing has been sold at what is now the Fred P. Stevens Store for 108 years.

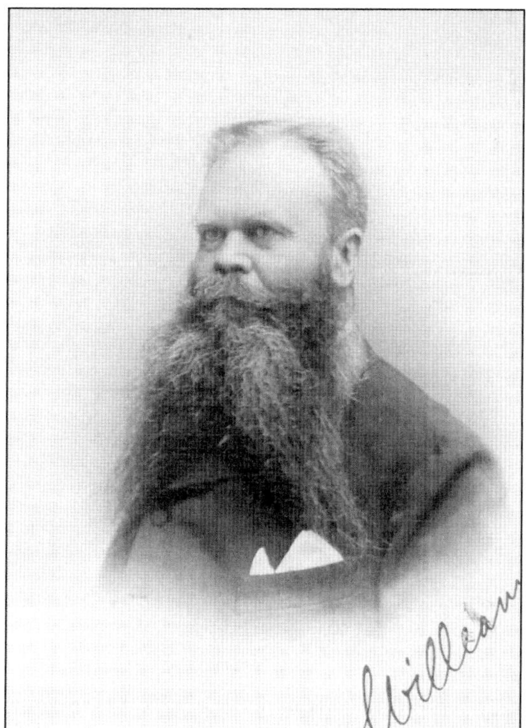

W.W. Thomas at the age of about forty-five or fifty in Stockholm, Sweden.

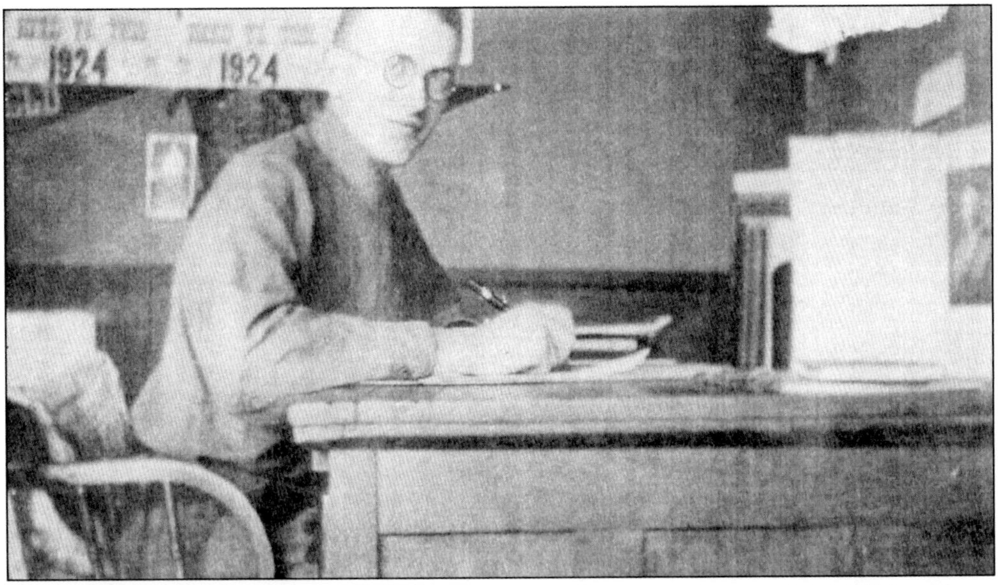

Frank Hussey of Presque Isle in 1924 at the University of Maine at Orono in his ROTC uniform. Only eight years later, Hussey was elected the first president of Maine Potato Growers Inc., the largest Maine potato growers cooperative. He was later named a high-ranking US Department of Agriculture official.

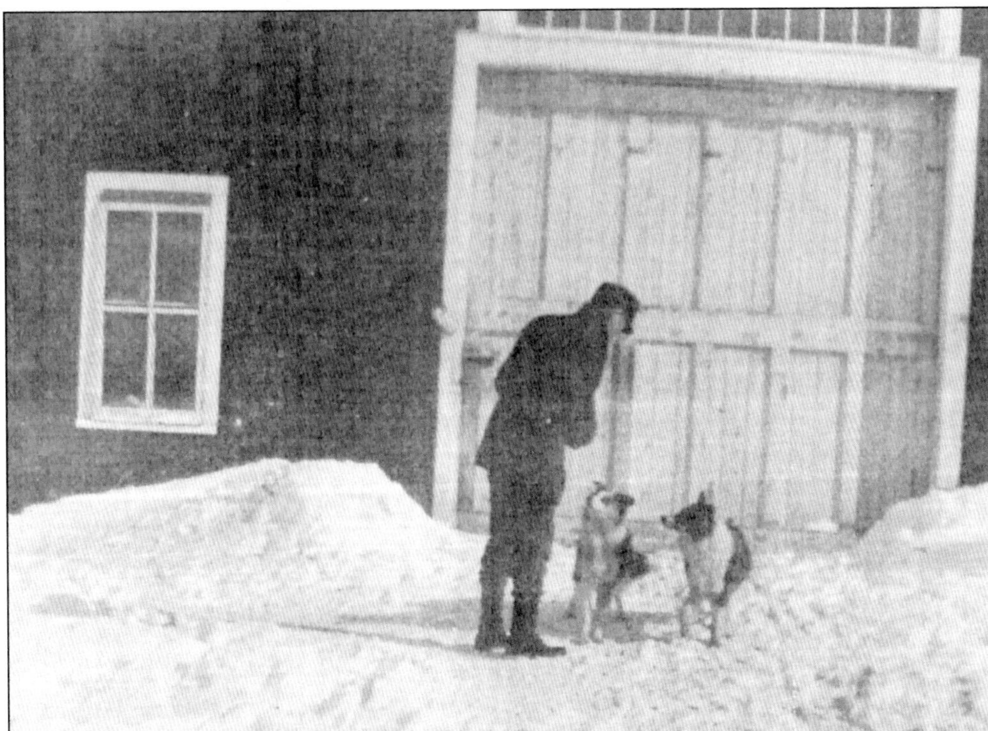
Thomas H. Phair and his dogs in Presque Isle about 1910. Phair, an extremely astute businessman, became known as the "Starch King of Aroostook County." He was one of the first directors of the Presque Isle Village Fire Department and served in the state legislature.

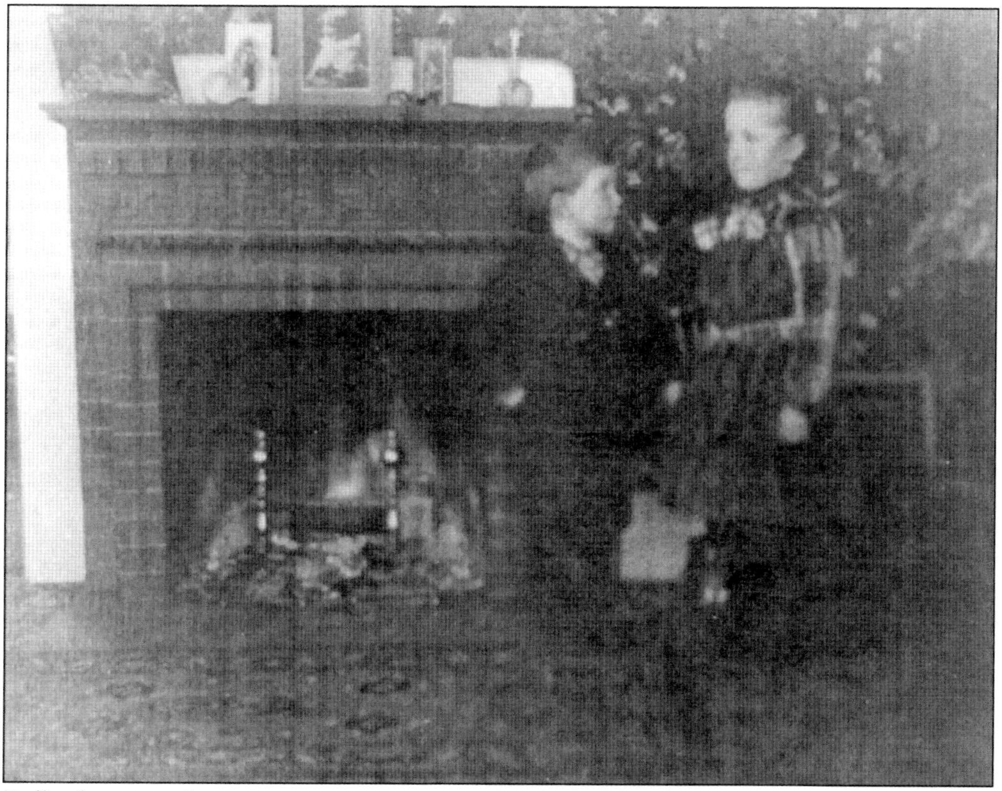

Sadly, the young from some prominent families in the area would leave, often when young. Maurice and Ruth Stevens (ages five and six respectively when this picture was taken, about 1900) left town when both were freshmen at college. They were probably the children of D.A. Stevens, the prominent Presque Isle businessman.

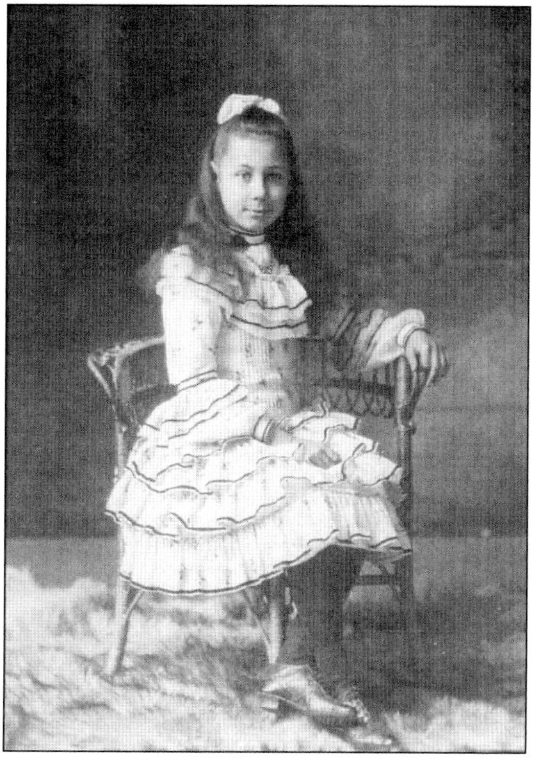

Vera Esty, who deeded a house on Third Street in Presque Isle to the city. That house is managed by the Presque Isle Historical Society. She is shown here in 1899 at the age of five.

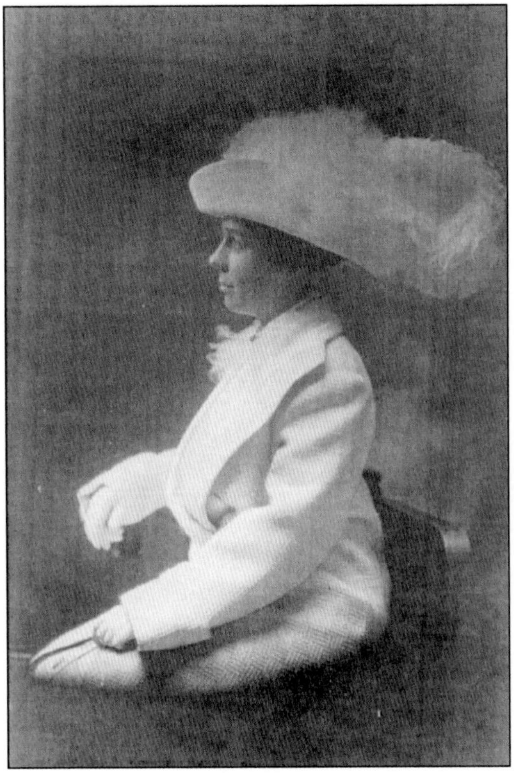

Vera Esty soon after her graduation from high school in 1912.

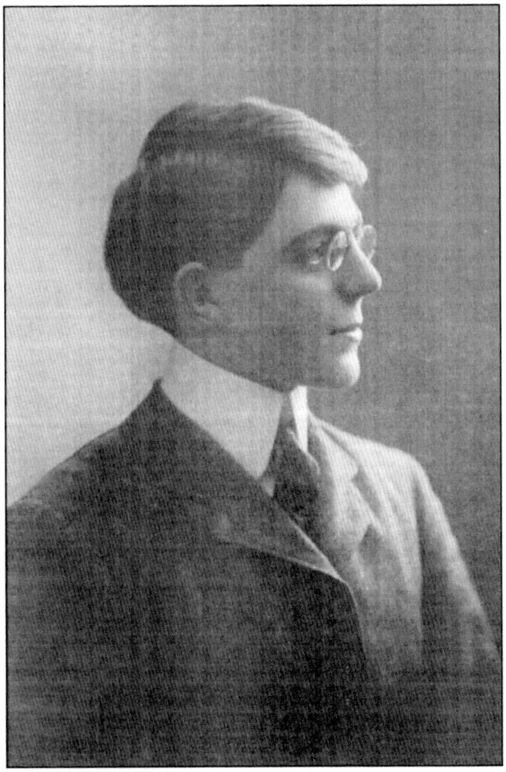

Fred Percival Stevens, the great Presque Isle retailer.

Seven

The Towns

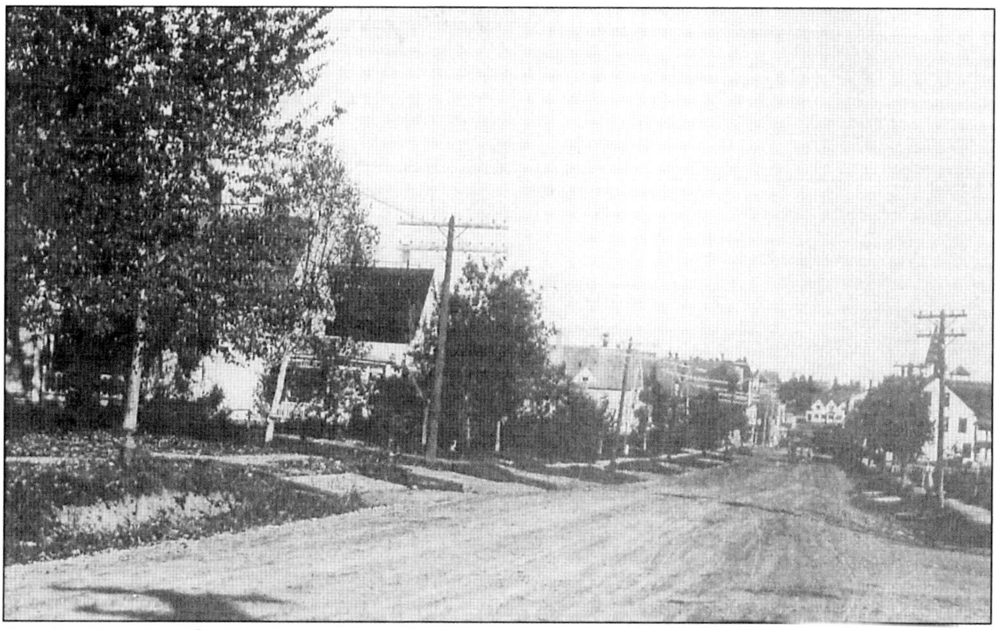

Sweden Street in Caribou about 1909, looking from the New Sweden side.

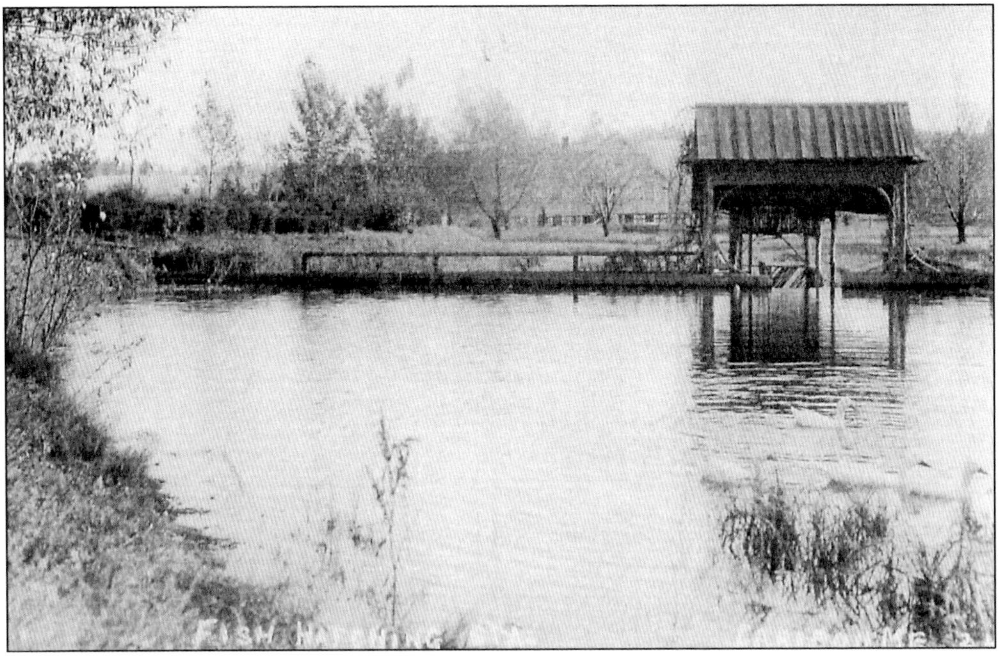

This is the Sweden Street fish hatchery in Caribou. This may have been taken before the state purchased it in 1895.

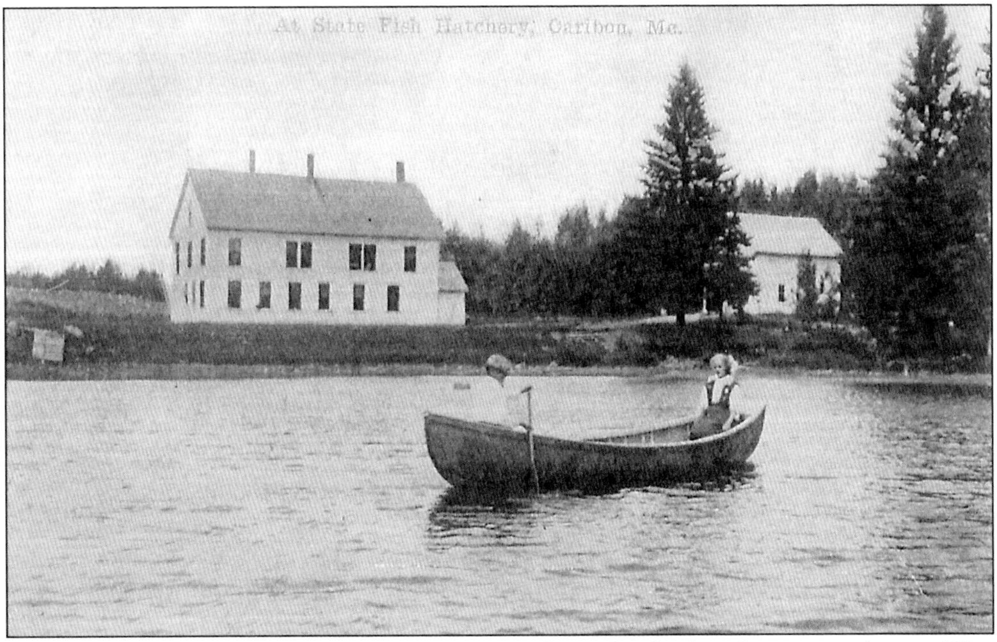

The hatchery was moved to Limestone Street on Otter Creek after the state took over. This may have been taken about 1910.

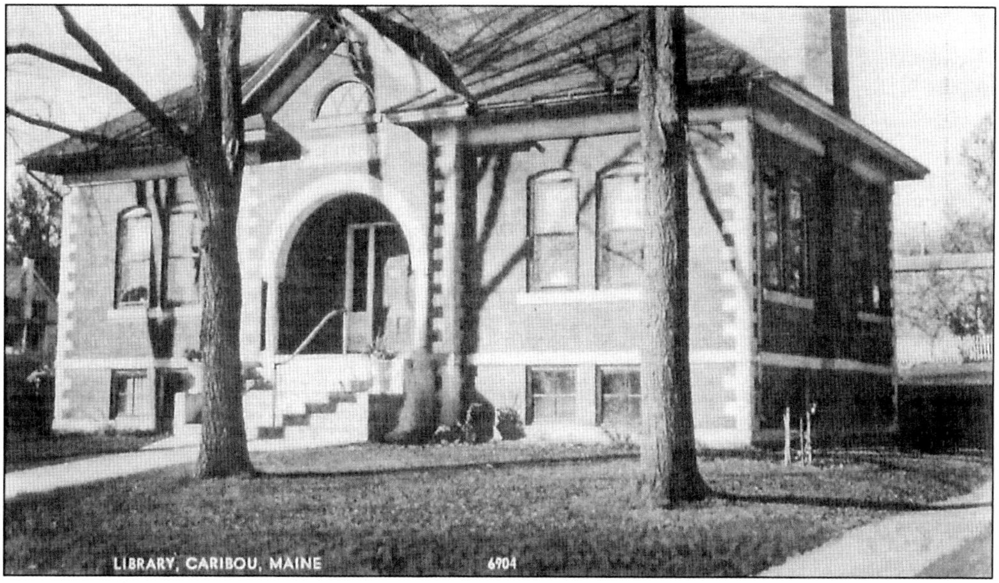

An early photograph of the Caribou Public Library in 1913. The library was started with a $10,000 donation from Andrew Carnegie.

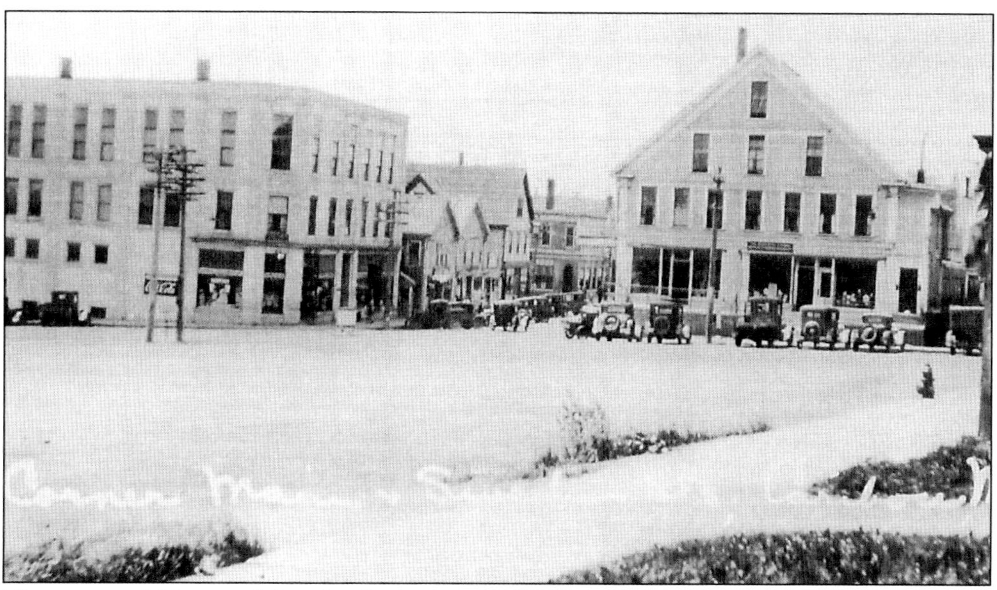

The corner of Main and Sweden Streets in Caribou in the 1930s. We are looking west. The Clark Block is on the left and the Skates Building on the right.

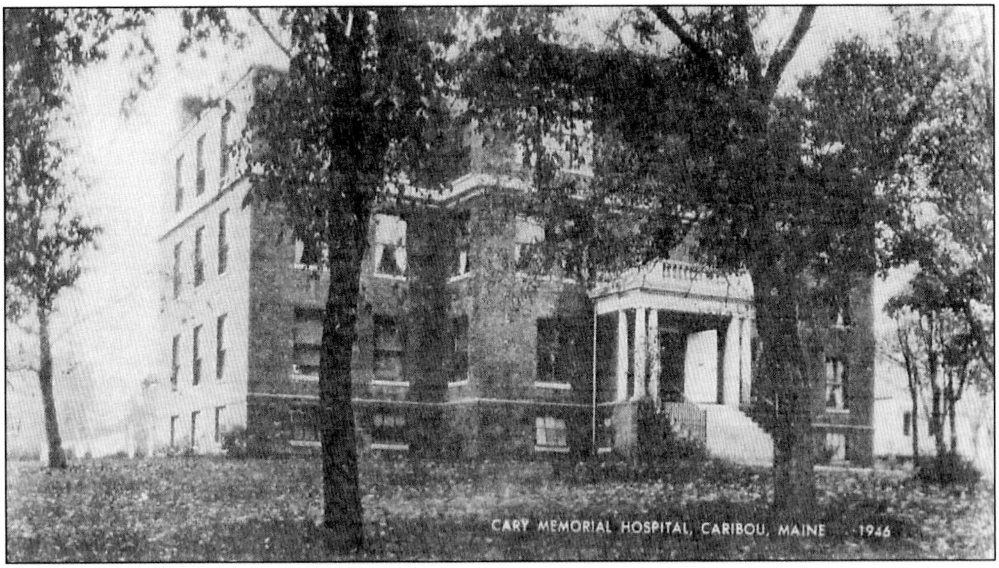

Cary Memorial Hospital in Caribou in 1946.

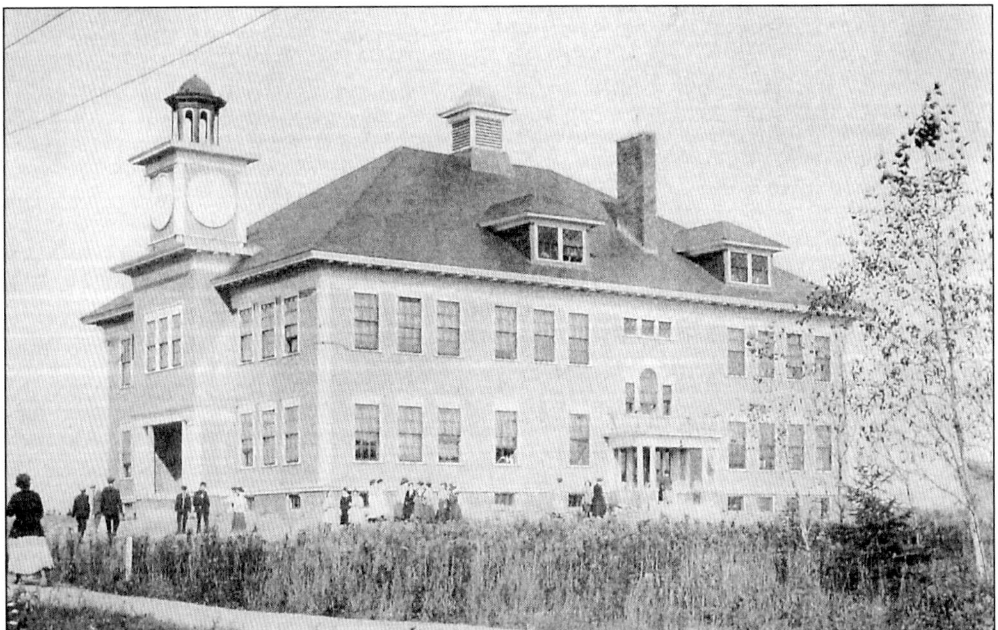

Caribou High School about 1920. The first high school had burned. A new high school was built in 1926.

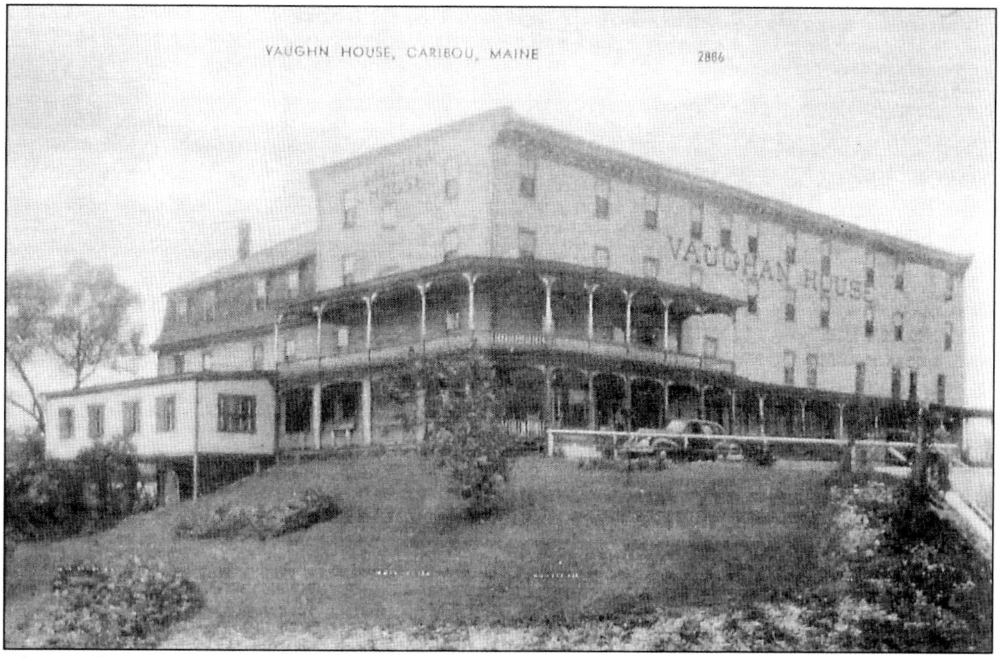

The third version of the Vaughan house in the 1940s.

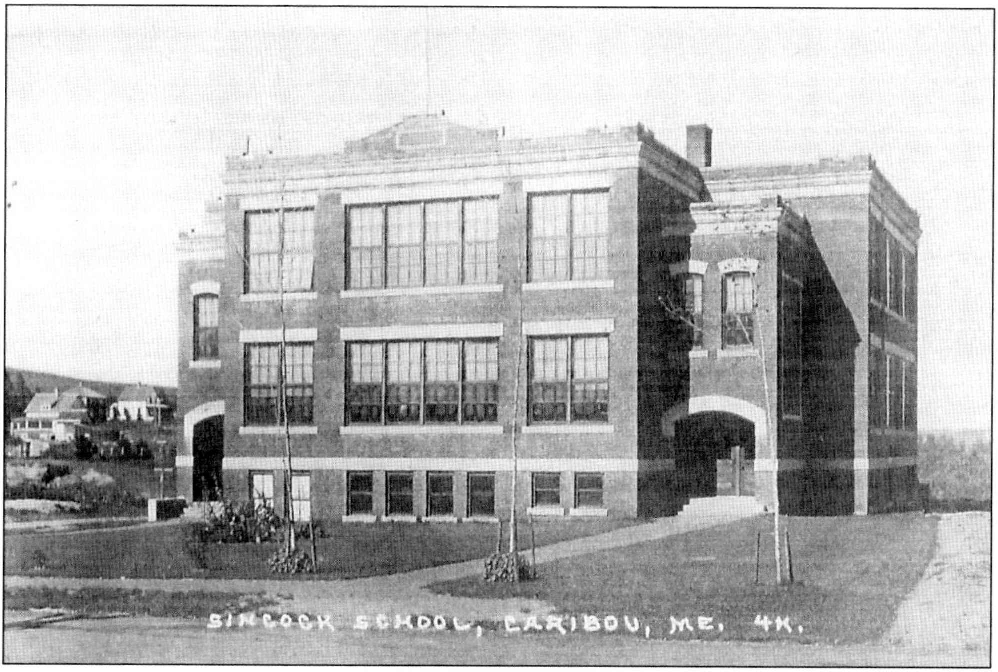

On with some of Caribou's buildings. The Sincock School was originally built for the education of Franco-American children and was operated by Dr. Sincock. Located on South Main Street, it became a public elementary school in the 1930s.

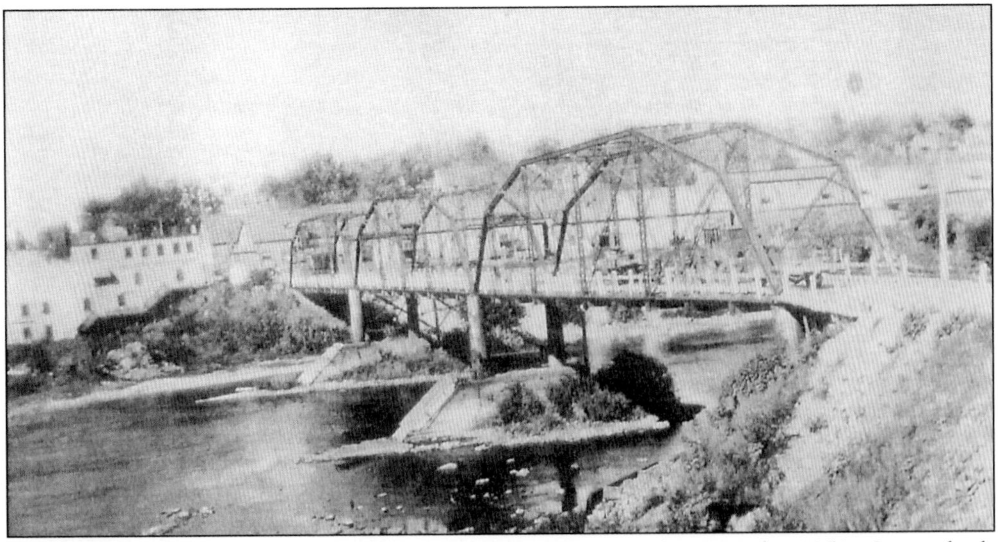

This bridge over the Aroostook River in Caribou was torn down in the 1950s. It was built around 1920 and replaced the "temporary" bridge engineered by Herschel Collins in four-and-a-half days.

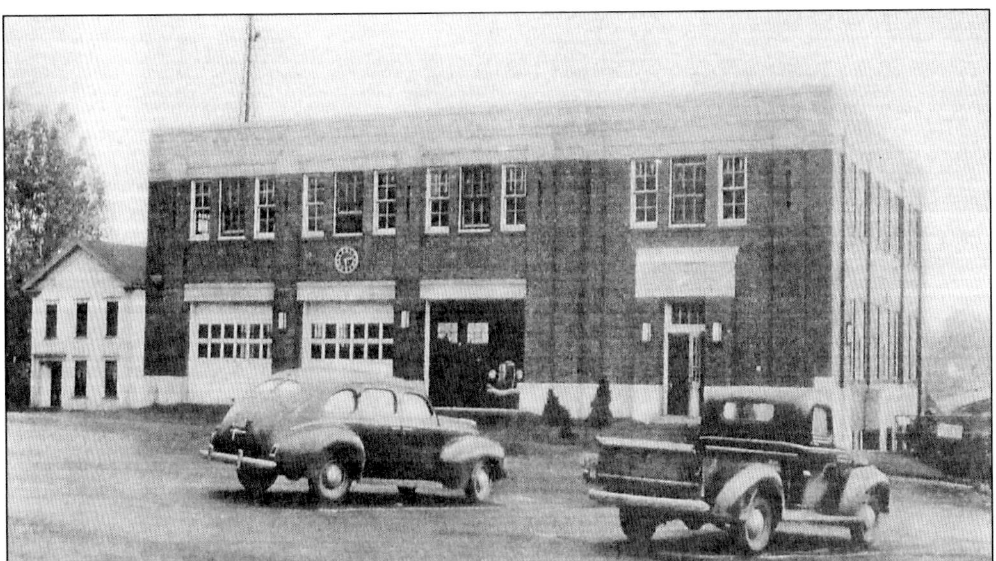

The Caribou Municipal Building was constructed in 1939. There is not too much to remind us of the frontier days in these buildings.

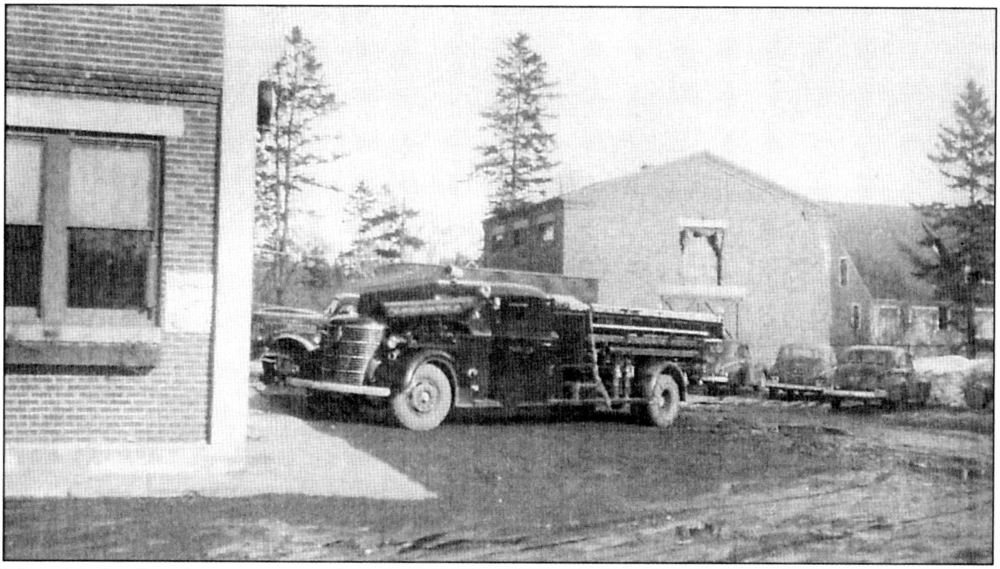

The old Caribou fire station in the 1940s with a fire engine behind it.

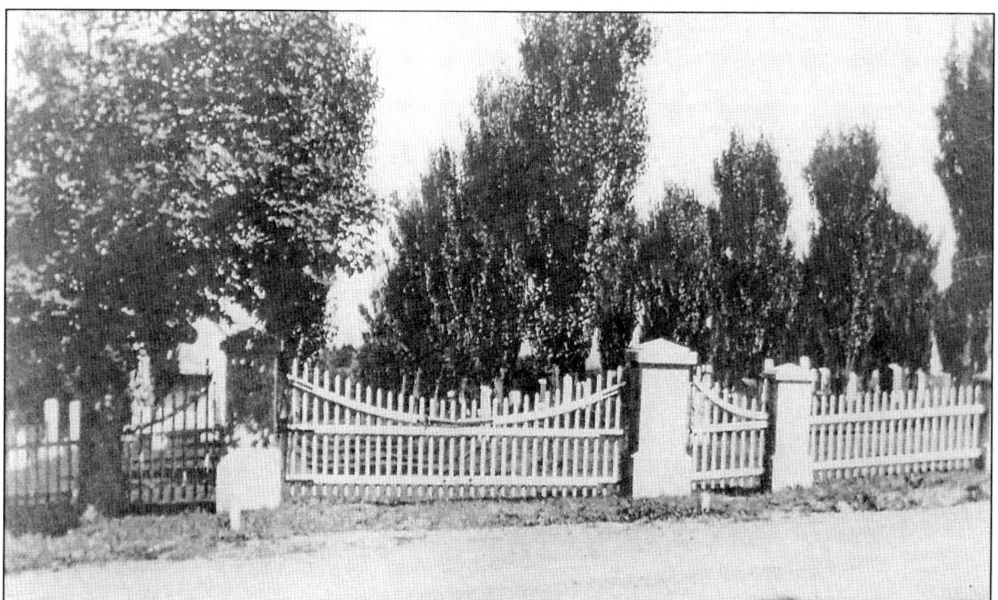

New Sweden's "new" cemetery was set up in 1876, six years after the community was founded.

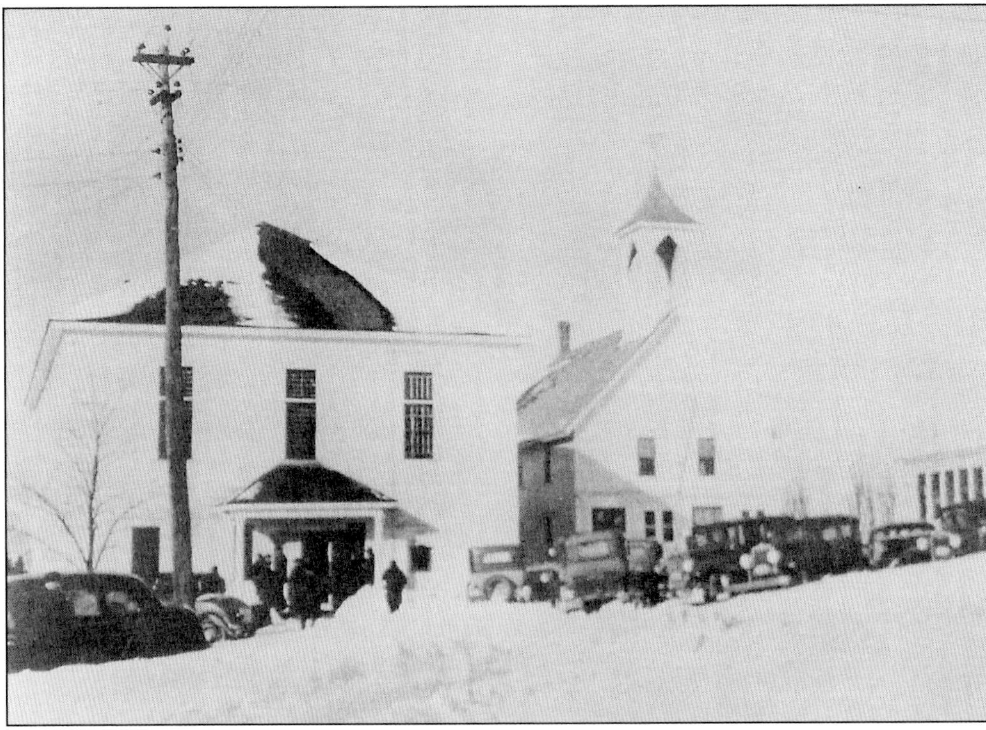

New Sweden's "new" town hall built in 1931; the old town hall, constructed as the Kapitoleum in 1970; and a school. Both town halls burned on June 30, 1971. Everything inside the Kapitoleum was saved. Even the doors were taken off. The building was rededicated as a museum on June 30, 1974.

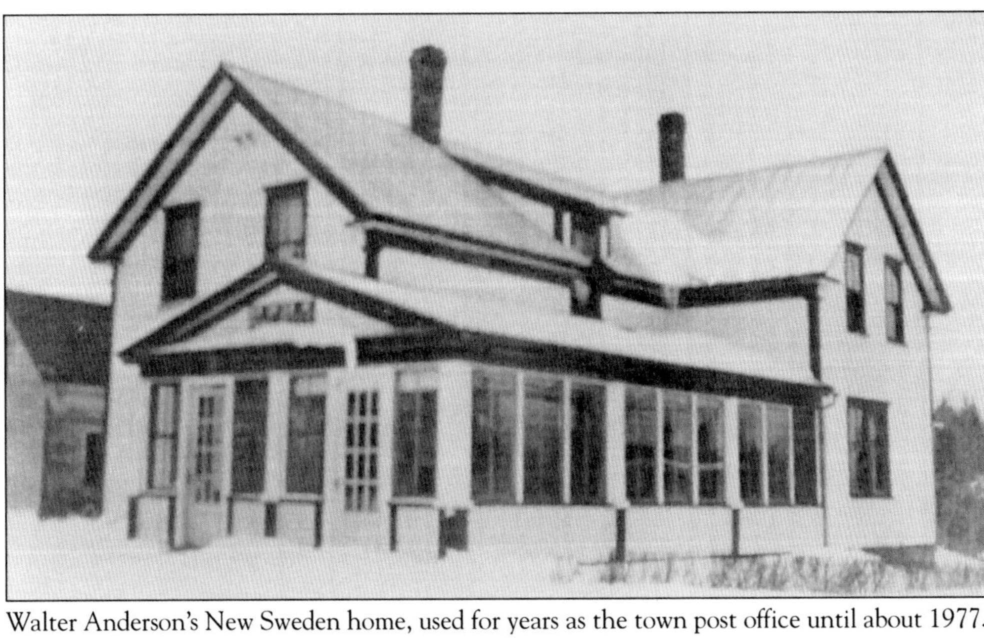

Walter Anderson's New Sweden home, used for years as the town post office until about 1977.

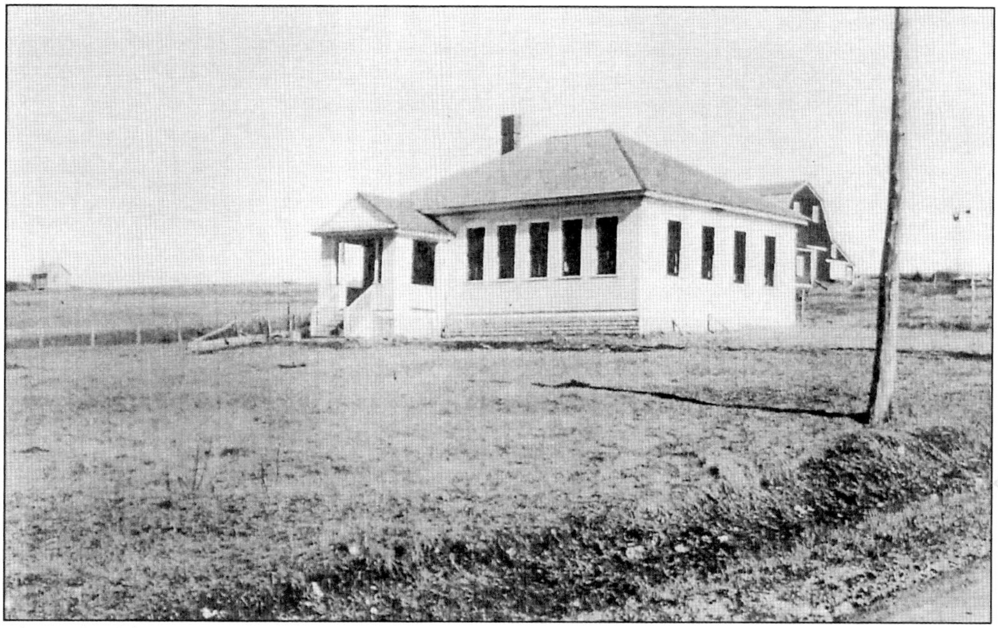

The only old schoolhouse of its type left in New Sweden. Once there were eight others like it.

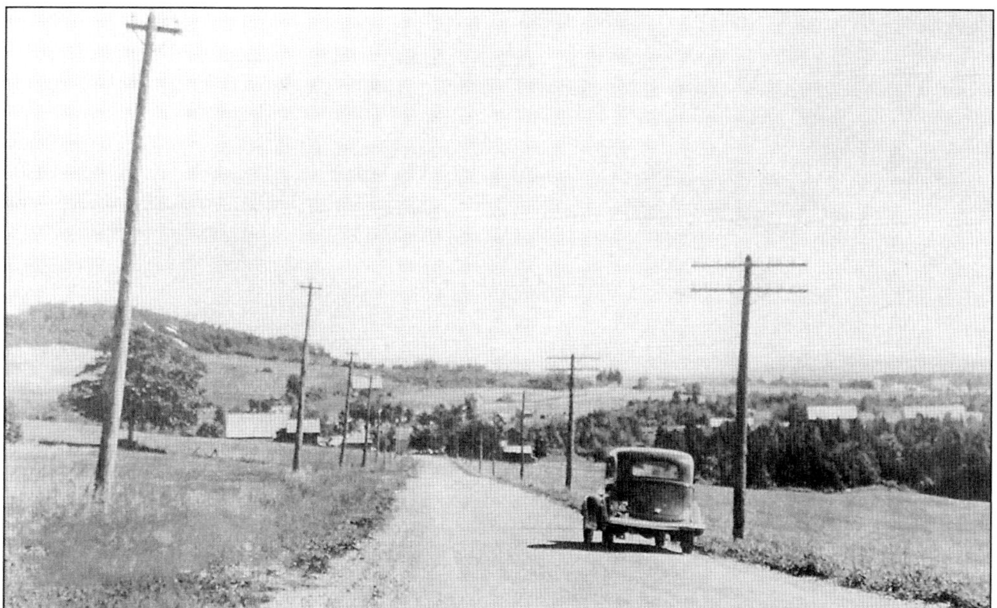

Looking down at New Sweden from Station Road with Ringdahl Hill on the left. It does have a frontier look about it in this photograph.

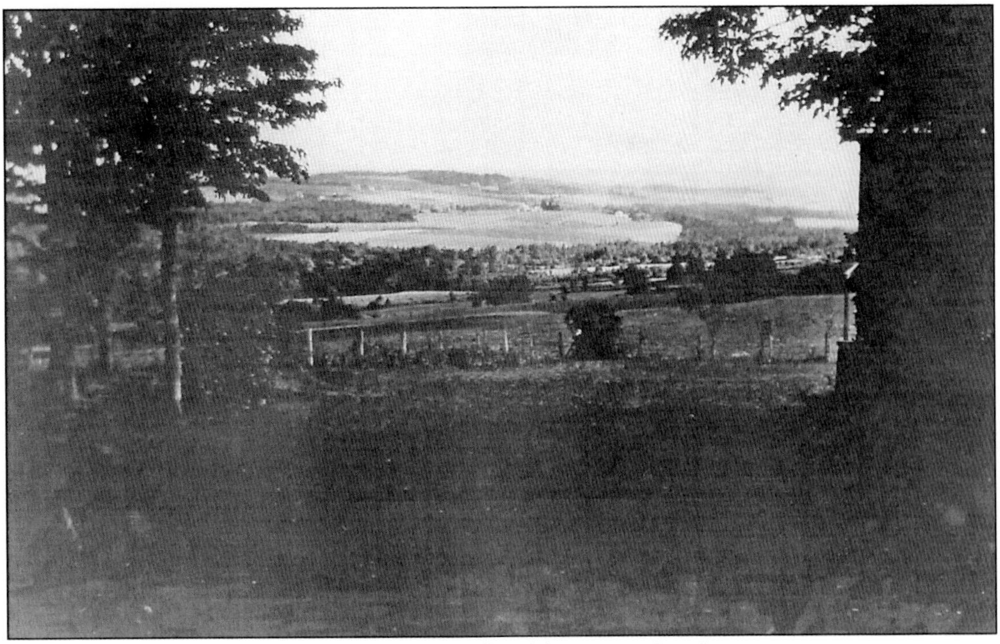

Looking in the direction of the town of Woodland from New Sweden.

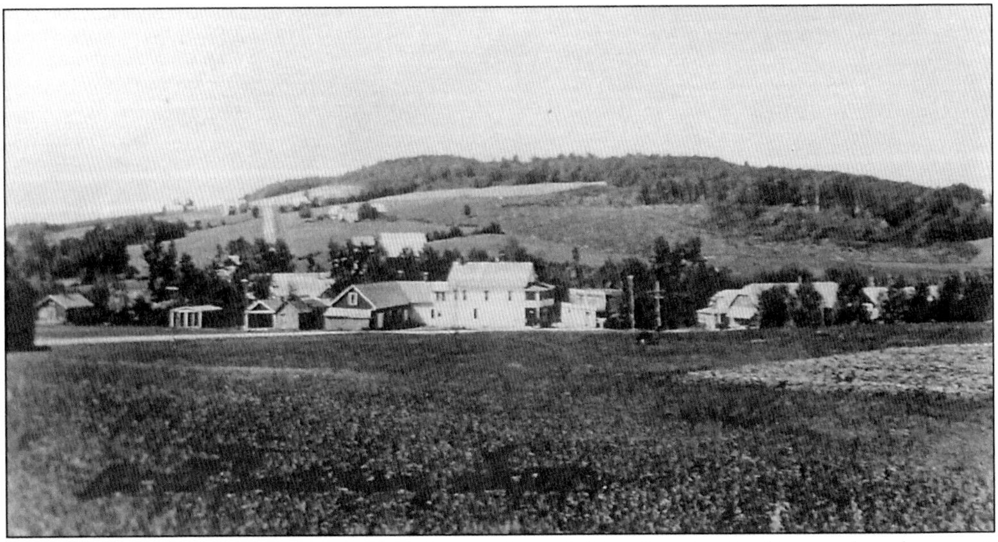

The Bangor and Aroostook Railroad tracks run through New Sweden in this area but they can't be seen in the picture. They are located in the populated section. Thomas Park is atop the hill on the left.

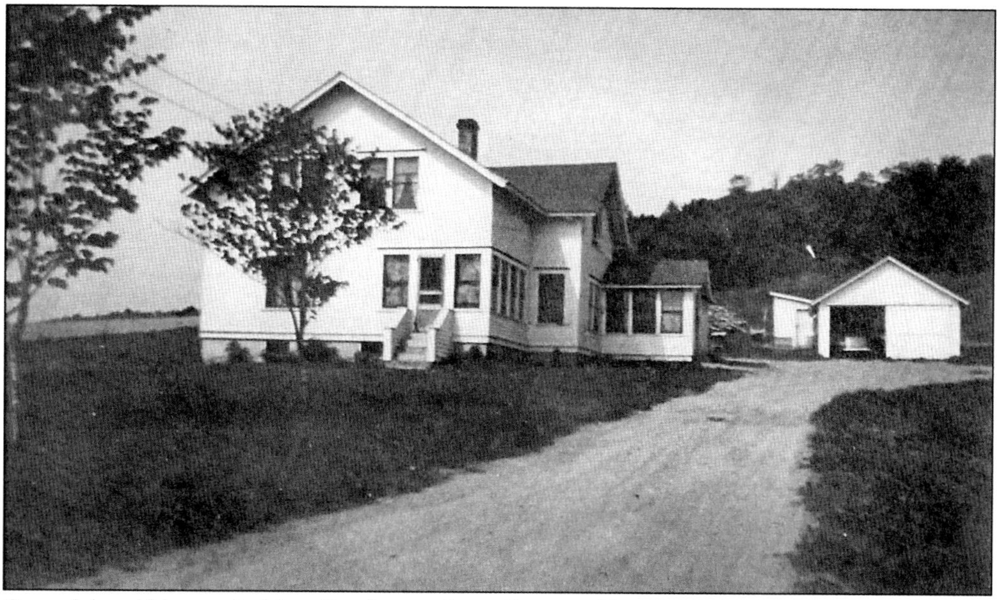

One of the old homes in New Sweden, perhaps Captain Clase's.

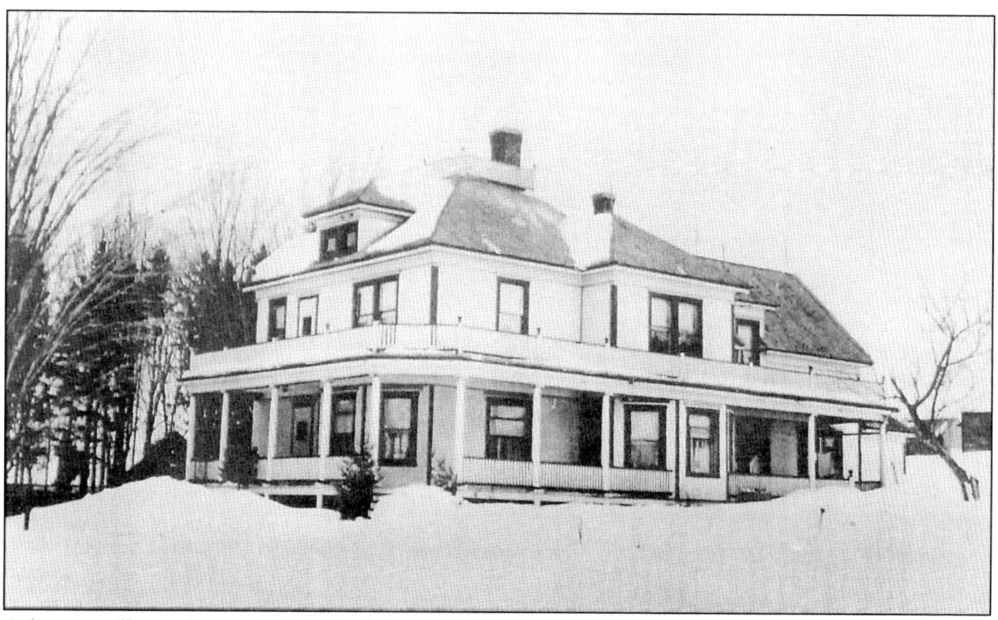

A home still standing in New Sweden, perhaps that of Almon McDougal or Auguste Peterson.

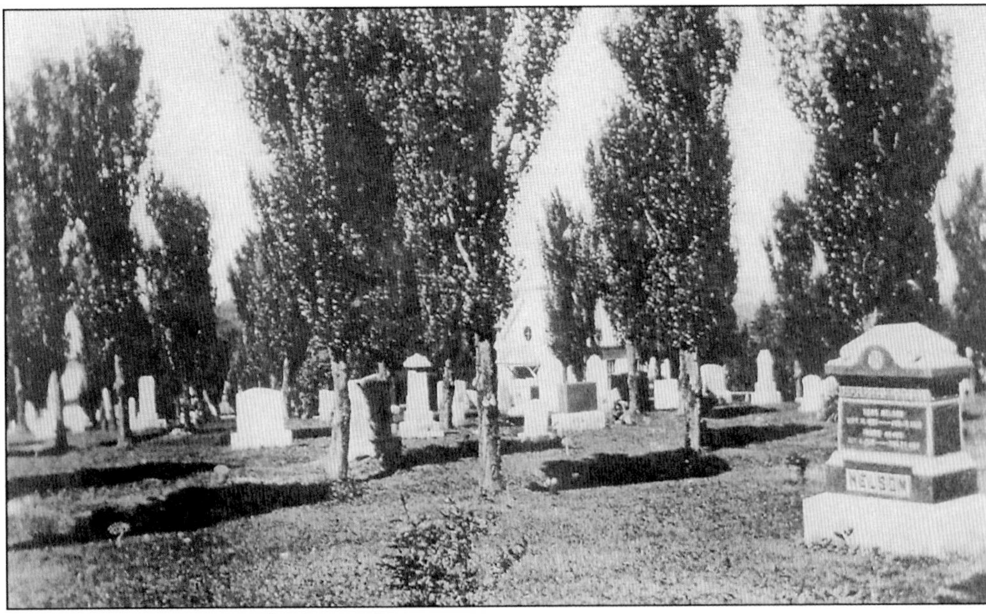

The poplars in New Sweden's "new" cemetery.

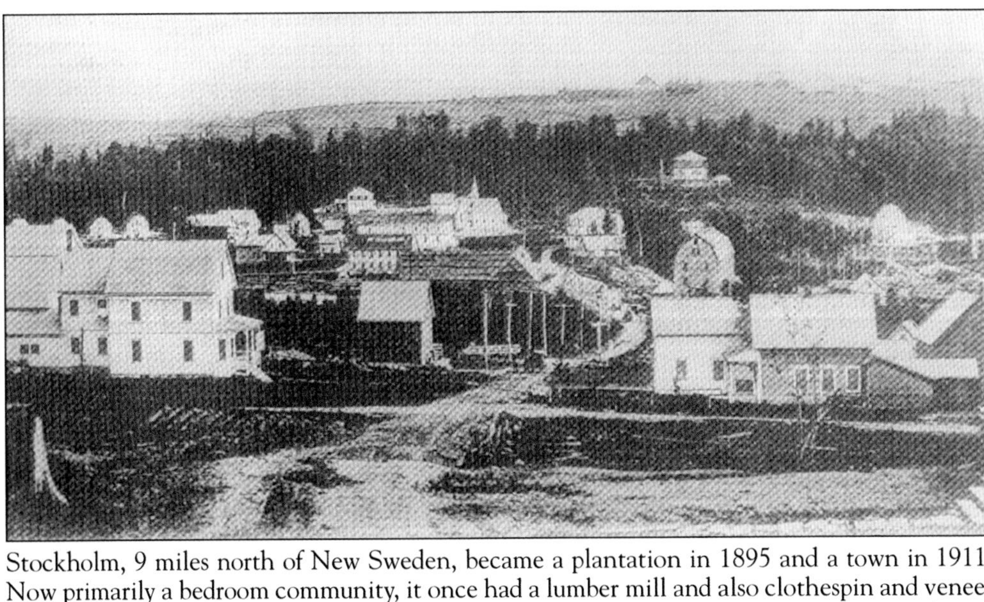

Stockholm, 9 miles north of New Sweden, became a plantation in 1895 and a town in 1911. Now primarily a bedroom community, it once had a lumber mill and also clothespin and veneer plants. Though settled by Swedes, it eventually developed a heavy Franco-American population which worked in the mills. It has two Swedish churches.

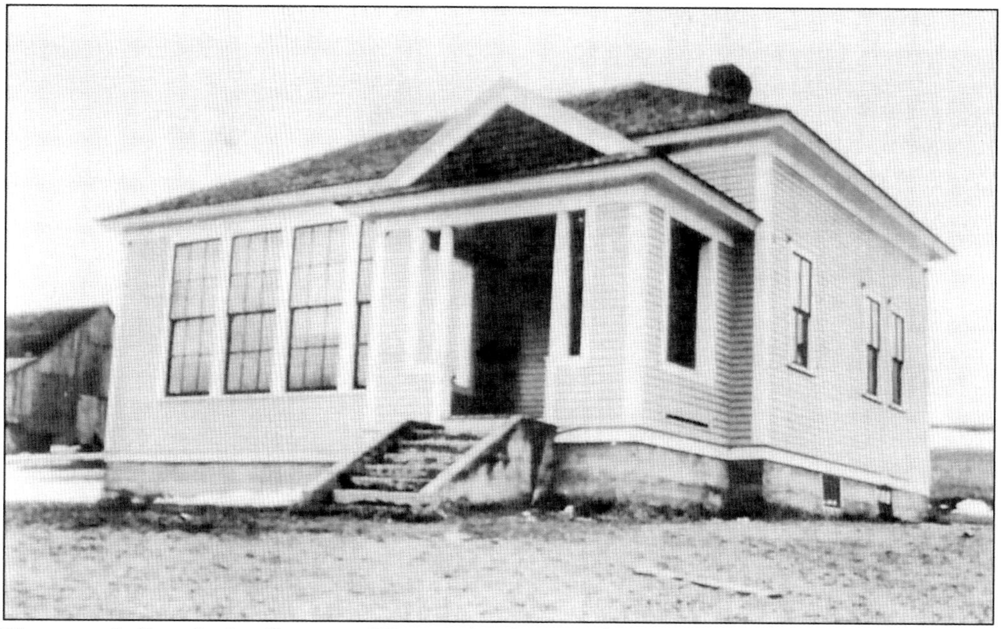

The town hall and schoolhouse at Westmanland, west of New Sweden, as its name implies. It too, was settled by Swedes. Westmanland became a plantation in 1892.

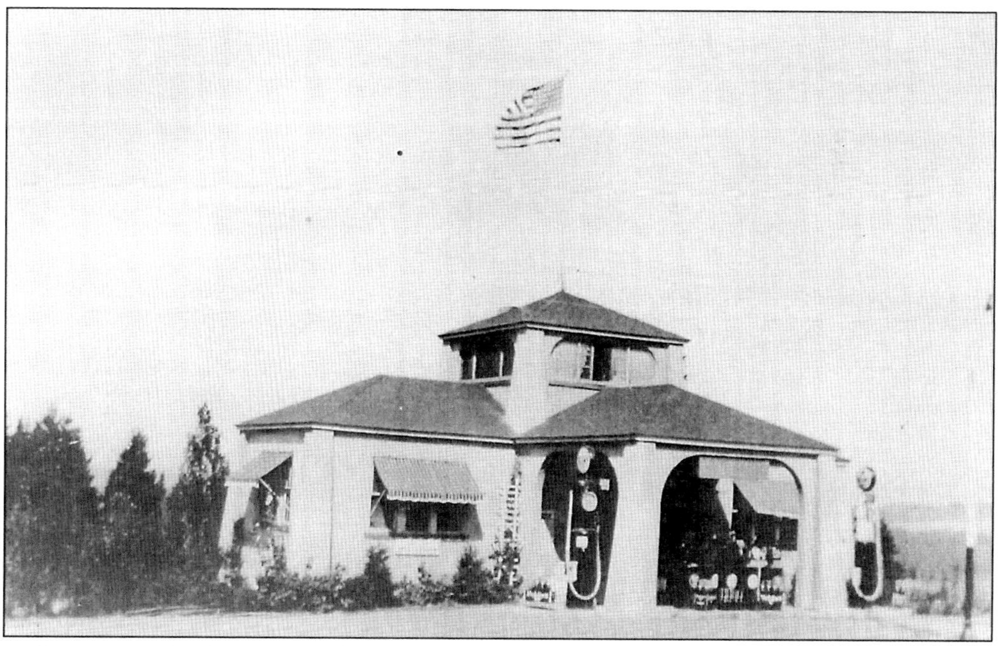

Kaffe Steegan, the former coffee house run by Mrs. Henry Anderson, is now a home.

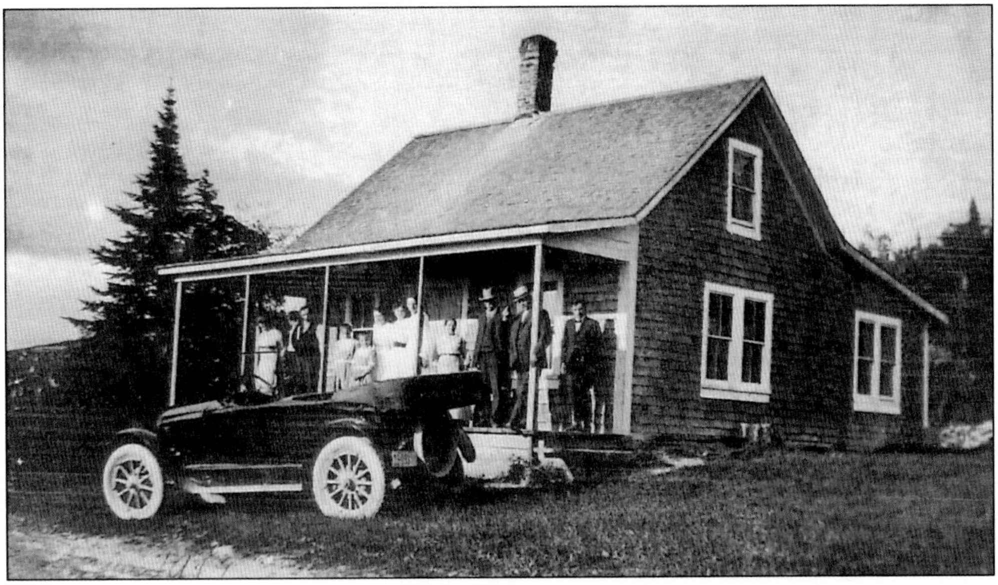

A more modern New Sweden home in the 1930s.

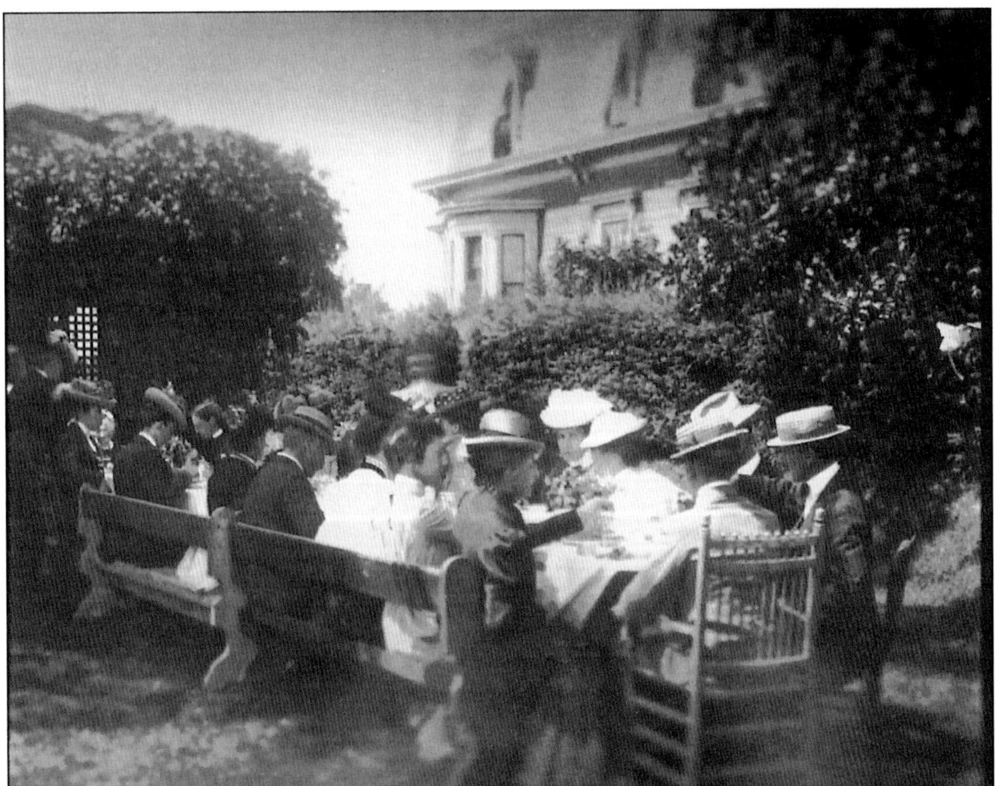

The corner of Chapman and Main Streets in Presque Isle with the Phair home in the background, probably around the turn of the century.

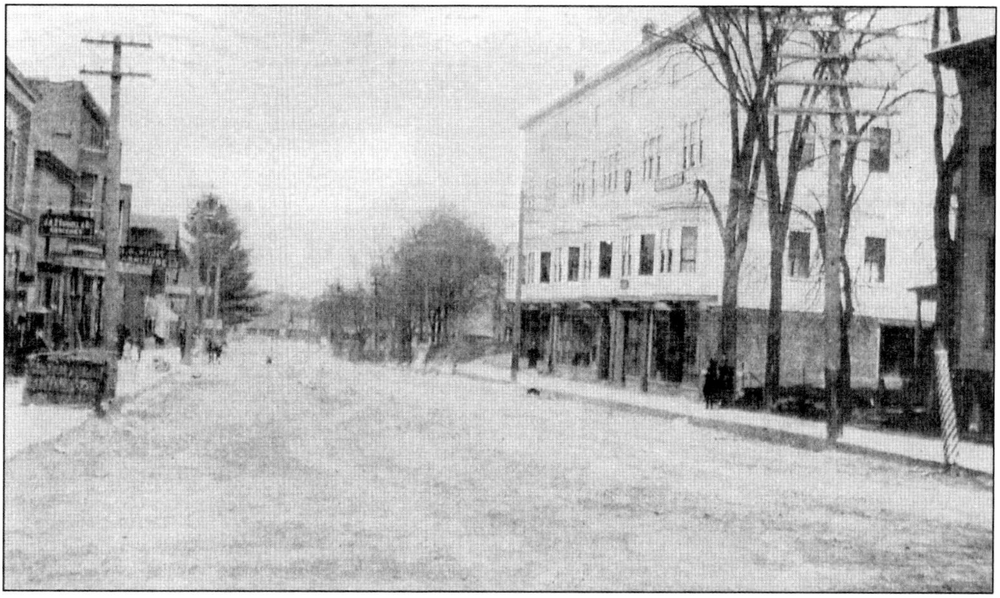

It's about 1910 in Presque Isle and these are the Higgins and Greenlaw Blocks on Main Street.

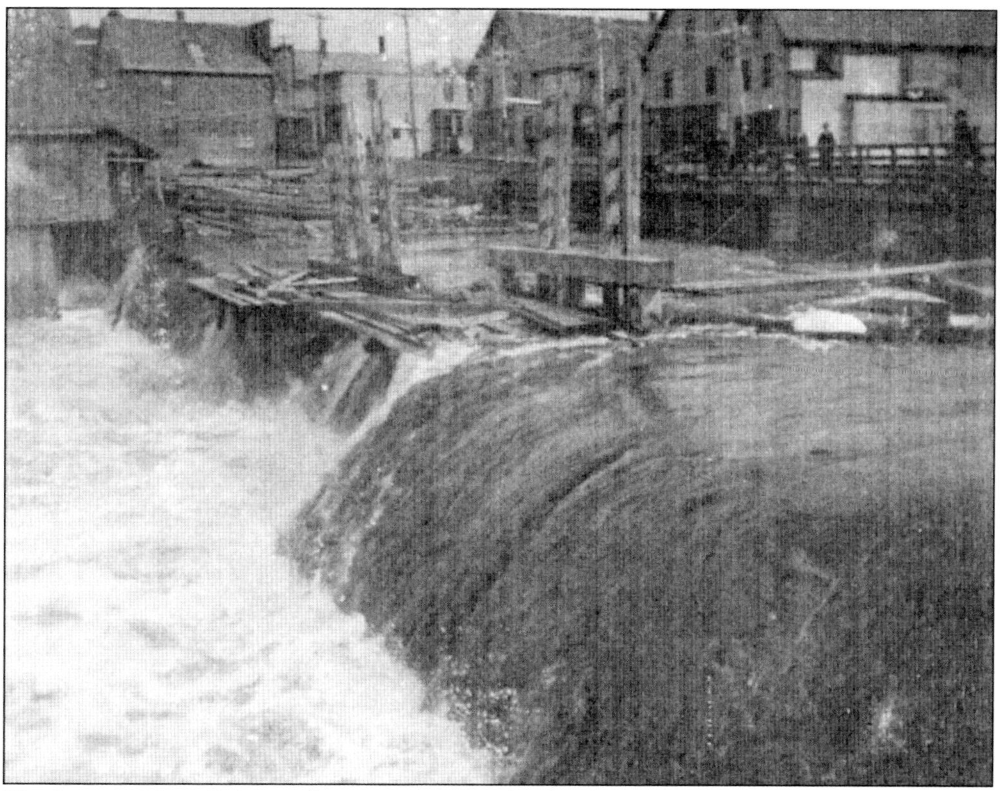

The Presque Isle mill dam and stream in 1900. The dam had to be strong and was washed out at times because there were ice jams each year.

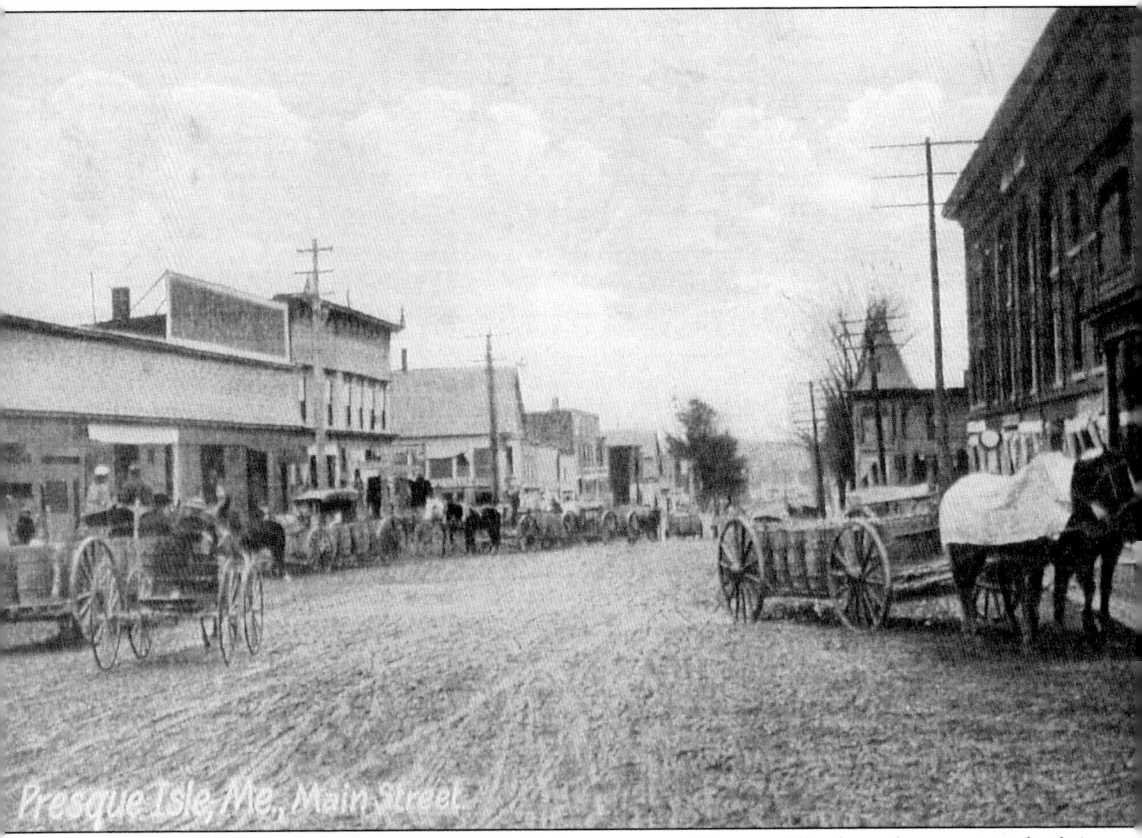

Main Street in Presque Isle about 1910 with wagons and horses. The horseless carriage hadn't yet made an appearance but was due shortly. Main Street remains the main drag in Presque Isle. When not blocked by construction, it's a fine, wide thoroughfare, reminding one of a wide street in a Texas town. There's that frontier again.

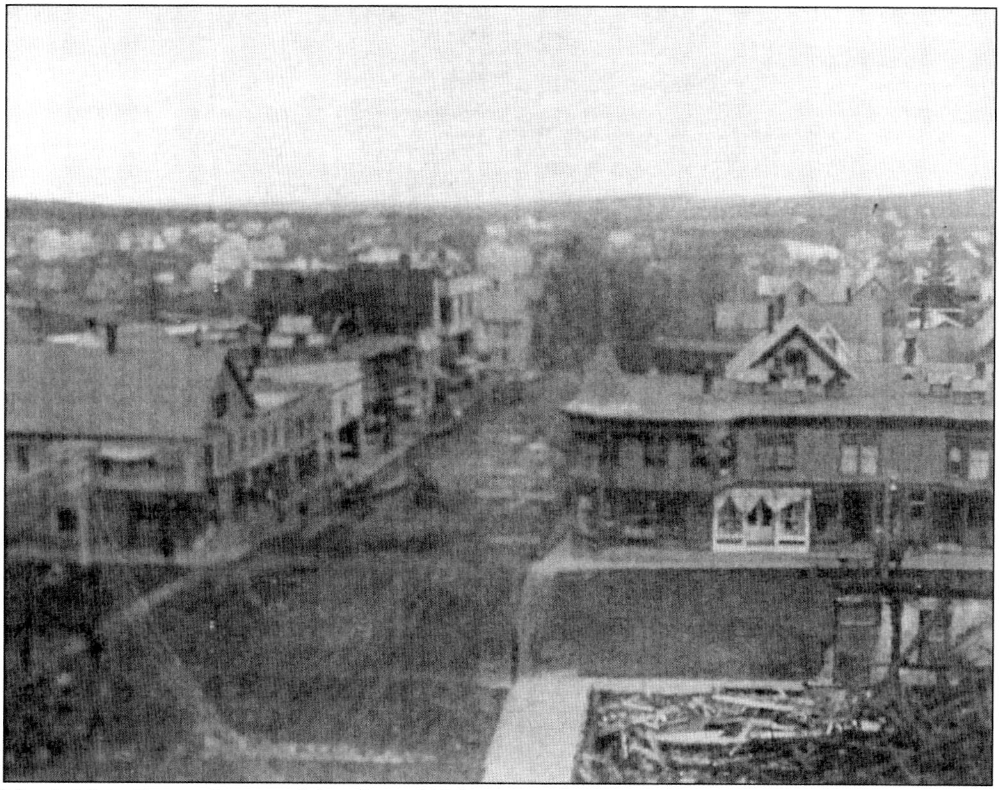

North Main Street, Presque Isle, about 1900.

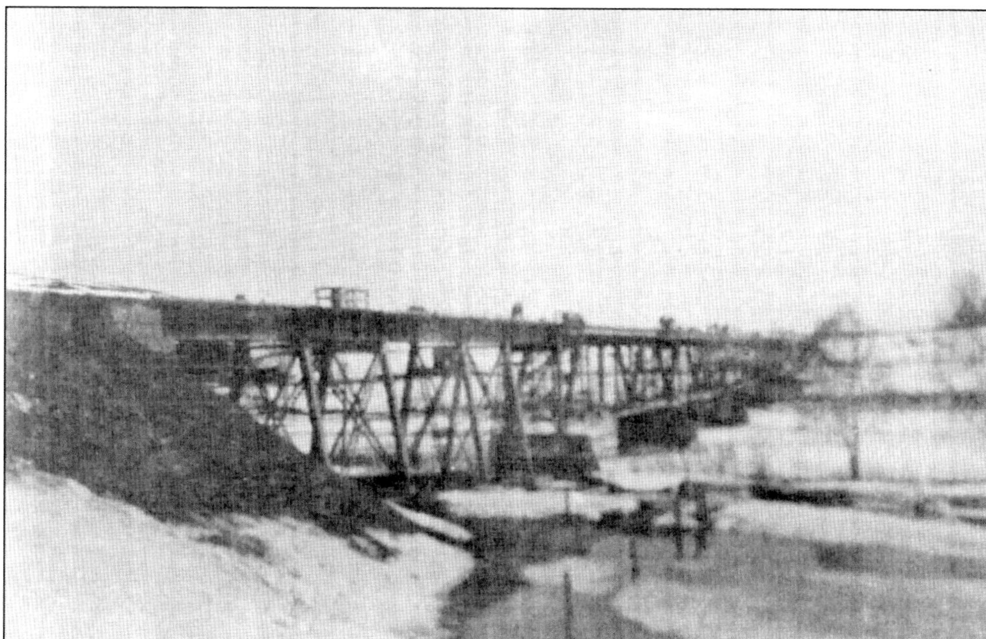

The Bangor and Aroostook Railroad bridge across the Aroostook River looks as if it would hold against the ice floes and log jams in this photograph.

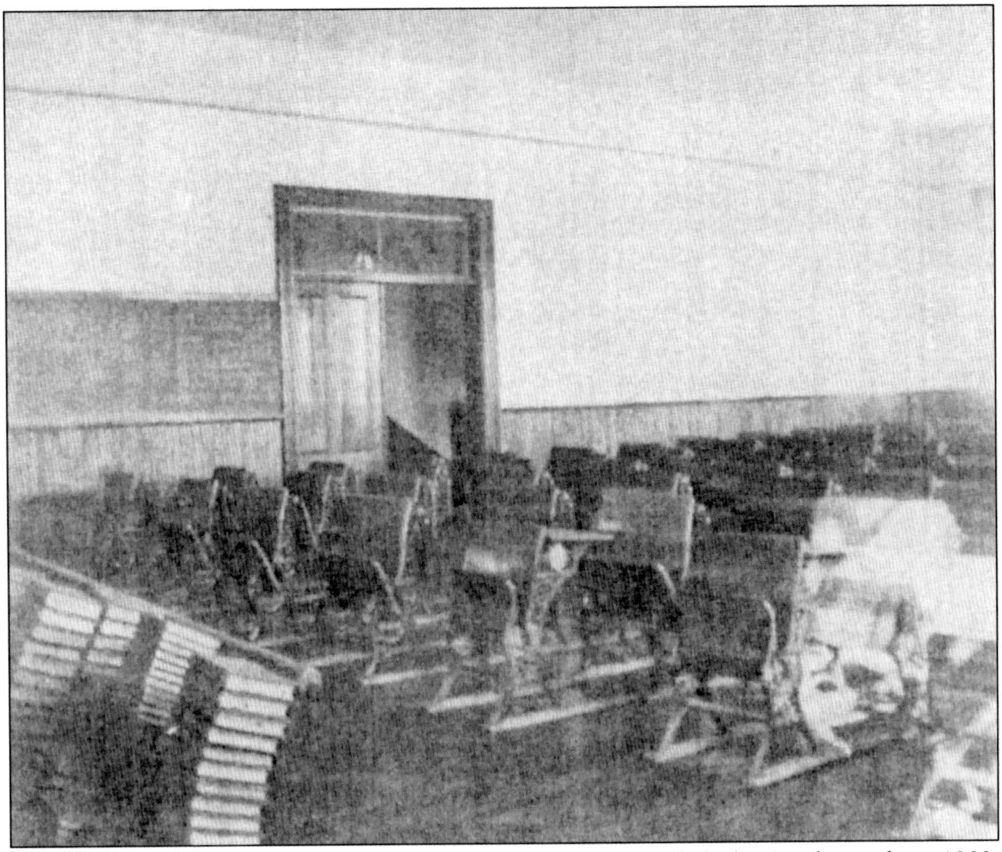

The interior of a Presque Isle High School room when it was called The Academy, about 1900. It later became part of Presque Isle Normal School and, still later, an elementary school. It's now an apartment house for the elderly.

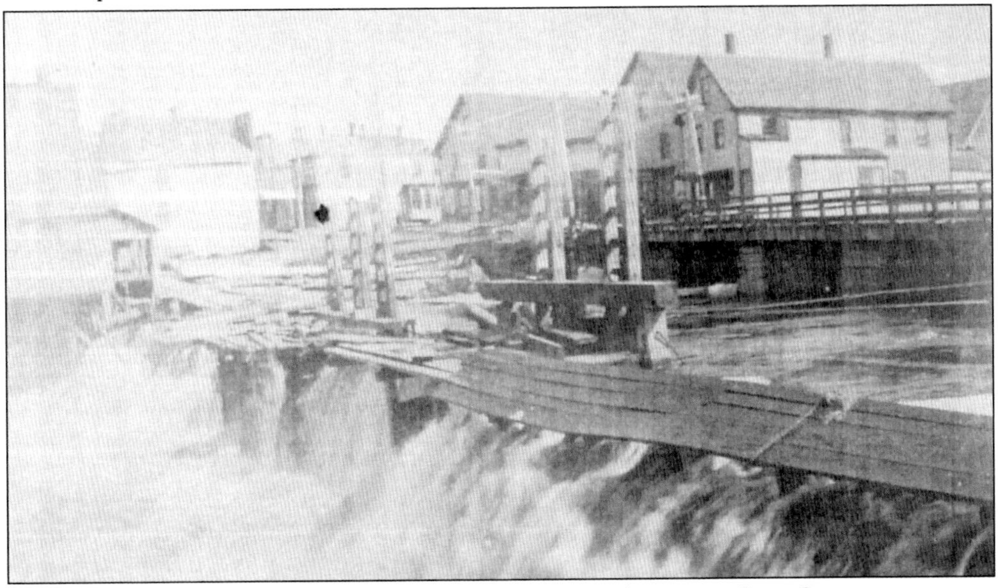

The Presque Isle mill dam in the spring of 1899, showing what is now State Street.

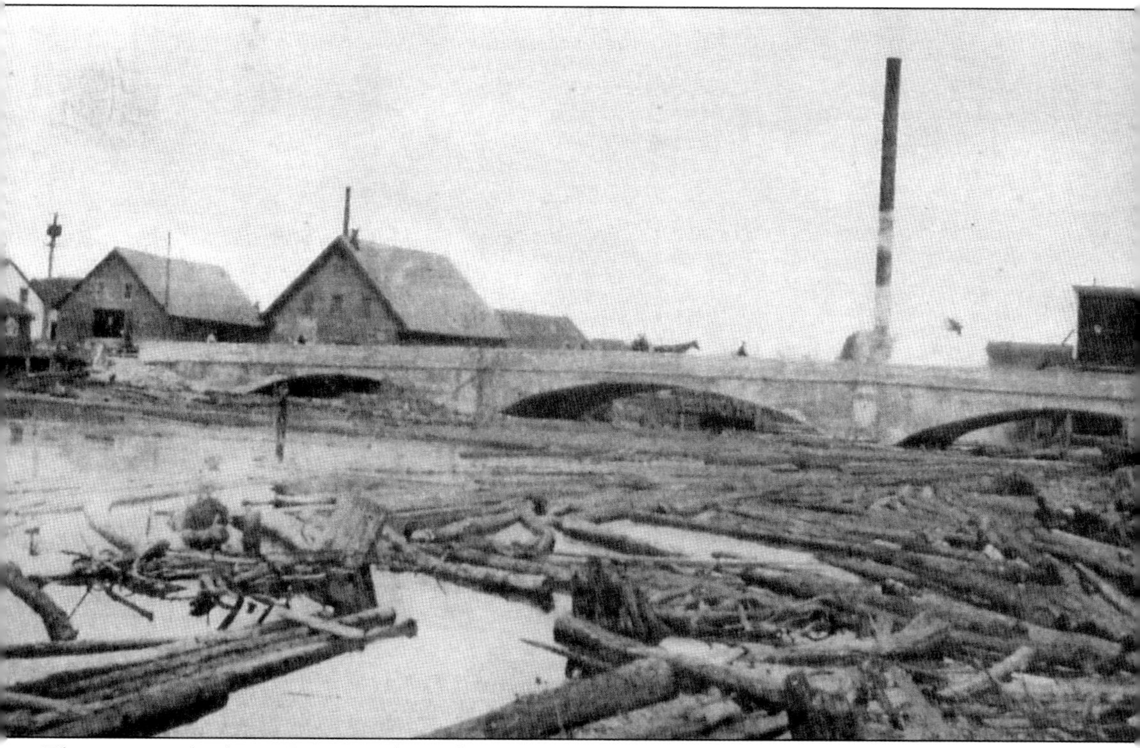

The concrete bridge in Presque Isle in the 1910s. There had been a wooden bridge but log and ice jams made concrete necessary. Logs for the sawmills are in the foreground.

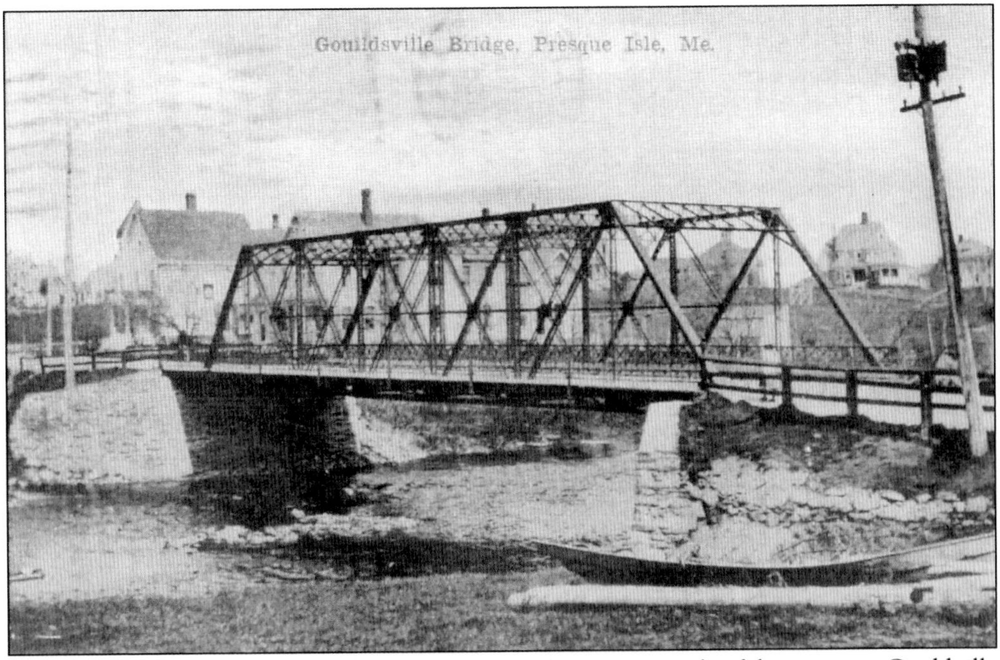

Gouldville Bridge in Presque Isle about 1900. Everything on one side of the river was Gouldville at one time.

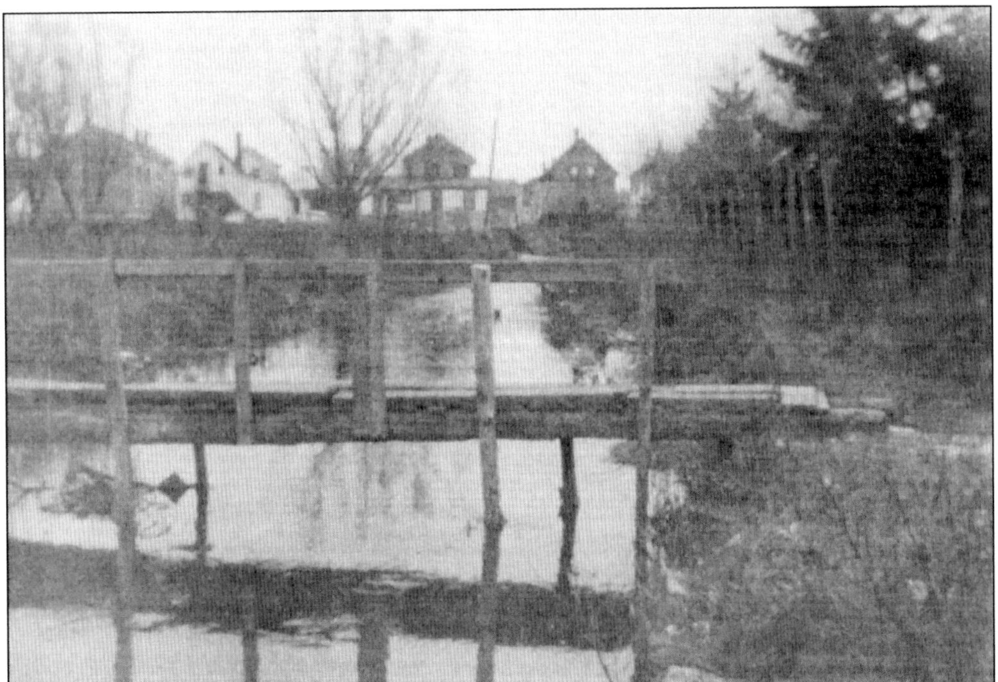

A footbridge and bicycle path near Chapman Street and Presque Isle Stream in 1958. A soccer field is on the left and the bike path on the right.

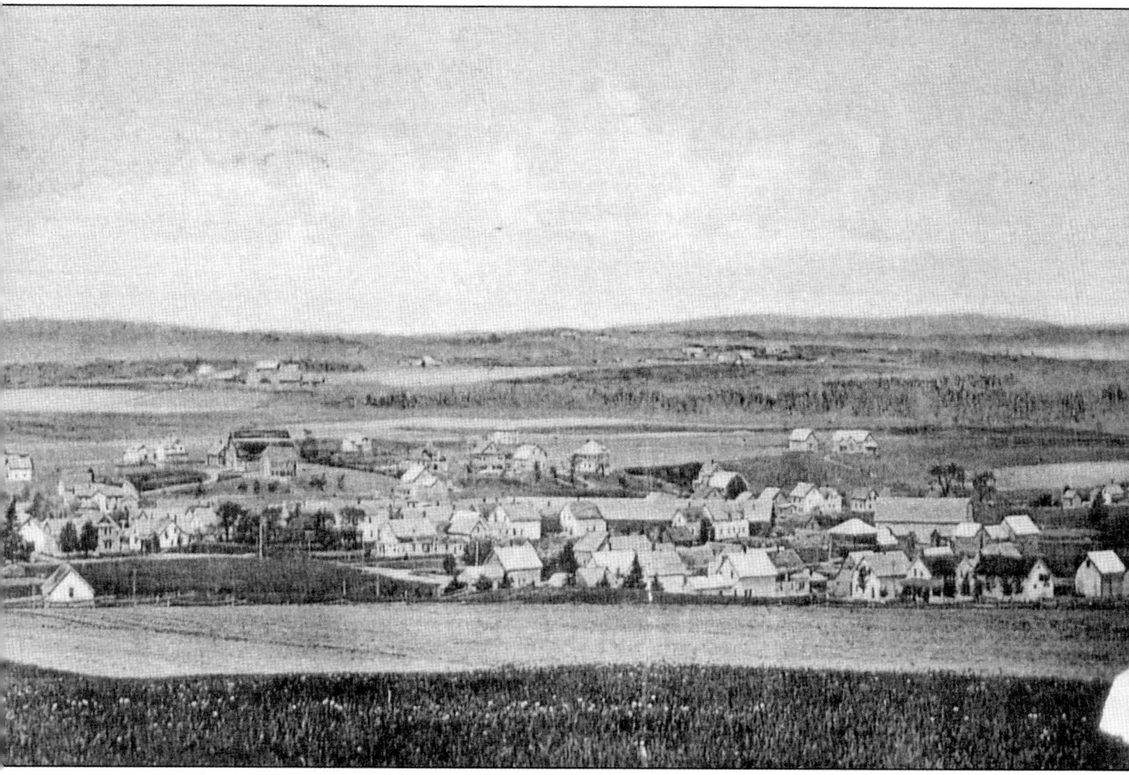

A view of Hardy Hill, Presque Isle, in 1910. The Hardy family owned a great deal of property in the town. We are looking northwest from the top of State Street Hill. Partly because of the great social mobility left over from the frontier days, the fortunes of families in the three communities sometimes ebbed and flowed.

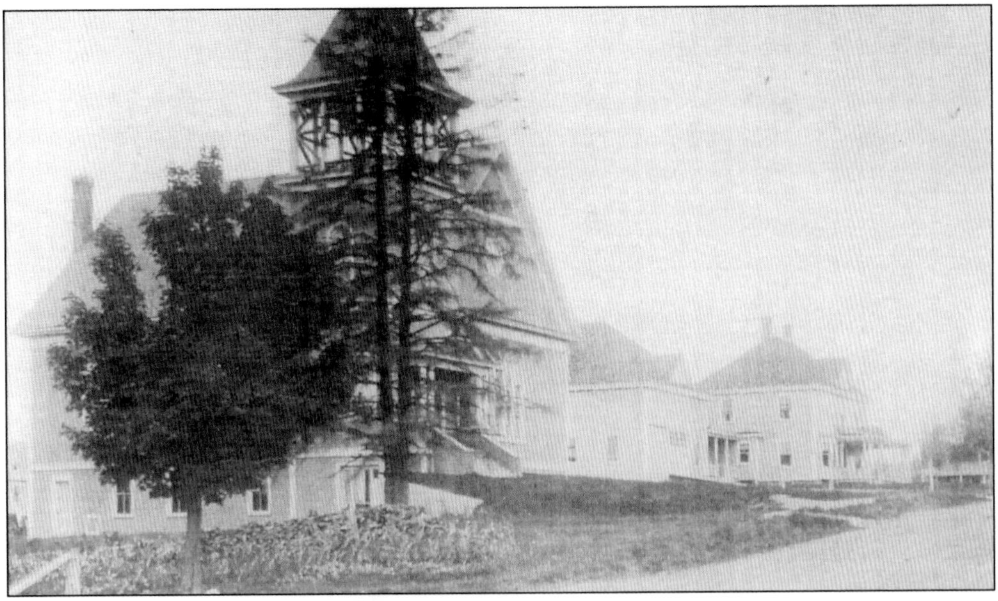

A view from the south of Presque Isle about 1900.

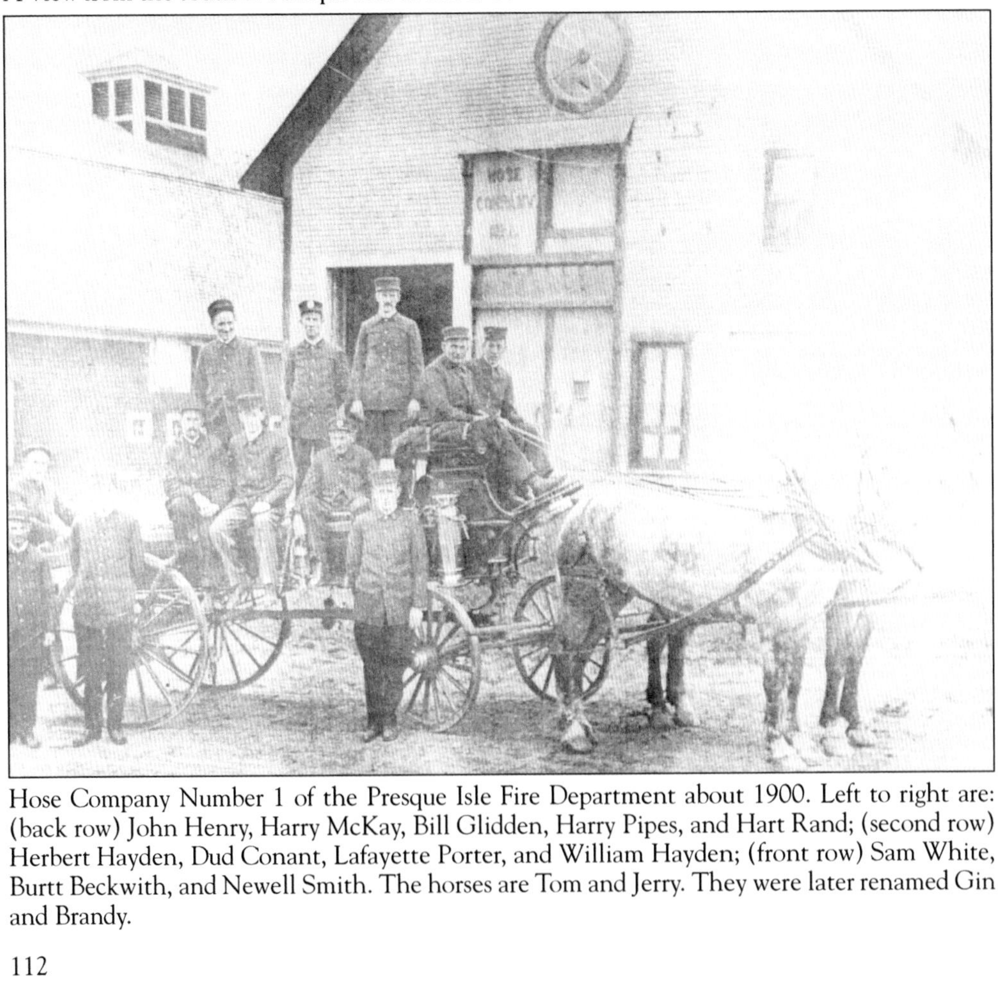

Hose Company Number 1 of the Presque Isle Fire Department about 1900. Left to right are: (back row) John Henry, Harry McKay, Bill Glidden, Harry Pipes, and Hart Rand; (second row) Herbert Hayden, Dud Conant, Lafayette Porter, and William Hayden; (front row) Sam White, Burtt Beckwith, and Newell Smith. The horses are Tom and Jerry. They were later renamed Gin and Brandy.

Eight

Faces of the North

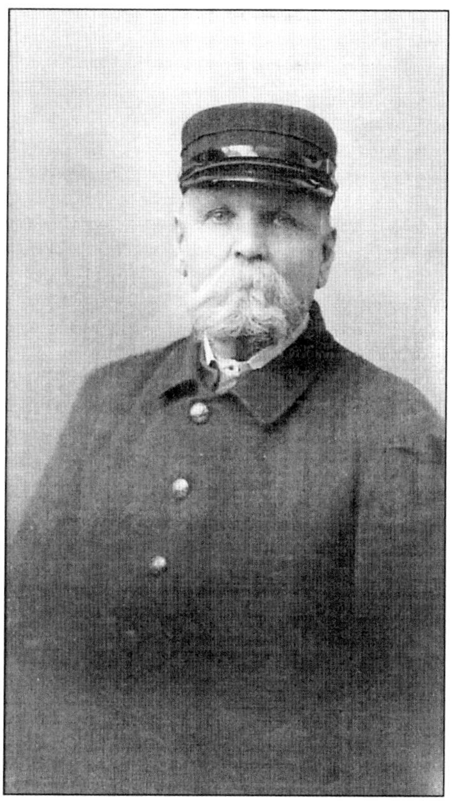

Stillman Wilson of Caribou in 1928, by Annie Stetson. We know nothing of the man but you can see that he has lived.

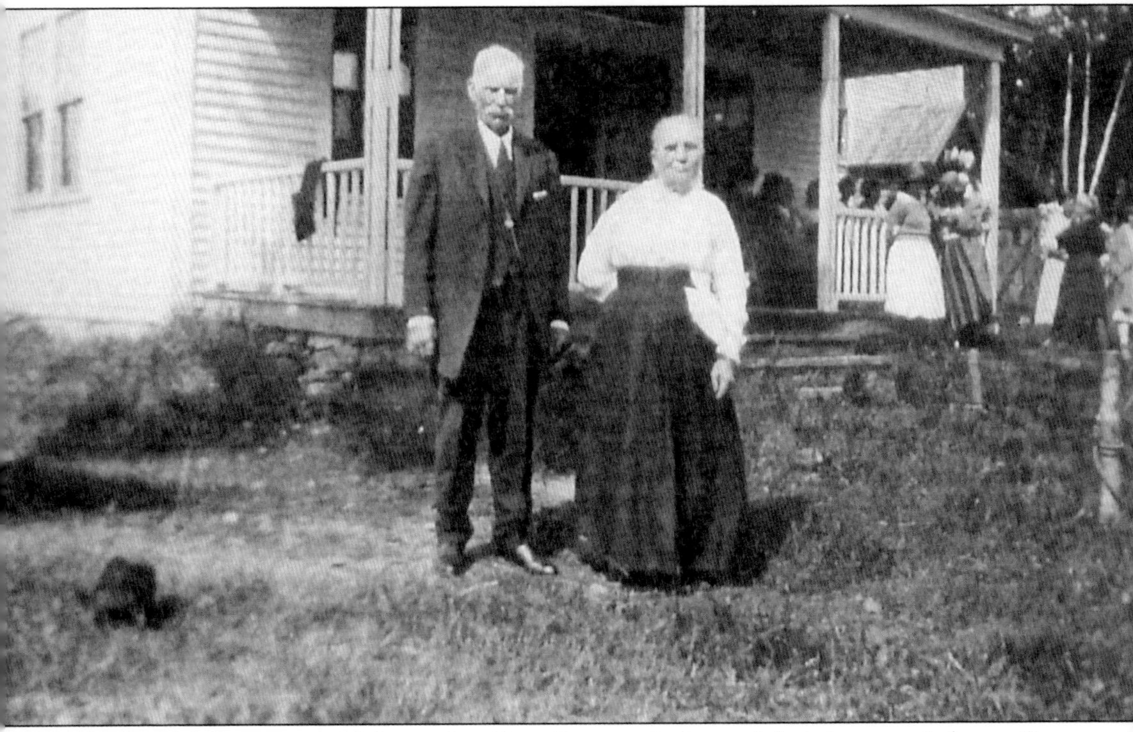

John Erik Peterson and Johanna Lundberg Peterson in front of their home on Lebanon Street, New Sweden, on July 15, 1922, the 50th anniversary of their wedding two years after New Sweden was founded. They look as if they are still of America's last frontier.

The Petersons, not too long after their wedding. They were both of sturdy stock. You can see that in their faces.

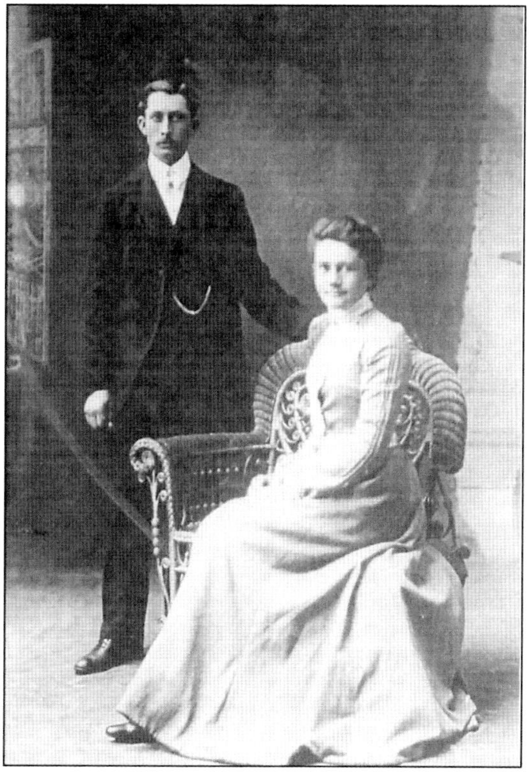

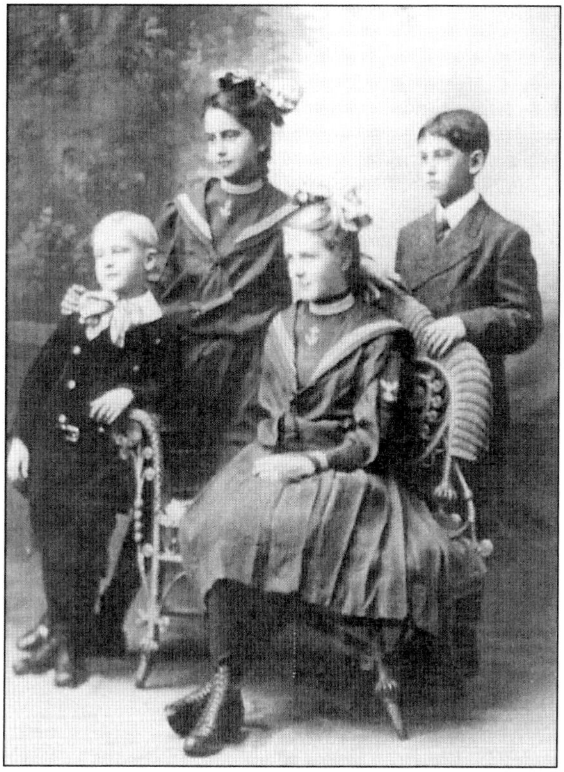

These are the Uhlrick children of New Sweden.

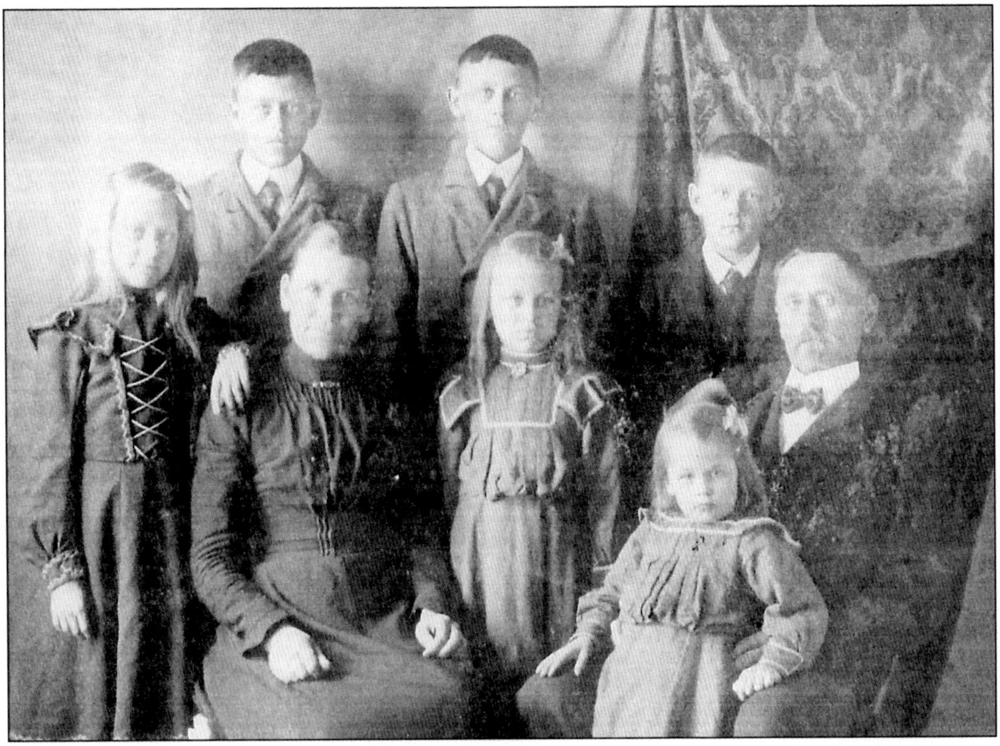

Another New Sweden family, the Olanders. Left to right are: (front) Anna Olander, Mrs. Elizabeth Olander, Lillie Olander Falk, Mabel Olander Hemberg, and Olof Olander; (back) John Olander, another Olof Olander, and Carl Olander.

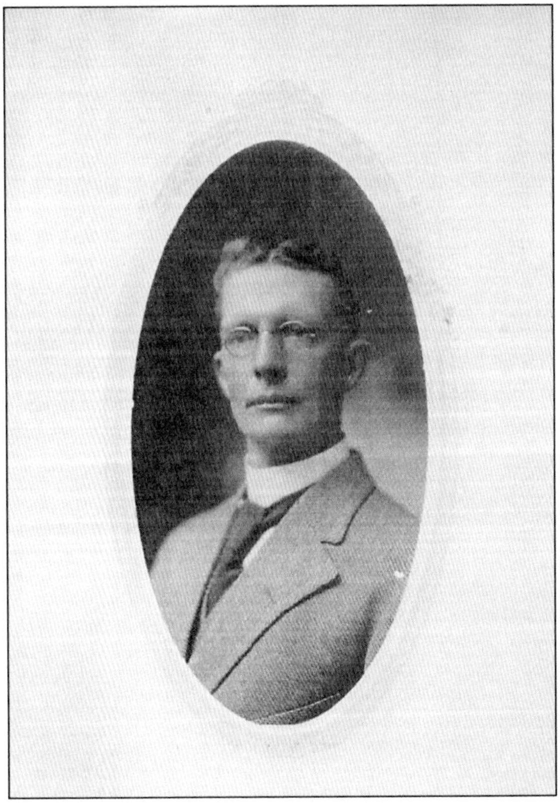

Dr. Victor Lagerson, a New Sweden physician.

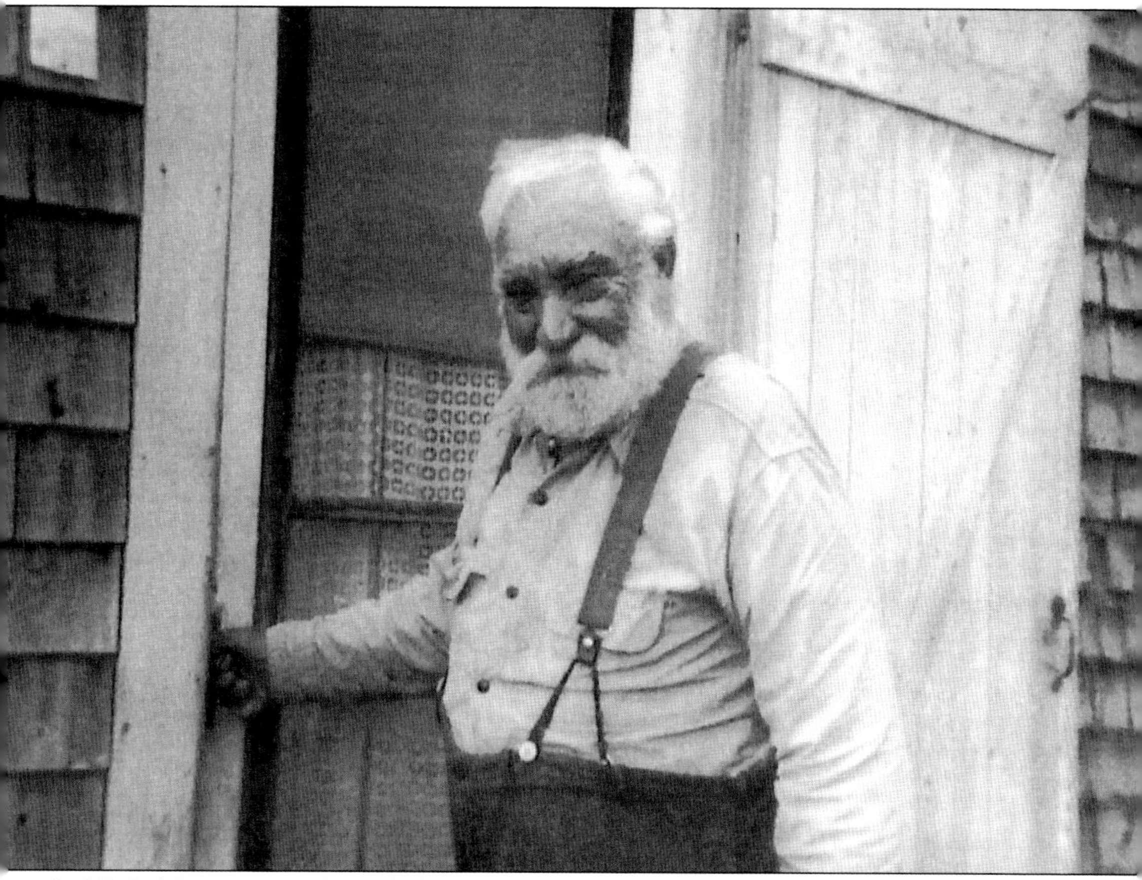

Carl Erik Adamson in 1950, with the face of a New Sweden farmer. Solidity shines through. These Swedes had something. Daily work on a farm up north is liable to weather your face a bit but despite the hardship, they endured and triumphed.

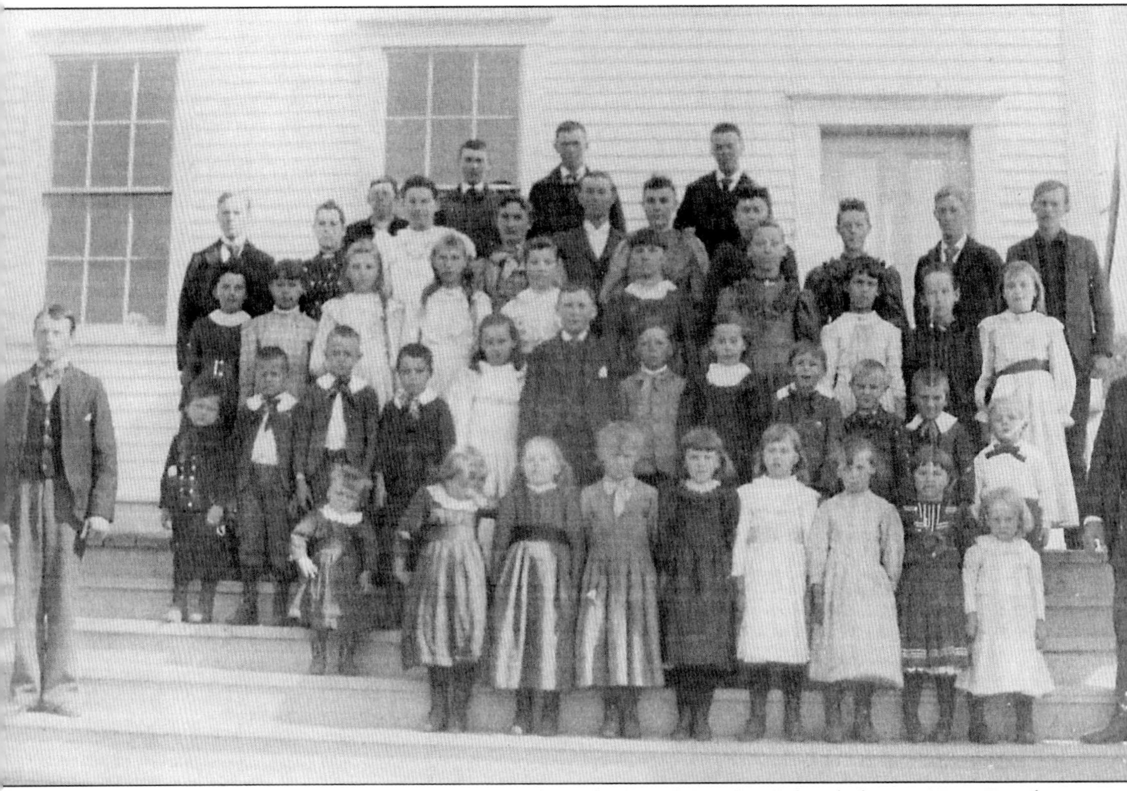

These are some of those attending the Madawaska Road Sunday School class in New Sweden in 1898. Their teacher was Eric Lundvall. In the first row, number one, is Mathilda Adler Peterson with Hannah Nygren Erickson as number two and Hannah Olsen Crockett as number three. Missing is number four while number five is Ellen Falk Pearson. Numbers six and seven are missing, while Signe Olson Espling is number eight. Nellie Adler is by herself on the left. In the second row, Oscar Adler is number one and John Olander, number two. Olof Olander is number three and the name of number four is missing. Adina Johanson Anderson is number five while Joe Johanson is number six. We find number seven is Robert Lindgren with Anna Olson Johnson as number eight. Johnny Halgren is number nine but the name of number ten is missing. Number eleven is Edward Olson and number twelve, Eddie Nygren. In the third row, Lydia Englund Johnson is number one with the names of numbers two, three, and four missing. Anna Nelson Weden is number five with number six missing. Sadie Lindgren is number seven and Helen Lindgren Anderson, number eight. Number nine is missing but number ten is Ida Johnson and number eleven, Lilie Falk. Number twelve is unknown. The fourth row is made up of: Ernest Falk, number one; Hilda Nelson Norberg, number two; Mina Johanson Neilander, number three; and Anna Johnson Anderson, number four. The names of numbers five, six, seven, eight, and nine are unknown but Willie Strid Pearson is number ten. Alone in the fifth row is Andrew Dygg. How these Swedish names come trippingly off the tongue.

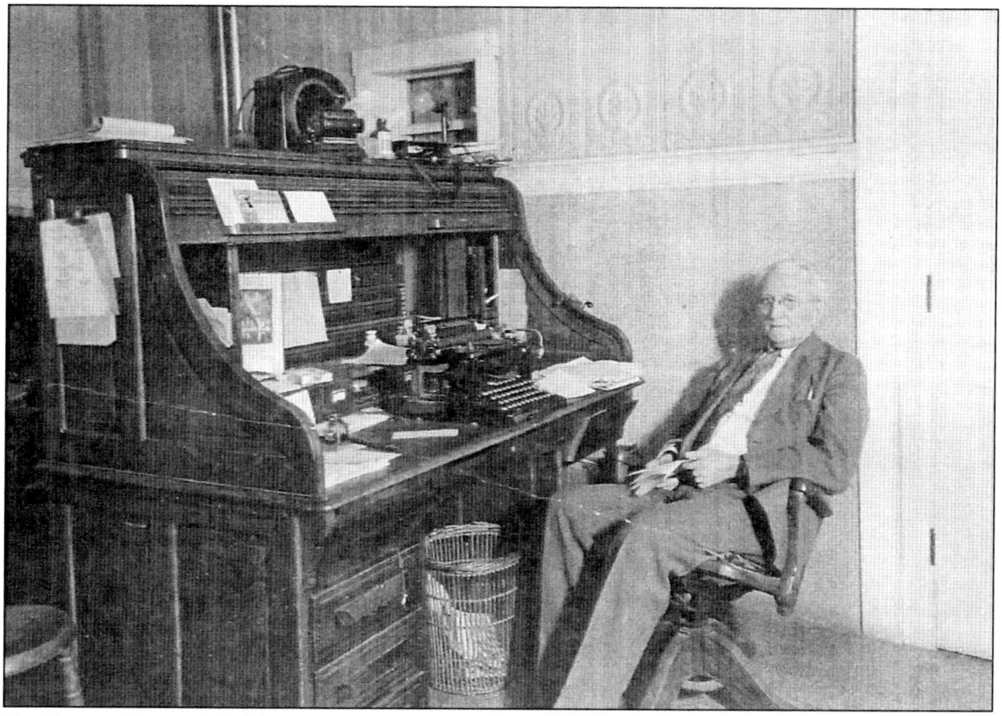

Dr. Eugene Howard Doble, 1876–1960, was a physician and radiologist in Presque Isle.

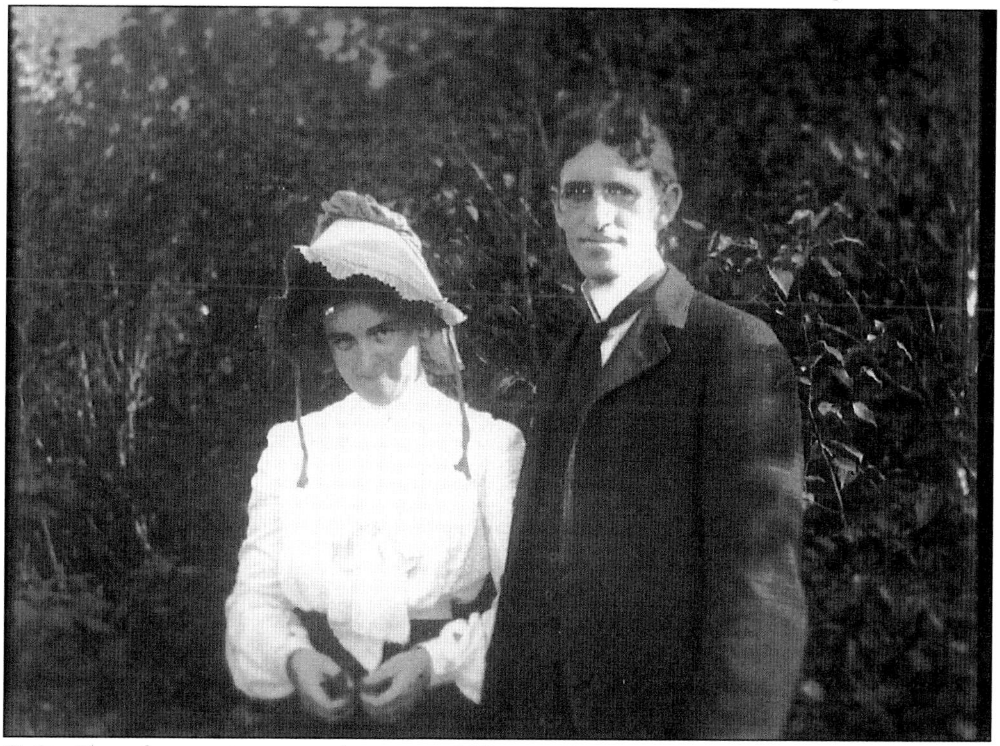

Philip Phair, later to become a lawyer, and Eleanor Ferguson are in Presque Isle about 1900. They were just friends.

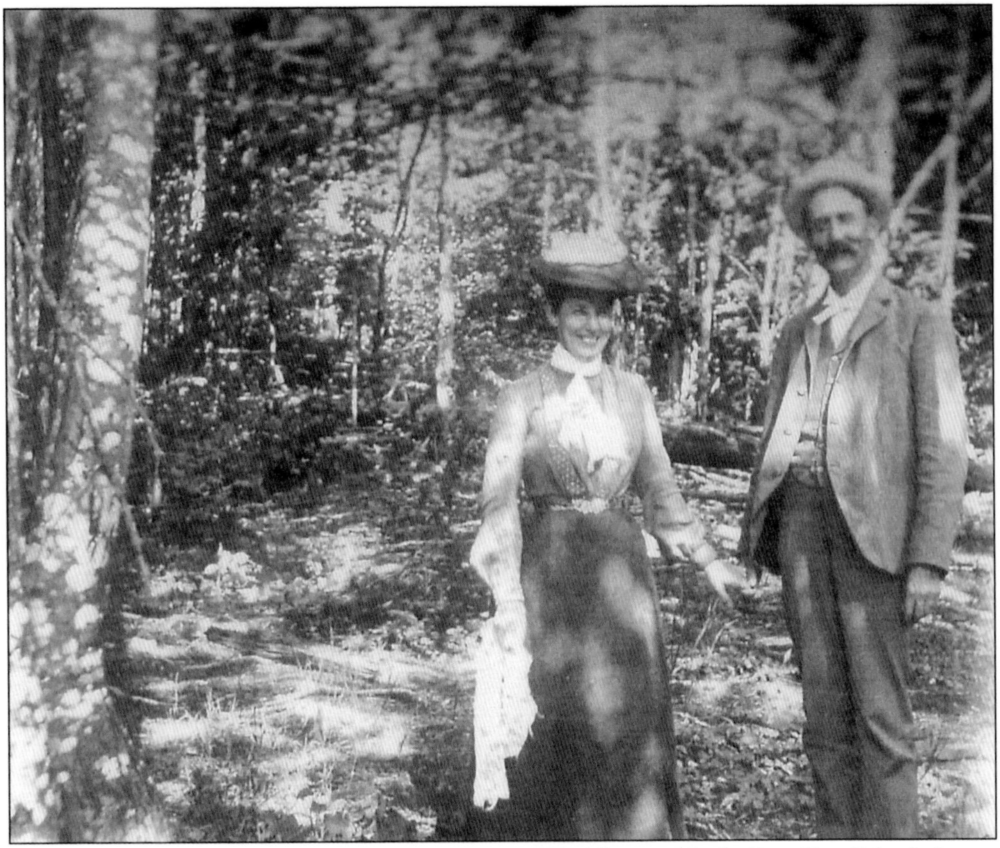

F.P. Allen and Lydia Rusell at Echo Lake, Presque Isle, on September 11, 1901.

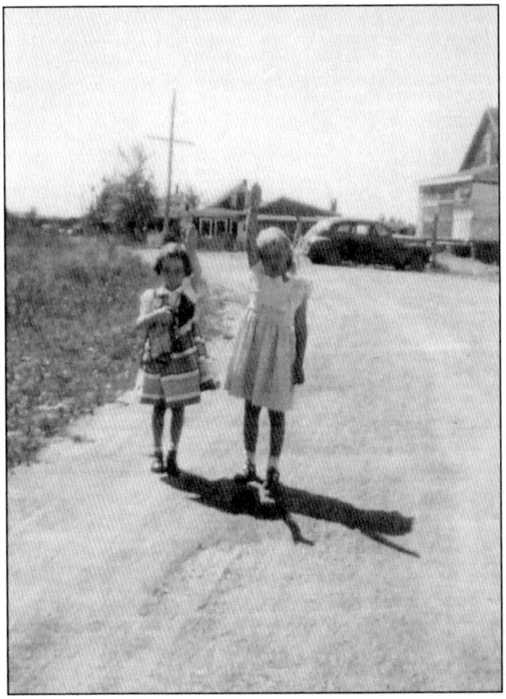

Christie Smart (left), and Barbara Doody wave goodbye on the first day of school in 1949. They were going to the subprimary class operated by the Presque Isle Normal School on Chapman Street.

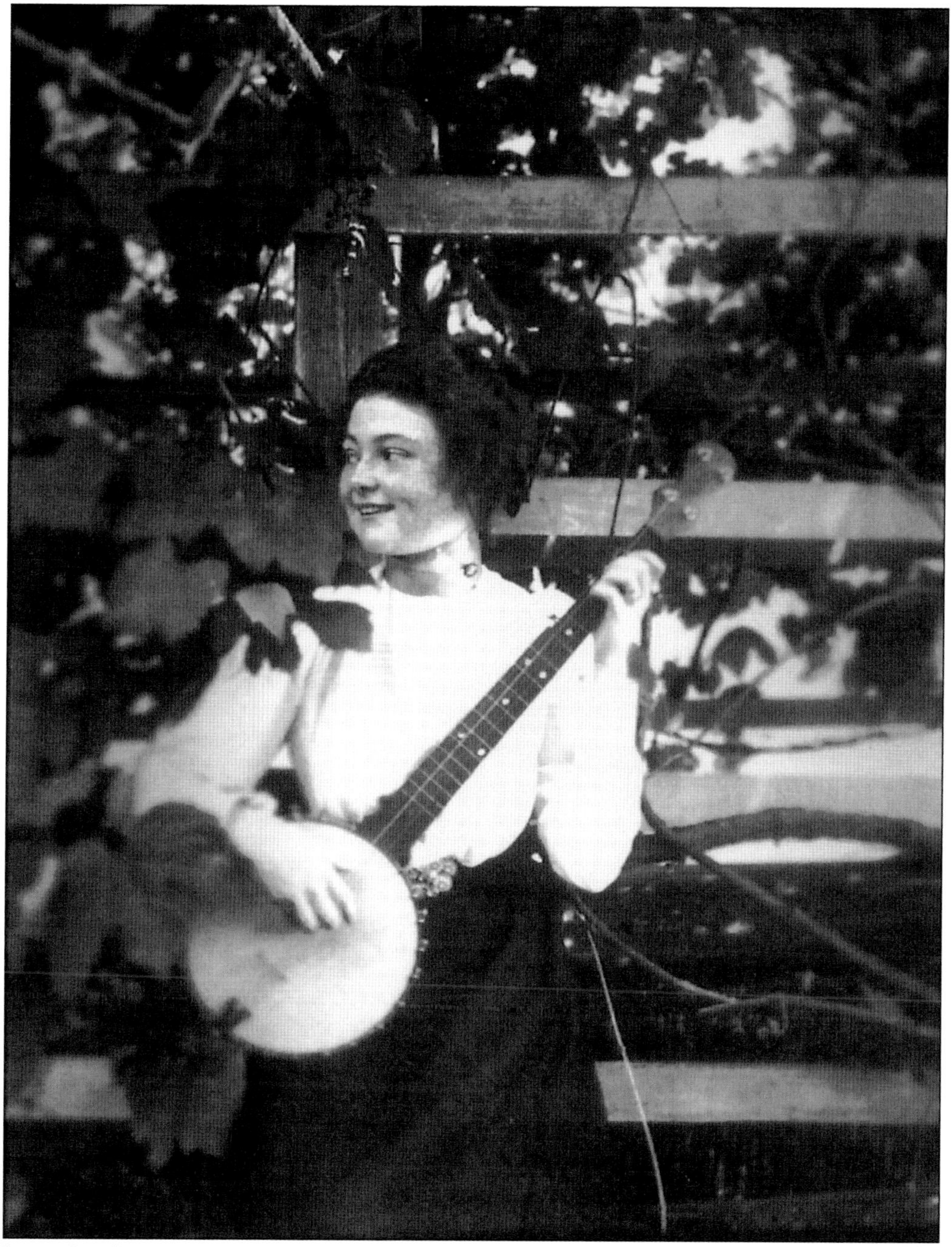

Jessie Goodwin strums her banjo in Presque Isle on June 26, 1899. The faces of the north were not all serious. In fact, the recreation section shows that there had to be both lightness and levity for survival in these parts.

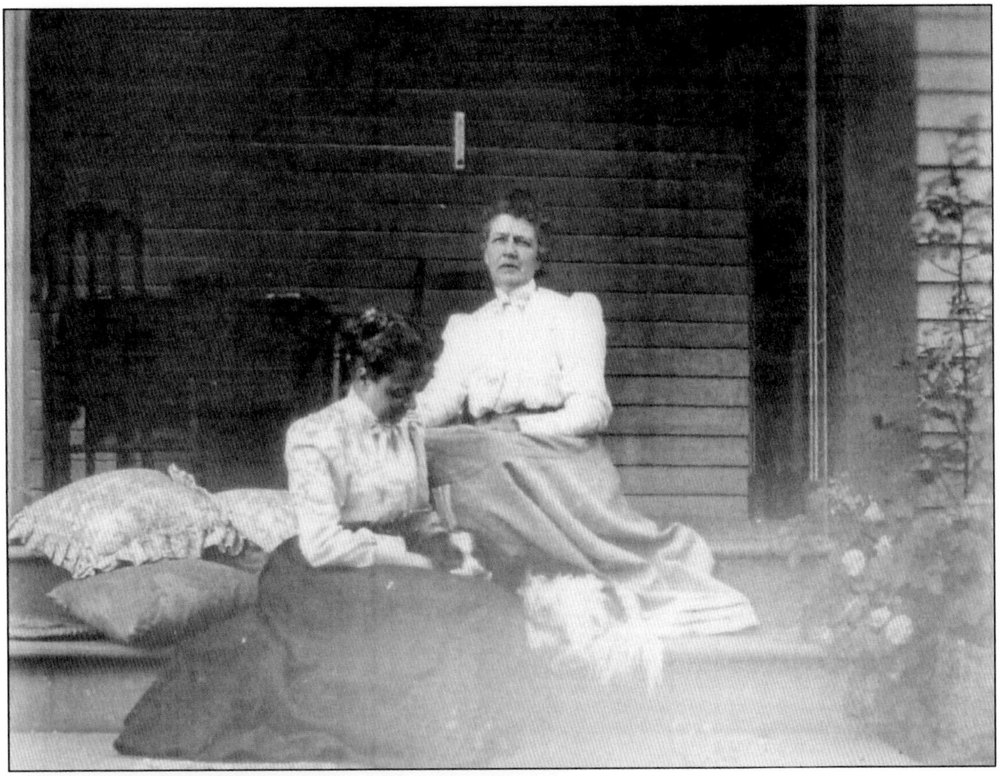

Two Presque Isle ladies in white relax with pillows about 1900. One has a springer spaniel on her lap.

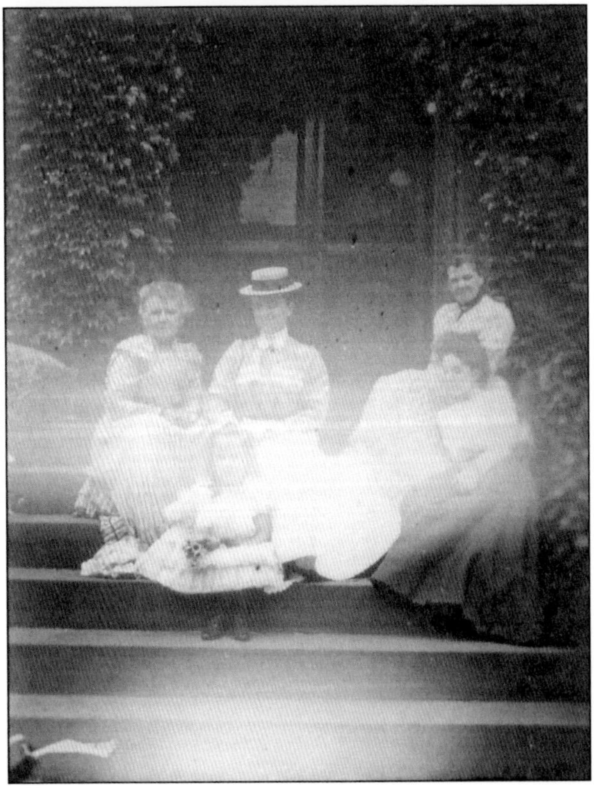

These are "The Little People," dwarves who moved into Presque Isle about 1900. They include Mrs. Smith, Mrs. Robeson, Mrs. Robb, Miss Hyatt, and Winifred Robb, the child in front.

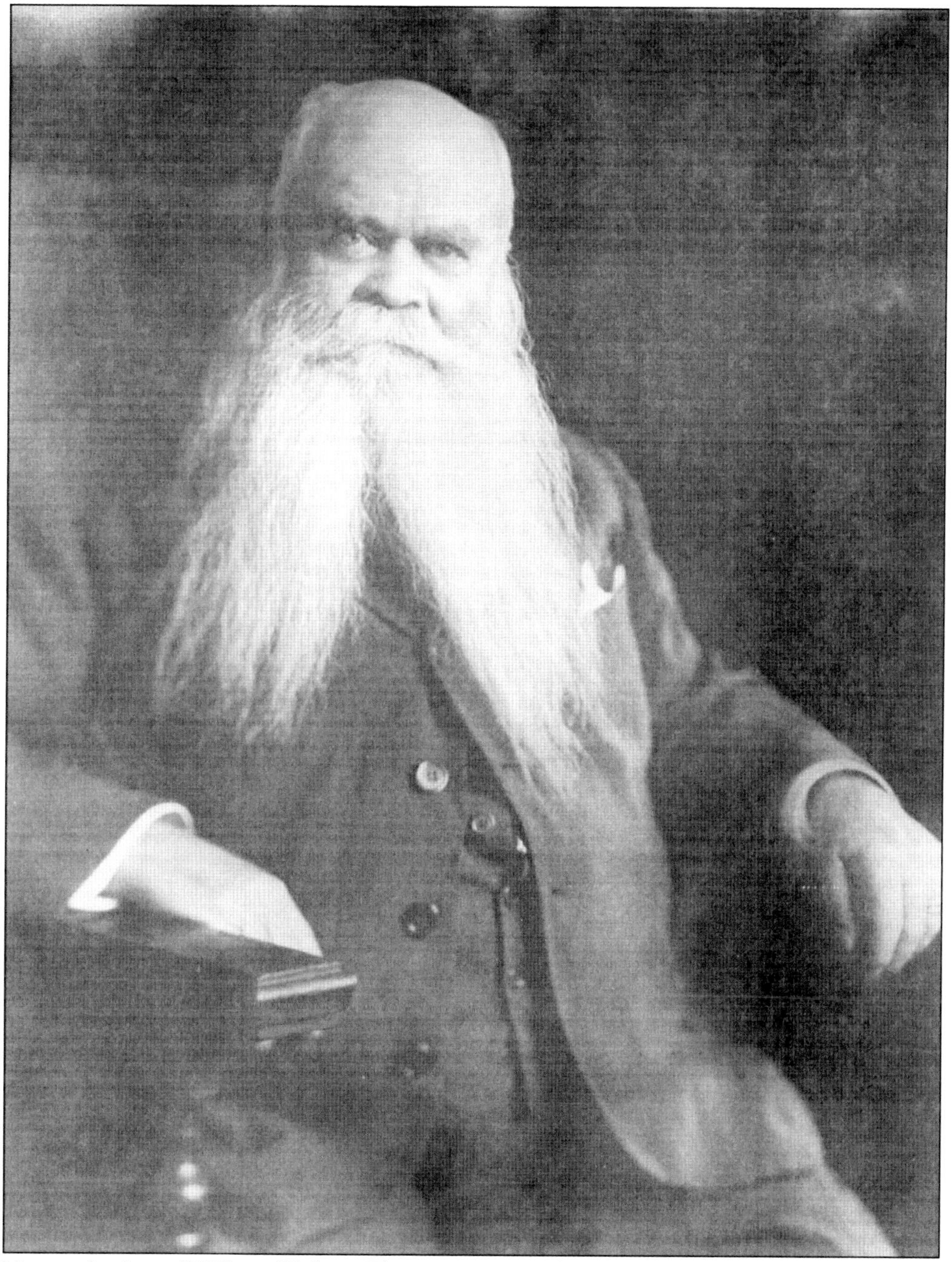

Here is the face of William Widgery Thomas again, in the 1920s. The man was just as colorful and as much of a leader as he looked. Aroostook County could use someone like him now.

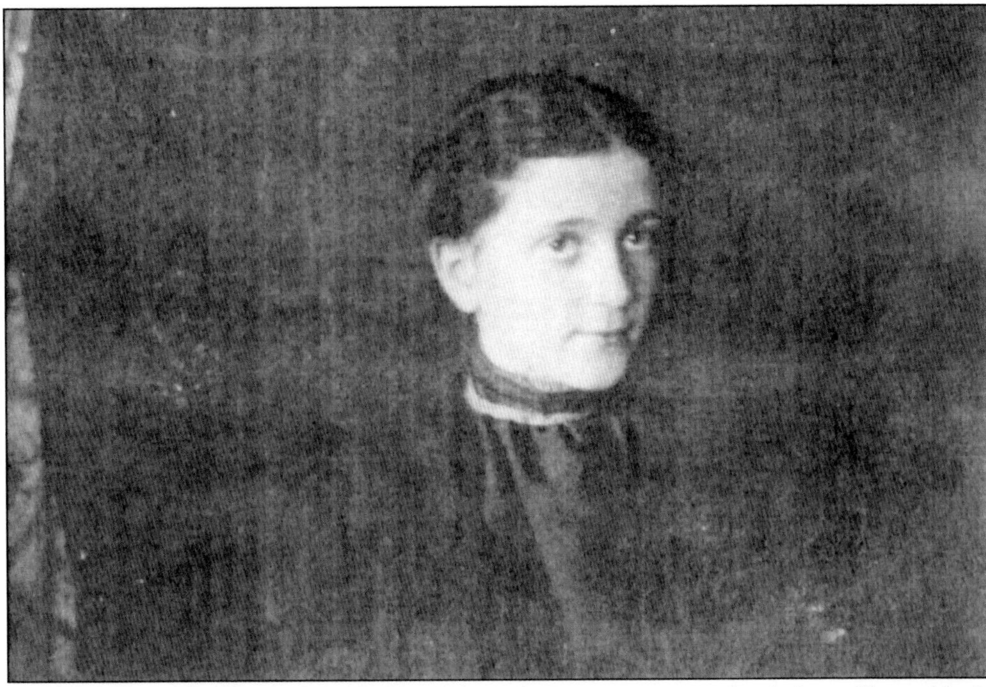

Theodate B. Stevens grew up in Presque Isle and went to nursing school there. She suddenly married John Ball and moved to Massachusetts. Growing up, Theodate was quite a tomboy, enough for many people to talk about it.

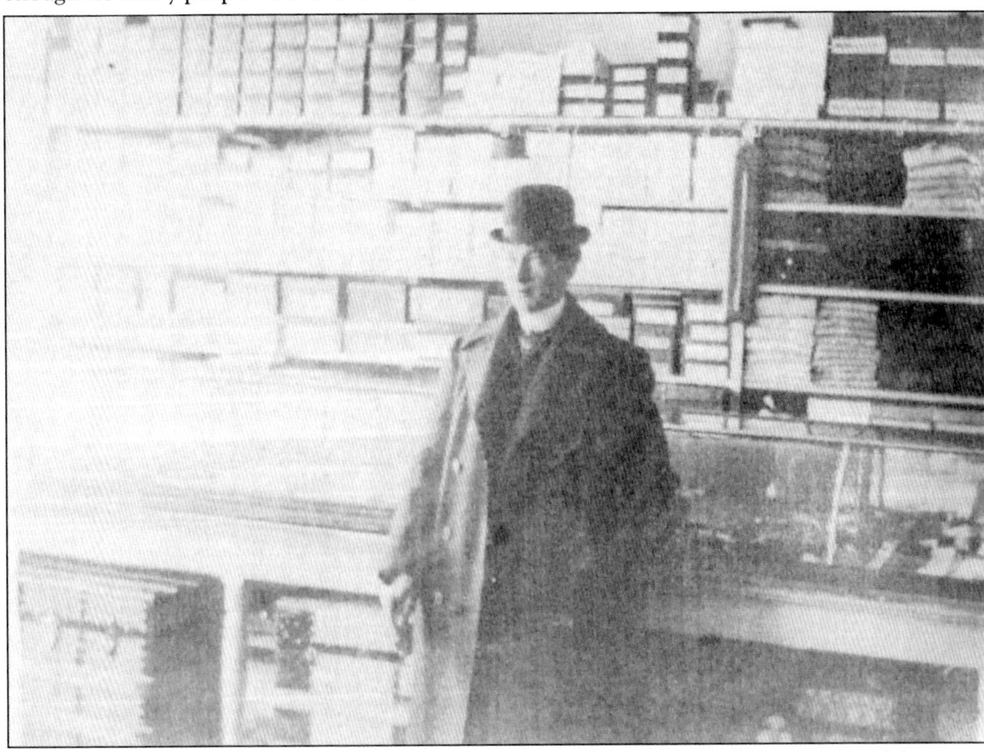

Warren P. Lindow was a great friend of Fred P. Stevens, the great retailer in Presque Isle.

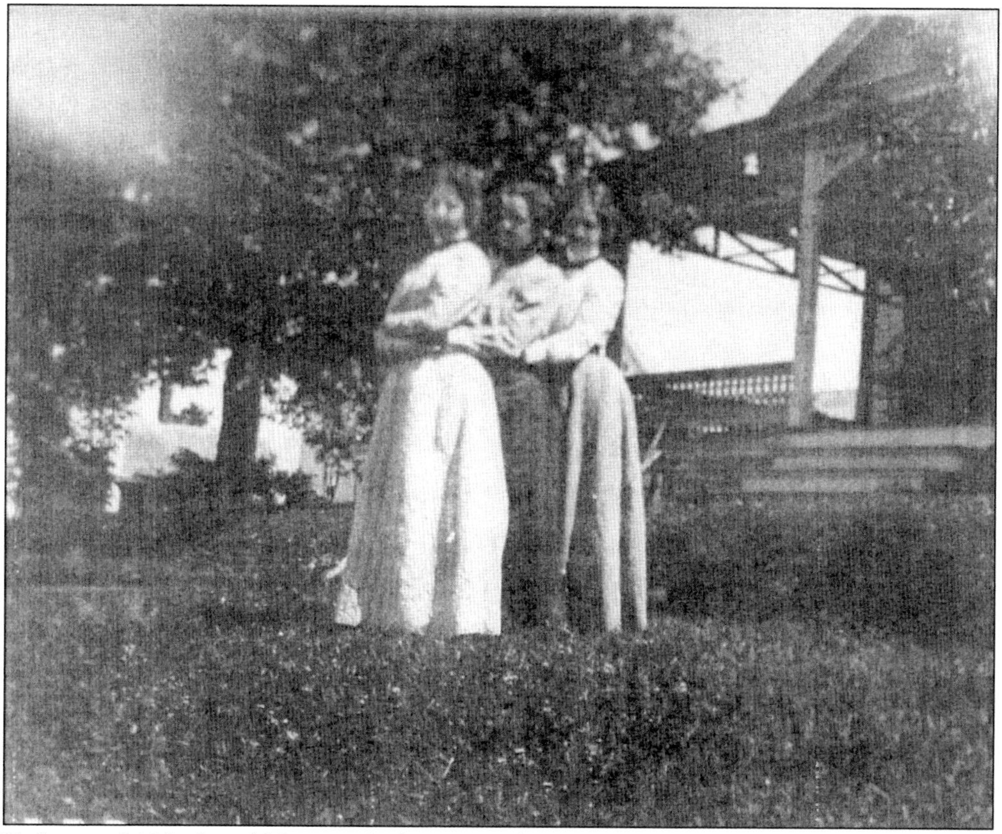
Katherine, Mildred, and Margaret Jenks get together in Presque Isle in 1900.

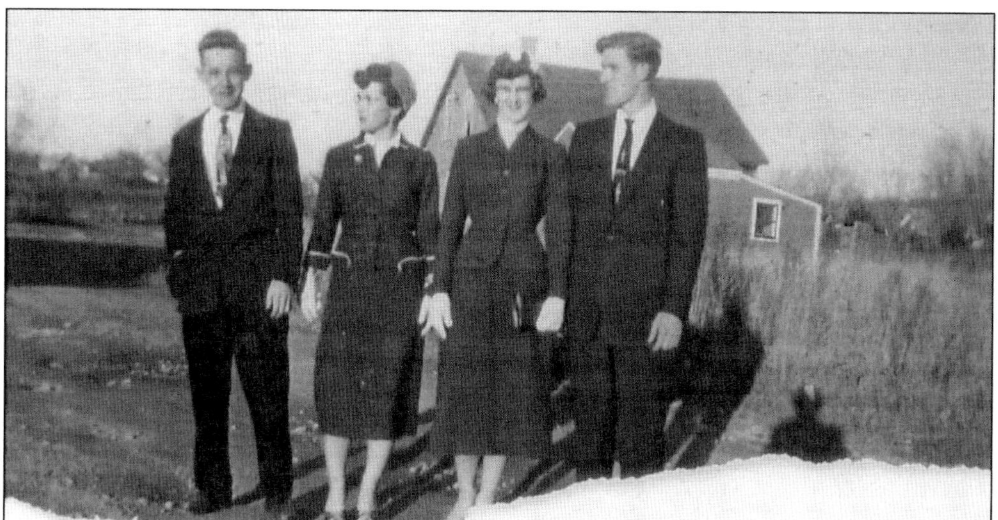
A 1956 private wedding on Bishop Street, Presque Isle. Left to right are: Darrell Harmon, Wilza Kelley, Charlette Hughes, and Gordon Hughes.

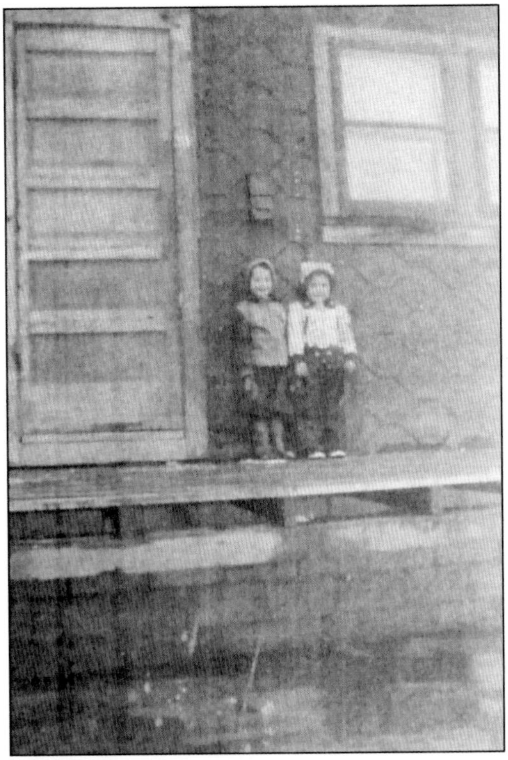

Danna Kelley and Christie Smart are waiting for the train in Caribou in 1951.

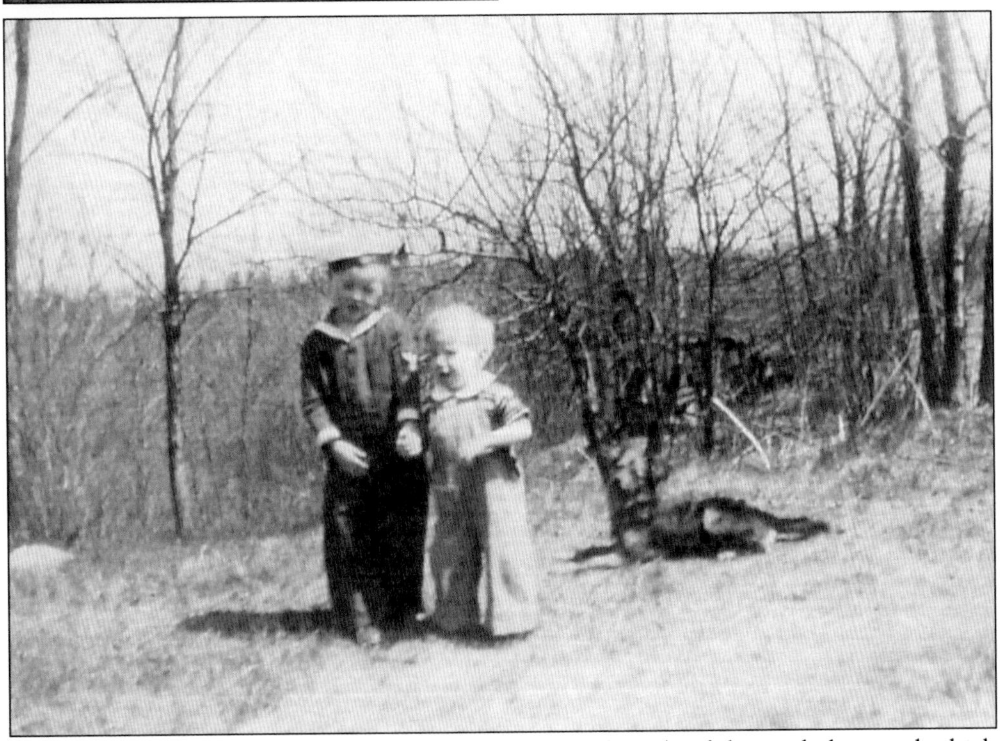

Bill Cochran, five, and Gary Cochran, three, stand by the side of the road close to the high school in Caribou in 1945.

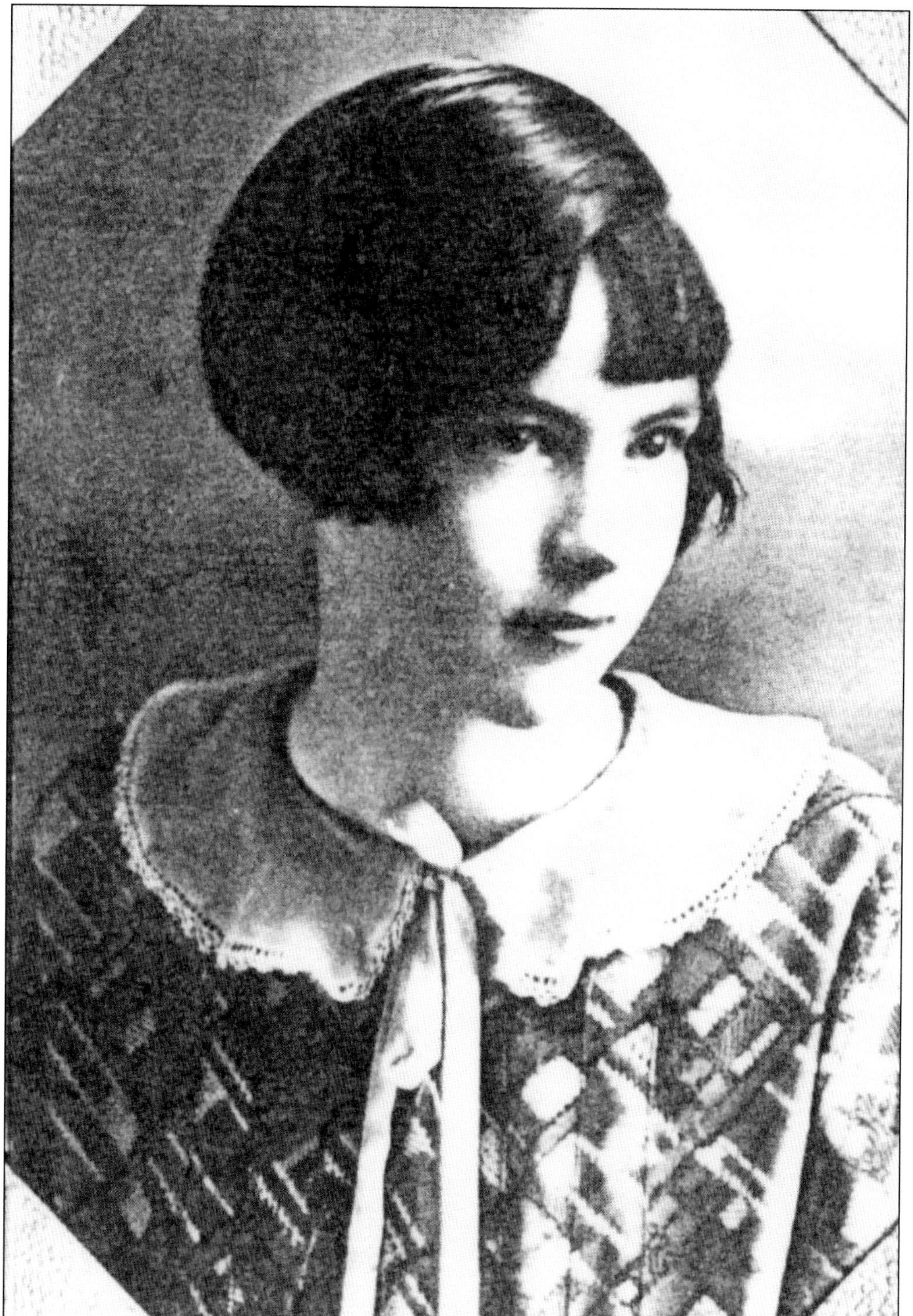

Mildred Kierstead Smart of Caribou taught school for many years before turning to business. She was the mother of Mrs. Christie Cochran of Washburn. She later went into both the hotel and taxi business, the latter owned by her husband. She died in 1991.

Acknowledgments

First thanks for this work must go to my co-authors, Jackie H. and Stan P. Greaves. Their invaluable contacts meant that the collection of these old photographs was speeded up greatly. It's very doubtful this could have been done without them. They earned their co-author status.

Based strictly on the size of the community, we give great thanks to Mrs. Audrey Thibodeau, president of the Presque Isle Historical Society, and Mrs. Joan Allen, that society's vice-president. Mrs. Allen, especially, went out of her way with aid, filling in for a hobbled Mrs. Thibodeau, who may have been more active than she should have been.

In Caribou, it was Mrs. Avis Armstrong and her husband, Ken, who were very, very helpful. Mrs. Armstrong is president of the Caribou Historical Society. Don Collins of S.W. Collins Co. was very helpful even as his daughter, Susan, was campaigning as Maine's first woman candidate for governor.

In New Sweden, Mrs. Mabel Todd, former schoolteacher and an officer of the New Sweden Historical Society and Museum, steered us in the right direction. Alwain Espling, president of that society, was also helpful. Paul Carlson, who teaches art at Presque Isle High, introduced the Greaves to New Sweden. Christie Cochran of Washburn, with the *Presque Isle Star-Herald*, gave us more help than anyone with more modern photos. Dr. Philip Turner helped with Caribou and in general. So did Frank Hussey of Presque Isle and Marilyn Clark, head librarian of the Mark and Emily Turner Memorial Library there. Debbie Sirois and Dana Rattray of Fitzgerald's in Caribou went out of their way in copying the photos. And officials of the Presque Isle and Caribou Chambers of Commerce were also helpful.

Frank H. Sleeper
October 1994